Cornell Studies in Political Economy

EDITED BY PETER J. KATZENSTEIN

Fair Shares

Unions, Pay, and Politics in Sweden and West Germany

Peter Swenson

Cornell University Press

Ithaca, New York

First published 1989 by Cornell University Press.

Library of Congress Cataloging-in-Publication Data

Swenson, Peter.
  Fair shares.

  (Cornell studies in political economy)
  Bibliography: p.
  Includes index.
  1. Trade-unions—Sweden. 2. Trade-unions—Germany (West) 3. Wages—Sweden.
4. Wages—Germany (West) 5. Profit-sharing—Sweden. 6. Profit-sharing—
Germany (West) I. Title. II. Series.
HD6757.S94 1989   331.88'0943   88-47768
ISBN 0-8014-2135-7 (alk. paper)

Contents

Acknowledgments

Many individuals did perhaps more than their fair shares on behalf of this book. Friends, teachers, and others who offered helpful views on portions and drafts were Fred Block, David Cameron, Youssef Cohen, Robert Dahl, Miriam Golden, Joanne Gowa, Roger Haydon, Peter Katzenstein, Peter Lange, Charles Lindblom, Juan Linz, Rianne Mahon, Andrei Markovits, Rudolf Meidner, Jack Nagel, Jonas Pontusson, James Scott, and Sally Swenson. All that bears resemblance to their influence may or may not be wholly coincidental and, in the latter case, may be inadequately acknowledged. To Axel Hadenius, Andy Markovits, Andy Martin, and Erik Åsard, I owe special appreciation, for readers will see how indispensable to me their research and publications were in the writing of this book. All translations from German and Swedish sources are my own. The Social Science Research Council, the German Academic Exchange Service, and Arbetslivscentrum of Sweden all contributed generously to the financing of my research. I owe special thanks to Rudolf Meidner in Sweden and Hans-Adam Pfromm, Karl Heinz Pitz, and Rudi Welzmüller in West Germany; they generously shared their time and expertise. The friendship and great hospitality of Måns and Lolita Arborelius, Helga Kleingeist and Jochem Poensgen, Ann-Christin and Hans-Åke Sjöquist, Ulrike Voss, and Christian and Marianne Voss made my visits to their countries personally as well as intellectually enriching.

There is no such thing as a finished book, it seems sometimes, only an abandoned one. In its long period of gestation a book is a source of great continuity in an author's life. For their loving interruptions, and advocacy of its abandonment, I dedicate this book to Pauline and our sons, Mattias and Samuel.

PETER SWENSON

Philadelphia, Pennsylvania

Abbreviations

SWEDEN

LKAB	Luossavaara-Kiirunavaara AB (State-owned iron-ore mining firm)
LO	Landsorganisationen i Sverige (Swedish Trade Union Confederation)
PTK	Privattjänstemannakartellen (Federation of Salaried Employees in Industry and Services)
SACO	Sveriges Akademikers Centralorganisation (Confederation of Professional Associations—merged with SR in 1974)
SAF	Svenska Arbetsgivareföreningen (Swedish Employers' Confederation)
SAP	Sveriges Socialdemokratiska Arbetareparti (Swedish Social Democratic Party)
SIF	Svenska Industritjänstemannaförbundet (Union of Salaried Employees in Industry)
SR	Statstjänstemännens Riksförbund (National Federation of Civil Servants—merged with SACO in 1974)
TCO	Tjänstemännens Centralorganisation (Central Organization of Salaried Employees)
VF	Verkstadsföreningen (Engineering Employers' Association)

GERMANY (FEDERAL REPUBLIC, UNLESS OTHERWISE NOTED)

ADBG	Allgemeiner Deutscher Gewerkschaftsbund (General German Trade Union Federation—Imperial and Weimar Germany)
AGVESI	Arbeitgeberverband Eisen- und Stahlindustrie e.V. (Iron and Steel Industry Employers' Association—Imperial Germany)

ix

BDA   Bundesvereinigung der Deutschen Arbeitgeberverbände (Federal Confederation of German Employers' Associations)

CDU/CSU   Christlich-Demokratische Union/Christlich-Soziale Union (electoral/parliamentary alliance of the Christian Democratic Union and the Christian Social Union)

DGB   Deutscher Gewerkschaftsbund (German Trade Union Confederation)

FDP   Freie Demokratische Partei (Free Democratic Party)

Gesamtmetall   Gesamtverband der Metallindustriellen Arbeitgeberverbände (Confederation of Metal Industry Employers)

GTB   Gewerkschaft Textil-Bekleidung (Textile and Garment Workers' Union)

HDA   Hauptstelle der Deutschen Arbeitgeberverbände (Central Confederation of German Employers' Associations—Imperial Germany)

IG Bau   Industriegewerkschaft Bau-Steine-Erden (Construction and Allied Industry Workers' Union)

IG Bergbau   Industriegewerkschaft Bergbau und Energie (Union of Mining and Energy Workers)

IG Chemie   Industriegewerkschaft Chemie-Papier-Keramik (Chemical and Allied Industry Workers' Union)

IG Druck   Industriegewerkschaft Druck und Papier (Printing and Paper Workers' Union)

IG Metall   Industriegewerkschaft Metall (Metalworkers' Union)

ÖTV   Gewerkschaft Öffentliche Dienste, Transport und Verkehr (Government and Transport Workers' Union)

SPD   Sozialdemokratische Partei Deutschlands (German Social Democratic Party)

VDA   Verein Deutscher Arbeitgeberverbände (Federation of German Employers' Associations—Imperial Germany)

VDESI   Verein Deutscher Eisen- und Stahlindustrieller (Association of German Iron and Steel Industrialists)

WSI   Wirtschafts- und Sozialwissenschaftliches Institut (the DGB's Economics and Social Science Institute, formerly WWI)

WWI   Wirtschafts- und Wissenschaftliches Institut der Gewerkschaften (the DGB's Economics and Science Institute, later WSI)

ZAG   Zentralarbeitsgemeinschaft (Central Labor Community—peak organ of union-employer collaboration in Weimar Germany)

ZDI   Zentralverband Deutscher Industrieller (Central Association of German Industrialists—Imperial Germany)

Fair Shares

Beyond the Wage Struggle

The union leader, in the words of C. Wright Mills, is a "manager of discontent." This notion will ring true to anyone familiar with institutionalized conflict between labor and capital in this century. Union leaders also manage conflicts within the working class. Though this idea might not have the same familiar ring, it is key to understanding the organizational and political success of unions. Their leaders do not just find working-class unity, they have to make it.[1]

The dual role of union leaders as interest brokers is a basic fact of the political economy of trade unionism. In reality, if not in rhetoric, labor leaders usually struggle to reconcile labor and capital to their mutual advantage. Working-class prosperity depends on the performance of capitalist enterprise, and union leaders ignore that fact at their peril. Meanwhile, they try to unify the working class organizationally and therefore manage real conflicts of interest within it. Division within labor upsets peaceable arrangements between labor and capital, often at a loss to labor if not capital too. Solidarity brings influence over employers. Solidarity also brings influence in politics and public policy, which can come to the aid of union leaders as they try to achieve balance.

Comparative evidence from advanced industrial democracies confirms that centralized, politically unified, and "encompassing" unions score greater social and economic policy successes through the demo-

[1]Mills, *The New Men of Power: America's Labor Leaders* (New York: Harcourt, Brace, 1948), 8–9. On working class unity, see Claus Offe and Helmut Wiesenthal, "Two Logics of Collective Action," in Offe, *Disorganized Capitalism: Contemporary Transformations of Work and Politics* (Cambridge: MIT Press, 1985), 170–220.

1

cratic process than their more fragmented counterparts in other countries. It also suggests that the economies they operate in perform comparatively well, if not consistently better than others, because of social and political mechanisms foreign to conventional economic theory.[2]

While trade unions in capitalist countries vary widely in structure and accomplishments, they appear to differ little in their failure to redistribute factor income between capital and labor. Their accomplishments vary considerably, on the other hand, in the redistribution of income received by those depending solely on wages, salaries, and family or state support. Strong compression of pay differentials, full employment, and universalistic social policy are clearly within the reach, in varying degrees and combinations, of only some labor movements, whereas others lack the influence to achieve these goals or to shape related government policies on their own terms.

In this book I aim to illuminate the ways in which unions try—and manage—to reconcile internal conflicts of interest that threaten organizational centralization, solidarity, and strength, and thereby enhance their economic and political influence. At the same time I want to show how and why unions try to use their political clout to win economic and social policies for neutralizing market forces that generate internal and external opposition. Union leaders and their organizations thrive only when they can reconcile internal (membership) and external (employer) conditions for "support." *Support* here means both consent from members and activists on the one side, and willingness if not eagerness from employers to maintain bargaining relations on the other. Unions, after all, are as dependent on employers as they are on their members. Without collective bargaining, unions are frail or short-lived affairs, lacking economic or political influence. By recognizing unions as legitimate partners in centralized collective bargaining, employers empower them in politics as well as in the labor market.

[2]Cf. David Cameron, "Social Democracy, Corporatism, Labour Quiescence, and the Representation of Economic Interests in Advanced Capitalist Society," in J. H. Goldthorpe, ed., *Order and Conflict in Contemporary Capitalism* (New York: Oxford University Press, 1984), 148–73; Manfred Schmidt, "The Welfare State and the Economy in Periods of Crisis: A Comparative Study of Twenty-three OECD Nations," *European Journal of Political Research* 11:1 (1983), 1–26; Peter Katzenstein, *Small States in World Markets: Industrial Policy in Europe* (Ithaca: Cornell University Press, 1985); Geoffrey Garrett and Peter Lange, "Performance in a Hostile World: Economic Growth in Capitalist Democracies, 1974–1982," *World Politics* 38 (July 1986), 517–45. On why this is so see Mancur Olson, *The Rise and Decline of Nations: Economic Growth, Stagflation, and Social Rigidities* (New Haven: Yale University Press, 1982), especially 89–92, and Lange, "Unions, Workers, and Wage Regulation: The Rational Bases of Consent," in Goldthorpe, *Order and Conflict*, 98–123.

UNION POWER IN SOCIETY AND POLITICS

To cultivate internal and external support, unions operate in two interactive spheres of influence—the "moral economy" and the "political economy." A *moral economy*, as I define it, is a pattern of economic exchange relations whose normative bounds are introduced in substantial part by economic (including labor) elites, incorporated into custom, and enforced by institutional and/or spontaneous collective intervention that overrides what self-interest and market power alone would dictate. In the moral economy, unions can play two roles limited primarily to the subsphere of wage determination. First, they actively and intentionally establish distributive norms for wage setting—that is to say, they help form the values underlying the moral economy as they shape it into a more or less uniform system and extend its influence into sectors dominated by either paternalistic relations or the cash nexus. Second, they are part of the institutional apparatus that enforces the moral economy when market forces disturb it. Union officials endeavor to use their tutelary and coercive influence in the moral economy in a way that bolsters their own organizational security, maneuverability, and power. In other words, they endeavor to use their power over pay norms and distribution in a way that fosters both membership and employer support.

A *political economy*, as I define it, is a pattern of state-society interaction in which interest coalitions of organized societal and state actors produce market intervention policies whose central purpose, whether these actors explicitly acknowledge it or not, is to foster the organizational security and collaboration of interest groups. A political economy may be static or dynamic, depending upon how well government policy reinforces prevailing interest coalitions in the face of uncontrollable market developments and the unintended market effects of policy itself.[3] In the political economy, union leaders help design market intervention policies and make coalitions behind them. The political economy is thus a sphere of political action that inhibits and re-

[3]This conception of political economy and the role of social and economic policy in shaping labor movements shares a perspective with but not the conclusions of Gøsta Esping-Andersen, *Politics against Markets: The Social Democratic Road to Power* (Princeton: Princeton University Press, 1985). Its focus on the role of interest coalitions shares some of the perspectives of Peter Gourevitch, *Politics in Hard Times: Comparative Responses to International Economic Crises* (Ithaca: Cornell University Press, 1986). On the state and interest group politics generally, see Theda Skocpol, "Bringing the State Back In: Strategies of Analysis in Current Research," in Peter B. Evans, Dietrich Rueschemeyer, and Skocpol, eds., *Bringing the State Back In* (Cambridge: Cambridge University Press, 1985), 21–27.

directs the play of market forces, whereas the moral economy is a sphere of societal action for the same purpose.

Union success in one sphere apparently depends on success in the other. In France and the United States, for example, important instances of "labor exclusion" from the political economy, national unions are politically weak, and especially in France, divided. They are also organizationally decentralized, with uneven and haphazard influence over wage norms and limited influence on economic policy.[4] By contrast, Sweden and West Germany are apparent success cases for modern unionism. Swedish unions in the peak confederation of blue-collar unions by all accounts are, or until recently were, extraordinarily successful in influencing both the moral and the political economy to their advantage. Union aspirations regarding wage redistribution and social policy have been realized to an exceptional degree. The electoral and parliamentary dominance of the Social Democratic party has of course facilitated union success, while union unity and success have in turn helped sustain the party's dominance.

Unions in postwar West Germany have not fared quite as well. In the absence of peak-level coordination of wage policy, and without a comparable electoral and parliamentary dominance by the Social Democratic party, they have lacked the unity, opportunity, and resources to influence systematically their moral and political economies to the same extent as their counterparts have in Sweden. But under less favorable circumstances they have nevertheless tried, and their efforts can be understood as rational attempts to maintain support in a hostile environment.

BEYOND THE WAGE STRUGGLE:
WAGE LEVELING AND FUND SOCIALISM

In illustrating my points about the moral and political economies of Sweden and West Germany, I focus on two interrelated issues. The first is what I call *wage leveling*, a wide variety of distinct processes that include compression of pay differentials, within or between enterprises and industries or throughout entire economies, and standardization of

[4]See H. A. Turner and D. A. S. Jackson, "On the Stability of Wage Differences and Productivity-Based Wage Policies: An International Analysis," *British Journal of Industrial Relations* 7 (March 1969), 1–17; Cameron, "Social Democracy." For an interesting study of labor inclusion and exclusion in Sweden and France, see Jonas Pontusson, "Comparative Political Economy of Advanced Capitalist States: Sweden and France," *Kapitalistate* 10:11 (1983).

pay rates, between occupational or skill categories within and between enterprises and industries or throughout entire economies. There is probably no union anywhere, even in socialist economies, that does not attempt to influence the structure of wages, usually in an egalitarian fashion, in the name of fairness and in the service of organizational self-interest. It is rare in the extreme for a union openly to advocate increased inequalities within its own organizational ambit, except as an emergency, concessionary response to economic crisis and the threat such a crisis brings to the existence of unions.

In his defense of trade unionism and the wage struggle, Karl Marx denied unions one of their central purposes: "To clamour for equal or even equitable retribution on the basis of the wages system is the same as to clamour for freedom on the basis of the slavery system."[5] Achieving fairness is one thing, but moving toward it is another, and if wage leveling is a measure of fairness, then unions everywhere make real if only modest progress. Equally important is how unions structure pay and shape norms in the service of organizational centralization and unity, thereby increasing labor's political influence, and even empowering workers in their occasional spontaneous defense of the labor movement's egalitarian results.

By focusing on pay leveling, often at the direct expense of high pay increases, unions thus transcend the important role that Marx would concede to the unions and what the Germans and Swedes, in the past, called the "wage struggle."[6] In those countries today—and in the United States as well—the cry of unionism has not simply been "more, more, more." In collective bargaining the net effect of American unions has been a compression of wage differentials within and across industrial sectors. Also, growing union-negotiated health and other benefits have leveled the value of total remuneration considerably within enterprises.[7] In West Germany, likewise, all unions try at various times to bring the earnings of low-pay workers up faster than the rest while actively promoting redistributional social policy. In Sweden, through "solidaristic wage policy," unions have helped bring about an

[5]This followed from the labor theory of value: "as different kinds of labour power have different values, or require different quantities of labour for their production, they must fetch different prices in the labour market." Karl Marx, "Value, Price and Profit" in Marx and Friedrich Engels, *Collected Works, vol. 20* (New York: International Publishers, 1985), 129.

[6]Marx defended unions against "wage-fund" theorists, and especially socialists among them like Ferdinand Lassalle, whose Malthusian premises led them to the conclusion that unions were useless in bettering the condition of the working class.

[7]See Richard B. Freeman and James L. Medoff, *What Do Unions Do?* (New York: Basic Books, 1984), especially 61–73.

astonishing compression of pay levels since the 1950s while at the same time actively designing an expensive welfare state financed by highly progressive income taxes.

How unions manipulate the moral economy of wage labor substantially affects their political strategies. Major differences in union political behavior between and within countries can be explained by different distributional strategies in collective bargaining. This I conclude after examining the differences among German and Swedish unions with regard to the second substantive issue on which this book focuses: *collective capital formation.*

German and Swedish unions in the 1970s, far overstepping the traditional bounds of the wage struggle, launched politically divisive plans for partial collectivization of privately generated profits in the hands of union-controlled capital market institutions.[8] Their legislative drives for what were variously termed "wage-earner funds," "collective profit sharing," and "workers' capital formation" all promised genuine transformations in state-sanctioned forms of capital ownership and control.

Why were unions calling for this peculiar brand of socialization at this time? The answer lies in what I call the "wage policy trilemma," the complex set of constraints and punitive mechanisms confining union action in collective bargaining. From the trilemma we can derive social and economic policy objectives (such as Keynesian and social policies) common to most if not all union movements, as well as significant departures from the norm. The trilemma helps us explain why unions seek to change the political economy, deriving explanations from the distributional tasks of unions in collective bargaining.

The trilemma thus integrates analyses of the moral economy with analyses of the political economy. It captures the systematic contradictions of (1) union interests in wage leveling, (2) the conflicting interests of unions in wage growth at the expense of profits, and (3) union interests in maintenance of tight labor markets with full employment. Trilemma analysis reveals that much of union strategy in the political economy aims at muting these contradictions or resolving them altogether.

Union proposals for collective capital formation promised such a resolution. They cannot be attributed to socialist tradition or the immanent drive of strong labor movements to transform capitalism. Indeed, the revival of demands for socialization were a sign more of weakness than of strength. "Fund socialism" appeared when Swedish and German unions were confronted with acute predicaments in collective bar-

---

[8]Some of these plans also called for payroll taxes not just taxes on profits.

6

gaining and, in particular, when they came under severe pressure to abandon the leveling policies that underpinned their management of the moral economy. Radical ideas for the fundamental transformation of the political economy became attractive to traditionally conservative union leaders when transformation of markets and industries threatened the standing of their organizations with members and employers. Transformative plans promised aid in fulfilling old reformist objectives under new and unfavorable conditions.

The troubles of Swedish and German unions in the 1970s were of course shared by other national unions. With the exception of Danish, Dutch, and Austrian unions, however, collective capital formation had little appeal elsewhere. The reason is fairly simple. Policy-making opportunities represented by the strong electoral and legislative presence of labor parties motivated unions to investigate statutory solutions to their troubles. Unions in labor-exclusionary political economies naturally turned their sights elsewhere, experimenting with militant mobilization, particularistic hide-saving, and contract "give-backs." To unions in Sweden and Germany, socialization by means of collective capital formation appeared at the time politically within reach, even if in retrospect this might seem to have been only wishful thinking.

In fact, the Swedish unions did succeed in obtaining "wage-earner funds" from a Social Democratic government in 1983. What they got, however, was only a watered-down version of original designs. By the late 1980s, both the unions and the Social Democrats lost interest in such ideas as conservative forces in both electoral and economic spheres demonstrated sufficient muscle to frighten the labor movement away from transformative policy.

In West Germany it was the opposition of the enormous Metalworkers' Union as much as employer and parliamentary opposition that took collective profit sharing off the political agenda by the late 1970s, a time when other unions had yet to lose interest. One of Germany's most radical and militant unions, IG Metall adopted a seemingly paradoxical stance against this brand of socialization. My explanation of the heated conflicts within the German labor movement on the issue again derives from the wage policy trilemma. As fully autonomous units in collective bargaining, German unions naturally experienced and struggled with the trilemma in different ways and thus regarded the new debate over socialization through different lenses. How IG Metall's experiences differed and why they mattered will become clear as the concepts of the moral and the political economy of labor are developed.

7

PART I

PAY STRUCTURE AND THE MORAL ECONOMY

CHAPTER ONE

Pay Norms and Union Leadership

Unions are built in a world of morals as well as one of markets and politics, and they help shape that world. In this chapter I focus on the moral sphere, where rank-and-file membership norms regarding wage distribution constrain and facilitate organized action. As constraints, these attitudes are part of the environment that union leaders try to change when they cannot adapt to them. The malleability of value orientations makes workers' pay norms a resource, not simply an obstacle, for union leaders.

The purpose of this inquiry into the moral economy of labor in industrial capitalism is to build an understanding of the political action of unions in knowledge about their power relations with both members and employers. In collective bargaining, unions do not concern themselves only with factor or functional income distribution—in other words, with what share of value added goes collectively toward wages and what share capital retains. Unions concern themselves with what individual workers earn and so by necessity with relative wages (the distribution of the wage share). They also concern themselves with what workers think they *should* earn. Hence unions can take active control in the moral economy of wage determination—by responding to it, by shaping it, and by administering it.

This conception of the moral economy, unlike earlier ones, focuses on workers and wage setting in industrial capitalism. E. P. Thompson introduced the idea to show that the supposedly spasmodic English bread riots in the eighteenth century were morally motivated and therefore restrained actions against capitalists whose pricing and marketing behavior violated traditional notions of the fair market place. James C. Scott used the idea to explain peasants' subjective experience

11

of exploitation at the hands of landlords and the state in the era of capitalist colonialism in Southeast Asia. There, according to Scott, violation of the peasants' redistributive moral economy through increasingly rigid and nonpaternalistic rent and tax practices, not relative or absolute deprivation per se, engendered rebellion. Charles F. Sabel in turn applied the idea to explain what he thought was the distinctively egalitarian behavior of unskilled workers of peasant background who migrated to the heartlands of industrial capitalism—places like Ford in Cologne and Renault in Flins.[1]

Sabel, in accordance with earlier notions, suggests that the moral economy of the wage-earning poor is a precapitalist phenomenon imported into the urban industrial setting and thereby implies its eventual disappearance.[2] But this kind of interpretation errs in portraying anger and rebellion based in traditions of fairness as the peculiar frictional heat generated when capitalism and the modern state roll over traditional society. On the contrary, the institutions of modern capitalism establish normative traditions of their own in adaptive response to expectations and demands from wage earners. The violation of modern traditions and its consequences are equally worthy of inquiry.

A "moral economy" in this book is therefore more than a set of precapitalist norms and behaviors, which is how the term is often loosely used by the above authors. Here I use it to describe a more or less stable pattern of relations between market actors in which market power is held in check. A moral economy is a pattern of exchange relations constrained by values and traditions that societal elites impose in interaction with subordinate groups; its violation often provokes spontaneous rebellion when elites fail to enforce the very norms that they established to sanctify their power.[3]

The focus of this renovated conception of the moral economy is an old one in the study of capitalist industrial relations. Since the days of Sidney and Beatrice Webb, a wide variety of sociologists, economists, and industrial relations specialists have been intrigued by the ubiquity and power of wage norms and workers' desire for pay equity. This

[1]Thompson, "The Moral Economy of the English Crowd in the Eighteenth Century," *Past and Present* no. 50 (February 1971), 76–136; Scott, *The Moral Economy of the Peasant: Rebellion and Subsistence in Southeast Asia* (New Haven: Yale University Press, 1976); and Sabel, *Work and Politics: The Division of Labor in Industry* (Cambridge: Cambridge University Press, 1982), 132–36.

[2]See also E. J. Hobsbawm, *Primitive Rebels: Studies in Archaic Forms of Social Movement in the 19th and 20th Centuries* (New York: Norton, 1959).

[3]Analytically, this concept excludes direct state involvement. Of course government policy affects the societal power relations that give rise to the moral economy of labor.

chapter builds on some of their insights in its analysis of union objectives in the moral economy of wage labor—an analysis that ultimately helps explain union actions in the political sphere.

"MORALITY" AND "RATIONALITY"

There has been a growing tendency in the social sciences, following economics, to build theoretical models of collective behavior as an aggregated form of individual means-ends rationality. In the study of unions, not surprisingly, it was economists who imported motivational assumptions about rational utility-maximizing behavior. Some, focusing on wage policy makers, assume unions try to maximize average wages or alternatively the wage bill. By implication, then, they tend to treat workers as an undifferentiated mass whose conflicts of interest and distributional values matter little in union policy making.[4] Others derive theories about institutions as collective actors bound by the cost-benefit calculi of union members as distinct individuals and of union officials as administrators of selective benefits and sanctions for inducing membership recruitment and cooperation. This approach, however, seems to offer little help in modeling causal explanations about the substance and variations of union policy in wage bargaining and politics.[5]

The arguments advanced here are a partial critique of this growing tradition, or at least of its more materialist and reductionist currents. As "rational choice" theories supposedly do, my analysis upholds the analytic importance and historical consequences of individual motivations, strategies, successes, and mistakes. But my argument differs in suggesting that individual moral commitments and materialist rationality will often be at odds, and that over time the actual behavior of individuals probably conforms only erratically to either. Contradictions begin at the individual level, and union leaders have to take account of this fact for their own success and the success of their organizations. To

[4]The classic in this field is John Dunlop, *Wage Determination under Trade Unions* (New York: Kelley, 1950). Some interesting recent variations are Donald L. Martin, *An Ownership Theory of the Trade Union* (Berkeley: University of California Press, 1980), and Peter Lange, "Unions, Workers, and Wage Regulation: The Rational Bases of Consent," in John H. Goldthorpe, ed., *Order and Conflict in Contemporary Capitalism* (Oxford: Clarendon Press, 1984), 98–123. See also Wallace N. Atherton, *Theory of Union Bargaining Goals* (Princeton: Princeton University Press, 1973).

[5]The seminal work is Mancur Olson, *The Logic of Collective Action: Public Goods and the Theory of Groups* (Cambridge: Harvard University Press, 1965).

the extent that they themselves act rationally, their actions will respond to—and shape—the moral responses as well as the instrumental motivations of their members.

A successful labor leader is one who anticipates workers' anger and knows the limits of solidarity, one who can harness the first and stretch the second. Action in anger or solidarity is not easily rendered intelligible as instrumentally rational behavior in the service of maximized wages (or perhaps of anything else). Of course anger may move someone to action that practically any reasonable person would see as instrumentally rational. Strikes begun in anger, however, have frequently brought immediate economic misery to unions and members, and not simply because workers lacked the information that a strike was likely to do so. Actions motivated by solidarity usually entail sacrifice, not benefits. That is part of the meaning of solidarity. Short-run sacrifice, of course, may be based on expectations of long-run payoffs, which in some cases might indeed suffice to motivate real manifestations of solidarity. Every period in labor history, however, has strikes that, at least in retrospect, appear suicidal.

Behind what might seem to be reckless disregard for consequences in industrial relations there are often value-bound emotional impulses mixed in with ostensible material objectives. Commitment to principles of fairness may motivate industrial action whose expected material consequences are too small by themselves to have justified that action and its costs. Feelings about entitlement, just deserts, or dignity may inspire self-serving action where the material rewards, in context, are symbolic of other things, and which out of context would meet with inaction or indifference. Likewise, similar feelings may incapacitate or morally disarm an individual in the face of golden opportunities. The objects of moral commitments and feelings of entitlement are often utterly material: a few cents per hour or a few dollars per week in wages. Actions that fulfill or express moral principles may have meaning—or value—in and of themselves, not just as value-free (or costly) instruments for achieving other values.

Workers do of course weigh the satisfactions from morally expressive behavior against things like foregone material satisfaction. They may also abstain from selfish behavior in anticipation of the heavy psychic costs of moral censure and ostracism. But admitting such considerations into our understanding of instrumental rationality probably robs the notion of its empirical utility if not its discriminative conceptual power. Attempts to reconcile rationalist assumptions with behavior rooted in solidarity and outrage lead directly into a wilderness of tautology and vain speculation. Human moral response is irreducible and not easily integrated into elegant theoretical models built on individual cost-benefit and means-ends rationality.[6]

Another problem in rationalist theory is its relative inattention to the sociological mechanisms and dynamics of value formation, as well as to the contexts and agencies that activate or cue individuals to respond to their moral or their material values. We know that people can act inconsistently, especially when principles of moral propriety are involved. This knowledge forces the rationalist to infer either instability in values, information, or perceptions over time. A useful alternative is to analyze the social contexts and cues that activate opposing modes of action in pursuit of contradictory interests and values.

In the case of labor relations, union leaders have the power to mold and cue workers' behavior. Hence it makes sense to examine how labor leaders act in both a tutelary and a communicative capacity to instill and activate the moral values underlying solidarity. In doing so one can steer a sensible course between unfounded assumptions about the individualistic instrumentalism of workers as the sole basis of collective action, on the one hand, and the perhaps equally undue romanticism of some "moral economists" with regard to the solidarity and egalitarianism of subordinate classes, on the other. Both possessive, rational individualism and communitarian norms matter, and they matter in both the capitalist and the precapitalist contexts. What matters most in determining how the dynamic interplay between them works is leadership and the exercise of power.[7]

FAIRNESS

What are the nonmaterial values of workers that matter for union leaders? The answer is revealed in what regularly makes workers indignant with the conditions of wage labor. Clearly, the answer cannot be found in objective measures of deprivation alone, for part of what

---

[6]Some grounds for this skepticism are presented by Amartya K. Sen, "Rational Fools," *Philosophy and Public Affairs* 6:4 (1977), 317–44; Albert O. Hirschman, "Against Parsimony: Three Easy Ways of Complicating Some Categories of Economic Discourse," *Economics and Philosophy* 1 (April 1985), 7–21; and Amitai Etzioni, "The Case for a Multiple-Utility Conception," ibid. 2 (October 1986), 159–83.

[7]For a critique of the moral economy literature and a rational-choice alternative, see Samuel Popkin, *The Rational Peasant: The Political Economy of Rural Society in Vietnam* (Berkeley: University of California Press, 1979), 1–82. In developing what he calls his "political economy" approach, even Popkin seems to veer in the direction of my analysis when he argues that leadership in peasant movements and its use of "cultural themes," "moral codes," and "visions of the future" proved necessary to counteract free-rider behavior on the part of rational peasants. Ibid., 259–66.

determines workers' choices and actions is their conception of what is fair—as well as what they think brings much and comes cheap. Capitalist culture nowhere extinguishes the desire for fairness, the capacity to feel inequity, or even the strong tendency to "rationalize" one's current condition as a fair one. For example, the meritocratic ethic of capitalist society responds to and shapes moral needs. In a meritocratic society, the anarchy of market wage setting can sow the seeds of rebellion just as it might in a paternalistic one.

Any individual worker has a given moral capacity as well as elastic material needs and desires. Practically all workers, furthermore, adhere to a rudimentary egalitarianism, in a multitude of parochial forms, that builds on the universalistic precept that "like should be treated like," a skeletal principle fleshed out in practice by varying grounds for identification and discrimination. If this is true, we should be able to trace much of worker militancy, and union leaders' understanding of it, to the power of this principle.

Morally grounded indignation disrupts the capitalist labor market frequently and systematically, and as any participant in industrial conflict or reasonably attentive witness can attest, anger at arbitrary and unequal treatment with regard to wages and other working conditions is often the cause. Taking offense at pay disparities is a phenomenon that cuts across ages and cultures.[8] It may not be true, as one author has argued, that "all industrial disputes about payments are differentials disputes," or in other words involve workers' and union leaders' attempts to rectify perceived unfairness in pay relations between different wage-earning groups.[9] There is no doubt, however, that wage differences, as much as or more than aggregate levels, cause virulent conflict between labor and capital. After all, the premise underlying conflict over wage distribution—that moral considerations should override the market—directly challenges the prerogatives of capitalists to price labor and manipulate its use.

In the workplace, pay differentials frequently generate spontaneous brushfire conflict between small groups of workers and employers. In British factories, Allan Flanders concludes, "the greater the inequities in [the] pay structure, the more unstable and a source of conflict it becomes." In a history of incentive pay systems in Germany, Rudi

---

[8]In the parable of the laborers, workers in a vineyard "grumbled" or "murmured" against the landholder for paying some laborers the same amount for fewer hours' work at the same job. The lesson presents their protest as mean-spirited rather than moral. Matthew 20:1–16. Here the discretionary benevolence of paternalism clashes with a competing morality of free wage labor.

[9]Elliot Jaques, "An Objective Approach to Pay Differentials," *New Scientist* 14 (1958), 313.

Schmiede and Edwin Schudlich cite the finding of a 1907 study of piecework: "Nothing upsets the workers so much and so easily leads to strikes, from which the factory has nothing to gain, as the issuing of variable piece-rates for the same work."[10]

Workers' desire for equity within the workplace can of course be an instrument to control labor as well as a stimulus to anger. Management can use workers' standards about "a fair day's pay for a fair day's work" to mobilize employee anger against others not performing up to standard.[11] Commonly, however, employers try to suppress the spontaneous norm-setting process. "Merit pay" systems atomize workers, exploiting individual vanities and shame to keep the wage structure veiled behind voluntary secrecy. Union leaders too find that they can play upon workers' moral sensibilities to regulate militancy and that regulation of pay standards is critical for maintaining membership support.

Pay disparities between as well as within firms are also a common source of worker militancy, which may be without coherent ideological underpinnings. In France early in this century, for example, worker militancy often attributed to a proletarian "syndicalist" culture was in many cases limited to the simple desire of workers for pay standards. As Peter Stearns notes, "syndicalist efforts to push workers toward relatively sweeping material goals were largely ignored," and "most workers who called in a syndicalist leader to help them with a strike did so for purely tactical purposes, remaining uninterested in the collective progress he would urge, or not convinced that it was possible." Workers struck, often in anger, with perhaps no more conscious justification than that of Lille weavers: "We want Pierre, Paul or Jacques to be paid the same price for the same work."[12]

Rapid changes in labor markets generate strikes. Flanders explains the postwar militancy of British workers as a reaction to the "seeds of disintegration in normative systems" brought on by the transition to a peacetime economy and the rapid structural changes associated with growth. Structural changes in the late 1960s brought an explosion of worker militancy in Italy, suggesting that Italians probably had fairness

[10]Flanders, "Collective Bargaining: Prescription for Change," in his *Management and Unions* (London: Faber & Faber, 1970), 192; Schmiede and Schudlich, *Die Entwicklung der Leistungsentlohnung in Deutschland: Eine historisch-theoretische Untersuchung zum Verhältnis von Lohn und Leistung unter kapitalistischen Produktionsbedingungen* (Frankfurt: Campus, 1978), 130.

[11]See Richard Hyman and Ian Brough, *Social Values and Industrial Relations: A Study of Fairness and Equality* (Oxford: Blackwell, 1975), 26.

[12]Stearns, *Revolutionary Syndicalism and French Labor* (New Brunswick: Rutgers University Press, 1971), 48–49.

17

issues on their minds. According to one important study, "In some factories conflict broke out in order to obtain equal pay between old and new employees or with other factories of the same company; in others to restore the dynamics of differentials frozen for years; in yet others to defend the traditional privileges of some groups of workers." Employers' arbitrariness "plunged [them] into a crisis from which they could not recover when their workers came to compare their own conditions, which had been guaranteed to be the best possible by the 'good employers,' with those of other workers in the same area or industry."[13]

Disparities in wage growth between industries probably explains a good deal of strike patterns also. Stearns notes the paradox that although overall strike levels in early twentieth-century France seem to have followed periods of strong economic growth (which we typically explain by decline in unemployment, increased bargaining power, and therefore expectations of success), "the industries and regions most rapidly advancing in prosperity and benefiting from the fullest employment were not the leaders in protest activity."[14] A solution to this puzzle may lie in the fact that rapid economic growth increases pay disparities in the short run, across firms and across industries, as high-growth sectors respond to bottlenecks in the labor supply with early pay increases. Workers in laggard firms and industries then strike, often closing the temporary gaps.[15] The case of the wildcat "revolts" in Sweden and Germany suggests as much. Growing pay disparities probably contribute as much to strike waves as generally declining unemployment and prospects of strike success.

Comparative as well as intertemporal differences in strike levels also suggest the importance of wage differentials stabilized around norms. The relatively low strike levels in the small democracies of Europe in the postwar years, compared with the high strike rates of Italy, France, Britain, and the United States, may be in part due to the presence of

[13]Flanders, "Collective Bargaining: From Donovan to Durkheim," *Management and Unions*, 262–63; Ida Regalia, Marino Regini, and Emilio Reyneri, "Labour Conflicts and Industrial Relations in Italy," in Colin Crouch and Alessandro Pizzorno, eds., *The Resurgence of Class Conflict in Western Europe since 1968*, Vol. 1 (New York: Holmes & Meier, 1978), 108.
[14]Stearns, *Revolutionary Syndicalism*, 44.
[15]In the long run, wage trends vary remarkably little between industries, despite differences in growth, productivity, employment—and therefore labor demand, which help explain some of the short-run variations. Organisation for Economic Co-operation and Development, *Wages and Labour Mobility* (Paris: OECD, 1965), 21–39. Economists find they must resort to sociological explanations for the lack of long-run differences. See for example Ashok V. Desai, *Real Wages in Germany, 1871–1913* (Oxford: Clarendon, 1968), 41–46.

well-institutionalized, centralized regulation of wage differentials and norms supporting them.[16] Centralized systems provide significantly more year-to-year stability in interindustrial wage differentials, which could help explain their low strike levels.[17]

IMPLICATIONS FOR UNION LEADERS

Strikes are complex events with many causes, and it may be that "comparison striking" explains only some of the dynamics of worker militancy while revealing little about fundamental causes. My objective is not to prove that the desire for wage distributional fairness lies at the bottom of all worker discontent and militancy. Rather, my objective is to understand *union* behavior—the behavior of union leaders—in the face of one irrefutable fact: that worker discontent is regularly aroused by violation of wage-distributive norms. Probably no other factor so systematically incites spontaneous conflict between workers and their employers. In the cross fire, union leaders can suffer.

For unions to regulate worker discontent, then, they must systematically focus their attention on equity issues. To do so, they have several complementary possibilities. First, through collective bargaining they can influence the structure of pay within and between enterprises and industries. Many costs and obstacles, analyzed later, prevent unions from accomplishing a great deal in this respect. Alternatively, or in addition, they can strategically control—and suppress—information about pay differentials. Third, and equally important, they can influence workers' perceptions about the power and objectives of employers, and hence about the chances of changing pay structures. Finally, as tutelary agents in the moral economy, they can influence what workers think they deserve—that is, they can create norms regarding pay differentiation.

Why might union leaders feel compelled to quell militancy and therefore regulate membership discontent about relative pay? Internal

[16]Recent literature argues differently, proposing that union centralization supports leftist party control in government, in turn providing substantial benefits that unions get in exchange for labor quiescence. See especially Walter Korpi and Michael Shalev, "Strikes, Industrial Relations and Class Conflict in Capitalist Societies," *British Journal of Sociology* 30 (1979), and David Cameron, "Social Democracy, Corporatism, Labour Quiescence, and the Representation of Economic Interest," in Goldthorpe, *Order and Conflict*, 170–74.

[17]See H. A. Turner and D. A. S. Jackson, "On the Stability of Wage Differences and Productivity-Based Wage Policies: An International Analysis," *British Journal of Industrial Relations* 7 (March 1969).

politics are a primary concern. Although unions may, as Friedrich Engels argued in 1845, neutralize competition among workers, they reconstitute competitive market relations over the distribution of jobs and wages as power conflict within their organization.[18] Membership groups within unions, stratified by the wage structure, form the latent or active basis for conflict over how to focus or apply their collective resources, including strike funds, against employers.

Although in all countries union leaders only rarely face the possibility of being unseated by challengers, they frequently battle credible attempts by internal critics to limit their decisional autonomy and to decentralize authority. Whether or not these critics have distributional objectives in mind, they may well be able to exploit distributional discontent to their advantage. The dangers of internal democratization for union leaders include an important loss of stature in the eyes of employers, whose willingness to engage them in collective bargaining varies with their speed and reliability in making pay agreements stick with members. Hence employer recognition rivals if not exceeds membership support as the leadership's motivation for quieting internal conflict over the structure of wage payments.

A problem for labor leaders also arises when inflamed wage rivalries cause membership groups to strike on their own in order to right perceived distributional wrongs created or left untouched by collective contracts. "Unofficial" or "wildcat" strikes, or the emergence as in Britain of powerful shop stewards who often are successful in producing unevenly distributed pay increases, can discredit leadership in the eyes of both members and employers. Employers ask, "Can't you control your people?" Members respond with "They got more," and "Why didn't you get us as much?"

For these reasons, union leaders have something to gain by controlling information about the pay structure that reaches their members. As a general rule they refrain from publishing more than crude aggregate statistics about wage differentials within their bargaining jurisdiction, and when they do, the information usually serves as an incitement to mobilization when bargaining strategy calls for it. Leaders more readily publicize favorable changes in aggregate differentials with respect to "rival" unions in order to prove their worth to members. They may also publicize differentials as a way of mobilizing membership anger against employers when, for example, under full employment, such a strategy is likely to bring members' pay up to standard. In a

[18]Engels, *The Condition of the Working Class in England* (Stanford: Stanford University Press, 1958), 248.

fragmented labor movement such as Britain's, with over one hundred autonomous unions, union leaders play a leading role in stimulating interunion wage rivalry. In Sweden, "official" wage rivalry is also open and intense but largely confined to relations between, not within, the large blue-collar and white-collar union confederations. In West Germany, where seventeen large unions make up the dominant union confederation, combining both manual and white-collar workers, the open and official wage rivalry characteristic of Britain and Sweden is rare.[19]

Union leaders do not always orchestrate wage rivalry openly, which suggests there are dangers involved. Officially sponsored wage rivalry between unions may legitimize divisive wage rivalry within them. Another risk is that union leaders may fail to "close gaps" that they themselves have pointed to. Failure can fuel internal opposition that can then use the leaders' own standards of judgment against them. For this reason, leaders try to influence membership perceptions not only about the existence of injustices but also about the relative power and ruthlessness of employers in defense of their unjust practices. The ideal, for them, is some balance of perceptions regarding both the extent of injustices and the organization's limited capacity to right them in a world of class conflict. Hence while unions depend on employers for recognition, they must also hold them at arm's length as antagonists, partly in ritual and partly in reality.

Finally, union leaders can also influence the normative standards members and subordinates apply to their situation. In their tutelary capacity, leaders try to implant norms that can be achieved and defended with collective bargaining.[20] Likewise, unions often must try to invalidate or counteract the appeal of norms that cannot be accommodated in an institutionalized process that reflects the power balance between unions and employers.

In doing so, unions "transmute the very nature of employee grievances, by defining issues within a narrow focus which shapes the parameters for potential resolution," according to Richard Hyman and

---

[19]It may be suggestive of the taboo against it that an "insider" in the German union hierarchy, IG Metall economist Adam Pfromm, wrote a book emphasizing the dynamics of wage rivalry and related phenomena without citing or analyzing a single specific case from Germany. *Solidarische Lohnpolitik: Zur wirtschaftlichen und sozialen Problematik tariflicher Lohnstrukturnivellierung* (Cologne: Europäische Verlagsanstalt, 1978).

[20]Elliot Jaques holds that workers' notions of fair pay are oriented to an objectively measurable attribute of jobs (the standard time units between necessary monitoring by superiors) and would therefore disagree with this argument. See *Equitable Payment* (London: Heinemann, 1961), and *Free Enterprise, Fair Employment* (New York: Crane Russak, 1982), especially 65–75.

Ian Brough's important leftist account of union wage policies.[21] Or as Barrington Moore might put it, unions, like other bureaucratic institutions, "expropriate moral outrage"—first by molding it, then by providing the mechanisms for alleviating it.[22]

UNIONS AS TUTELARY AGENTS

In any workplace and throughout many trades or industries, parochial norms of fairness and derivative notions of individual rights tend to evolve about relations among workers and their managers, about workers' relations with machines, and finally about the relations of economic reward to the quantities and varieties of labor performed.[23] These norms often arise out of "custom" but may as often result from the instrumentally conceived managerial practices of employers. Even when these customs are established by market forces or an informal bargain or power balance, they can acquire an "ethical aura" if followed repeatedly.[24] Even when they lack this aura, tradition may nevertheless assume a kind of "neutrality" that makes a moral issue out of disadvantageous departures from tradition, especially when employers represented what had prevailed as normal or even fair.[25]

Wage traditions are, in the usual absence of a deeply shared class ideology, the most important common moral "front" shared by workers against capitalist authority. As such they have the automatic ability

[21]Thus, they argue, unions strengthen capitalism by confining conflict to the details of its operation and not its foundations: "Trade unionism permits debate around the terms of workers' obedience while not challenging the fact of their subordination." Hyman and Brough, *Social Values and Industrial Relations*, 64, 71, and 74–92.

[22]Moore, *Injustice: The Social Bases of Obedience and Revolt* (White Plains, N.Y.: Sharpe, 1978), 500–505.

[23]Some traditional nineteenth-century "work rules" protecting skilled workers' autonomy appealed not to explicitly anticapitalist ideas but rather cultural values asserting workers' intelligence, independence, dignity, and self-respect—all inherent in the parochial (and sexist) principle of "manliness." See David Montgomery, *Workers' Control in America* (Cambridge: Cambridge University Press, 1979), 11–18.

[24]Michael J. Piore, "Fragments of a 'Sociological' Theory of Wages," *American Economic Review* 63 (May 1973), 378. This is much more likely to occur, as Piore points out, in certain segments of the labor market—namely, the "lower tier of the primary sector," dominated by skilled or semiskilled blue-collar males with secure employment within established corporations or within their crafts.

[25]People tend to see existing practices not as historical outcomes of unequal power conflicts but rather somehow as "normal" or "natural," and if they do perceive them as power outcomes then as a kind of stalemate in which the sense of equilibrium also suggests neutrality. By this token, when unions make major gains, they then appear to be "stronger" then employers.

to generate solidarity and mobilize militant action where individual action is risky and collective action is hard to initiate, coordinate, and sustain.[26] Shifts in traditional relationships—most commonly, disruptions in relative wages—confront affected workers directly with their impotence in the face of market or other forces that can erode their status and well-being. As their collective status sinks, groups of workers coalesce on the high ground of tradition, with its immediate moral appeal and ability to bind them in collective action against morally arbitrary change. When traditions are violated, traditionalism and militancy go hand in hand. Ideological radicalism may or may not spread, depending importantly on the rigidity of elite reaction.

Tradition does not militate against all change. Increases in wages are always welcome, but when they upset existing distributional patterns, they often disturb industrial peace. Attempting to negotiate wage adjustments that win moral approval because of their structure, unions therefore usually apply a limited principle of equality: *impartiality or equality of change.*[27] Some degree of equality in pay practices—if only those concerning allocation of pay increases—is thus for unions a fundamental corollary of "fairness as tradition," assuring them some degree of membership approval of union-regulated wage adjustments.

The principle of equality of change is not so strong that it cannot be contravened by another rudimentary but powerful principle of equality—that like is treated like and similar similarly, where relevant "likeness" is defined according to values workers themselves apply to rank their jobs (e.g., difficulty, training, skill, responsibility). Where equal or "comparable" work is not equally or comparably remunerated, as is often the case within or between enterprises, regions, or industries, unions can apply the idea of pay equity to justify intentional deviations from "equal" distribution of income changes.

The universalistic proto-egalitarianism of workers based on these two simple principles—equality of change and like is treated like—is a fact of enormous significance for union organizations trying to harness and direct the collective power of wage earners. It is also, I argue, *their greatest resource.* By generalizing, unions distill more expansive principles of fairness to be applied to more encompassing member groups, thereby tapping and harnessing workers' moral sensibilities for broader purposes. Unions can, in the words of Seymour Martin Lipset and

26See Piore, "Fragments," 379.

27H. A. Turner, "Trade Unions, Differentials and the Levelling of Wages," *Manchester School* 20 (1952), 237 and 241. See also Hyman and Brough, *Social Values and Industrial Relations,* 47, where they cite evidence that workers are more exacting in their demands for equality in change than equality of condition.

Martin Trow, "manipulate the reference groups" of their membership in attempts to influence their "sense of pertinent similarity" with other groups.[28] In doing so, they can alter and develop the underlying traditions in the moral economy of wage earners, if only by giving workers a group identity that extends their universalistic orientation to larger numbers and a greater variety of workers.

Unions thus reformulate what workers consider to be desirable pay relations throughout regions and industries and help loosen traditional pay structures supported by parochial norms of fairness in individual enterprises or separate crafts. Broadly encompassing unions expand parochial, myopic bases of comparisons that inform workers' perceptions of injustice. The norms of dominant unions tend to spill over into others that bargain for allied and neighboring industries.[29] Union-sanctioned pay structures become the norm to be defended against employer power and market disturbances, while the collective power of individual wage earners is aggregated and refocused in defense of new principles of fairness.

THE DRIVE FOR EQUALITY

Hard evidence that unions shape workers' normative orientations regarding distribution is more difficult to find than is evidence about their influence over the objective distribution of wages. Some evidence does suggest that unions succeed in changing wage structures, largely in an egalitarian direction. Indeed, it would be rather surprising if they failed, for it is still true, as Sidney and Beatrice Webb asserted in 1897, that "among trade union regulations there is one which stands out as practically universal, namely the insistence on payment according to some definite standard, uniform in application. Even so rudimentary a

[28]This is often brought on by the dynamics of inter- and intraunion competition over recruitment of members or member support in union elections. Lipset and Trow, "Reference Group Theory and Trade Union Wage Policy," In Mirra Komarovsky, ed., *Common Frontiers of the Social Sciences* (Glencoe, Ill.: Free Press, 1957), 403. Related points about the "structure of comparisons" have been made in William Brown and Keith Sisson, "The Use of Comparisons in Workplace Wage Determination," *British Journal of Industrial Relations* 13 (March 1975), 23–53; Arthur Ross, *Trade Union Wage Policy* (Berkeley: University of California Press, 1948), 6 and 49–57; Hyman and Brough, *Social Values and Industrial Relations,* 74 and 84–89; and Piore, "Fragments," 380.

[29]See W. G. Runciman, *Relative Deprivation and Social Justice* (Berkeley: University of California Press, 1966); Richard Scase, "Relative Deprivation: A Comparison of English and Swedish Manual Workers," in Dorothy Wedderburn, ed., *Poverty, Inequality and Class Structure* (Cambridge: Cambridge University Press, 1974), 197–216; and Turner, "Trade Unions, Differentials and the Levelling of Wages," 260.

form of combination as the 'shop club' requires that all its members shall receive, as a minimum, the rate agreed upon with the foreman for the particular job. The organized local or national union carries the principle further, and insists on a Standard Rate of payment for all its members."[30]

In the United States, for example, "pattern bargaining" has generated a great deal of wage uniformity within skill categories, even though by European standards collective bargaining is highly decentralized. In answering the question "What do unions do?" Richard Freeman and James Medoff conclude that despite the relatively small size of the union sector in America, unions' net effect on the whole U.S. labor market has been an equalizing one.[31]

The history of the evolution of trade unionism suggests that a union's expansion and growing strength in collective bargaining tends to equalize wage income between skill groups in the sectors it organizes. Between 1939 and 1951 in Britain, H. A. Turner argues, other plausible explanations for the leveling that took place do not suffice: "What is clear is that trades unionism—whatever its effect on the relative shares of workers and employers—has the profoundest impact on the distribution of income among the organized working class itself."[32] A fairly broad consensus holds, on the other hand, that unions do relatively little about the overall "functional" distribution of income between wages and profits.[33]

Turner's explanation for wage leveling is the "downward expansionism" of craft unions during the twentieth century, which caused unions to apply leveling policies to attract recruits from among low-pay, badly organized, unskilled workers. As the Swedish case shows, membership recruitment is certainly not the only motivation for leveling. There it was union leaders' desire for organizational unity against employer power that caused blue-collar unions to equalize wages within and

---

[30]Webb and Webb, *Industrial Democracy* (London: Longmans, Green, 1902), 279.

[31]Richard B. Freeman and James L. Medoff, *What Do Unions Do?* (New York: Basic Books, 1984), 78–94.

[32]Turner, "Trade Unions, Differentials," 232ff., 250, 270, 275.

[33]Cameron, "Social Democracy," 172–73. See also Allan M. Cartter, *Theory of Wages and Employment* (Homewood, Ill.: Irwin, 1959), 167–72; Michael Kalecki, "Class Struggle and Distribution of National Income," in his *Selected Essays on the Dynamics of the Capitalist Economy* (Cambridge: Cambridge University Press, 1971); Albert Rees, *The Economics of Trade Unions* (Chicago: University of Chicago Press, 1977), 94–96; Charles Mulvey, *The Economic Analysis of Trade Unions* (New York: St. Martin's Press, 1978), 140. Cf. Barry T. Hirsch and John T. Addison, *The Economic Analysis of Unions: New Approaches and Evidence* (Boston: Allen & Unwin, 1986), 175–76. Debate continues on the varying microeconomic impact of unions on profits. See Freeman and Medoff, *What Do Unions Do?* 181–90.

across firms and industries to an extent unparalleled elsewhere.[34] By the late 1970s, for example, hourly earnings for women in Swedish manufacturing came closer to those for men than anywhere in the world, despite Sweden's international leadership or near-leadership in (1) the degree of sexual segregation in the industrial division of labor, (2) the participation of women in the labor force, and (3) the proportion of women in part-time employment—factors that would lead one to expect relatively low pay for Swedish women. By contrast, in the late 1970s American women earned around 62 percent of what men made, whereas European women ranged between 66 percent in Switzerland and 87 percent in Sweden.[35]

As regards interindustrial pay leveling, the evidence suggests that peak-level centralization has had a strong effect in Sweden. However, comparative evidence, especially from Austria and Italy, suggests that other factors, including market and governmental, must also affect the movement of interindustrial pay differentials.[36] Formative experiences and moral commitments made in the historical process of centralization in Sweden were decisive in shaping later union policy and successes. The explanation of trends elsewhere has to take the same things into account.

The socialization of officials in the value of internal leveling in centralized industrial unions is part of the historical process. Although interoccupational leveling is not as universally compelling as the drive for pay standardization within skill and occupational groups, practically all national unions at one time or another, or even perennially, call for compression of skill differentials.[37] This is most surprising

---

[34]Ingvar Ohlsson, "Den solidariska lönepolitikens resultat," in LO, *Lönepolitik och solidaritet: Debattinlägg vid Meidner-seminariet den 21–22 february 1980* (Stockholm: LO, 1980), 216–27. On the weaker influence of unions before peak-level centralization, see Gösta Rehn, "Unionism and the Wage Structure in Sweden," in John T. Dunlop, ed., *The Theory of Wage Determination* (London: Macmillan, 1957), 222–37.

[35]See Patricia A. Roos, *Gender and Work: A Comparative Analysis of Industrial Societies* (Albany: SUNY Press, 1985), 38–66. Statistics from Earl F. Mellor, "Investigating the Differences in Weekly Earnings of Women and Men," *Monthly Labor Review,* June 1984, 17–28, and Ohlsson, "Den solidariska lönepolitikens resultat," 216–27.

[36]In Austria, institutionalized wage setting is highly centralized, yet interindustrial differentials increased consistently in the postwar period; in Italy, fragmented, decentralized industrial relations brought considerable leveling. Peter Hedström and Richard Swedberg, "The Power of Working-Class Organizations and the Inter-Industrial Wage Structure," *International Journal of Comparative Sociology* 26 (March–June 1985), 90–99.

[37]An informative but dated comparative international study is Lloyd G. Reynolds and Cynthia H. Taft, *The Evolution of Wage Structure* (New Haven: Yale University Press, 1956), especially 185–86 and 365–67 on unions' success in interoccupational leveling. Negotiated nonwage benefits also have a leveling effect. Vertically organized industrial unions in the United States, such as the United Auto Workers and the United Steel

when one considers the universal dominance of better-paid skilled workers in blue-collar union hierarchies. Some support for leveling comes of course from the interests of skilled workers in reducing employers' incentives to replace them with cheaper unskilled labor, by making the latter more expensive. Ideological forces also may help erode traditional defenses of pay differentials by sensitizing the entire active membership to low-pay workers' appeals for extraordinary consideration. For example, in applying what Arthur Ross calls "coercive comparison" against employers as a way of elevating their members' wages with respect to other groups' wages, union leaders often reach beyond the principle of equal pay for equal work and activate more humanitarian and egalitarian sensibilities of those disturbed by the financial plight of low-pay workers. By extension, such appeals give the official stamp of approval to demands by low-pay groups *within* the union for special increases of their own.

In this example, egalitarian socialization is a process initiated by the union leadership itself, but the process probably occurs in a spontaneous fashion from below as well.[38] Across time and cultures, spontaneous mobilization at the level of the workplace is commonly accompanied by demands for egalitarian compression of pay differentials by means of absolute, across-the-board increases. Increases calculated as percentages based on the existing structure often strike workers as unfair. This was as true for American workers early in the century as for European workers in the spontaneous mobilization of the late 1960s and early 1970s.[39]

Thus when union leaders officially sponsor mobilization, pay egalitarianism is a likely though not inevitable call to arms. In inflationary times, the need to mobilize against the uneven erosion of real wages and erratically widening wage differentials often triggers the

---

Workers, increased their insurance-type benefits between 1947 and 1963 from less than 1 percent of straight-time wages to as much as 15 percent. Negotiated improvements in pension, health, and welfare plans from the 1950s to the 1960s for members of the Pulp, Sulphite, and Paper Mill Workers increased progressively from 5.6 percent to 35.5 percent of total gains for each of five three-year contracts for the period. Richard A. Lester, "Benefits as a Preferred Form of Compensation," in Richard L. Rowan and Herbert R. Northrup, eds., *Readings in Labor Economics and Labor Relations* (Homewood, Ill.: Irwin, 1968), 292–93. On the statistical connection between unionization and the share of benefits in total compensation see Arnold Strasser, "The Changing Structure of Compensation," *Monthly Labor Review* 89 (September 1966), 953–58.

[38]Karl-Olof Faxén, writing from considerable knowledge as an economic expert for employers in Sweden, believes the leadership is the dominant if not the only source. "Wages and the Community," in OECD, *Wage Determination: Papers Presented at an International Conference* (Paris, 1974), 256.

[39]Montgomery, *Workers' Control in America*, 21 and 122–27.

egalitarian impulse as unions try to shore up their crumbling authority. During inflation, rigidly centralized bargaining often comes under spontaneous rank-and-file pressure for decentralization. Union leaders then frequently reaffirm their egalitarianism and raise egalitarian demands to restore support for centralization. Centralization, they vehemently insist, is indispensable for the systematic restoration and long-term protection of earlier differentials or the achievement of egalitarian objectives.[40]

Union leaders often see egalitarianism as promoting solidarity for the sake of restraint as well as for the sake of militancy. In response to government pressure for voluntary "incomes policies" to control inflation, unions will frequently demand that low-pay groups not be held back as rigidly as the better-paid. As Flanders argues, "One of the strongest appeals of an incomes policy to many wage and salary earners is the prospect which it offers of bargaining about a fairer distribution of incomes; ethical arguments are on the whole likely to be more persuasive than economic ones in gaining their consent for restraints on the play of self-interests."[41] Lloyd Ulman and Robert Flanagan, in a comparative study of wage restraint, found that unions and governments frequently act in the belief that this is the case.[42] When unions restrain wages, at least under conditions of inflation and full employment, the egalitarian drive is not held in abeyance. On the contrary, unions frequently take advantage of the situation to raise wages for low-pay workers faster than for the rest.[43]

In conclusion, there are good reasons to think that trade unionism has a built-in ratchet mechanism that pushes in egalitarian directions. Also, unions' formative experiences of conflict and cooperation with

[40]On inflation and leveling demands, see Reynolds and Taft, *Evolution of Wage Structure*, 185–86.

[41]Flanders, "Collective Bargaining: Prescription for Change," in *Management and Unions*, 191–92. A. K. Das Gupta makes a similar case for egalitarian incomes policy in India: *A Theory of Wage Policy* (Delhi: Oxford University Press, 1976), 38–39. In England, according to Hyman and Brough, "recent experience . . . suggests that . . . some reference to social justice is apparently an essential element in the public relations which surround incomes policy." This, they argue, is a "more or less cynical attempt to achieve worker and trade union support for restrictions on their bargaining activities. In this respect, notions of fairness and social justice are used for unashamedly ideological purposes." *Social Values and Industrial Relations*, 105–6.

[42]Ulman and Flanagan, *Wage Restraint: A Study of Incomes Policies in Western Europe* (Berkeley: University of California Press, 1971), 226–27. See also Paul William, *Fairness, Collective Bargaining, and Incomes Policy* (Oxford: Clarendon, 1982).

[43]Colin Crouch, "The Drive for Equality: Experience of Incomes Policy in Britain," in Leon Lindberg et al., eds., *Stress and Contradiction in Modern Capitalism* (Lexington, Mass.: Heath, 1975), 223, 229, and passim. Also Robert J. Flanagan, David W. Soskice, and Lloyd Ulman, *Unionism, Economic Stabilization, and Incomes Policies: European Experience* (Washington, D.C.: Brookings, 1983), 673–75.

employers may be critical in explaining differences in the degree to which they now push for and attain leveling. The drive for equality represents a confluence of workers' universalistic, proto-egalitarian, moral predispositions and union leaders' ability and desire to shape distributive ethics as a way of forging organizational unity and external support in varying historical circumstances.

Unions frequently call for a leveling of wages, sometimes on one dimension, sometimes on another, but it is rare in the extreme for unions to advocate increased inequality in wages or to espouse principles that call for the same. Often leveling in one direction may increase differentials in another, but rarely is the increase in differentials officially welcomed. Even when union policy sanctions inequalities by negotiating standard pay levels scaled according to skill and occupation, it also sets in motion forces to compress their spread. In action and ideology, sometimes intentionally and sometimes unintentionally, unions advance equality as active agents in the moral economy.

EMPLOYERS AND THE STATE

Nothing could be further from the truth than the idea that employers have little to gain from union pressure for leveling or that employers themselves always fight it. The history of employers' relations with one another and with unions shows that at times, *some* employers favor leveling, especially interfirm wage standardization within a particular industry and even interindustry standardization. Unions help those employers achieve it. For employers, therefore, unions are a resource with which to control the behavior of other employers competing in the same labor and product markets.[44]

Union-negotiated wage standards "take wages out of competition," as the common expression puts it. By establishing a floor on wages, unions restrict the leeway of product-market competitors to reduce prices without losing profits and thereby benefit employers facing a tight local labor market who have to pay relatively high wages. When unions reduce upward wage pressure on high-wage employers for the sake of leveling, so that industry- or economy-wide wage increases do not threaten aggregate employment, they may also help medium-pay employers hold on to workers who would otherwise be attracted away by higher wages elsewhere. High-wage employers themselves benefit

[44]John Bowman makes an interesting case for this idea, applying game theory, in "When Workers Organize Capitalists: The Case of the Bituminous Coal Industry," *Politics and Society* 14:3 (1985), 291.

from relaxed labor-cost pressures on profits. These are only some of the more important benefits to employers of active union engagement in the moral economy.[45]

It follows that structural change disturbing stable competitive relations and market shares among employers in labor and product markets will also upset the coalitions of union and employer interests that underpin stable, centralized collective bargaining. Just as a firm's long-term economic success fosters stable labor relations and the development of parochial shop-floor traditions, so relatively static competitive relations among employers provide the most stable foundations for the moral economy of labor.

This perspective on the historical background and structural underpinnings of the moral economy suggests that the instrumental behavior of union leaders in the political sphere might derive in large part from their need to foster market conditions suiting their "established forms of organization and action" in collective bargaining with employers.[46] The state, after all, can promote the development and maintenance of the moral economy by manipulating the legal and market determinants of industrial power relations.

This general proposition only suggests the more detailed analytical and historical treatment in Part II of how and why unions try to influence government policy in order to facilitate the achievement of wage distributional objectives and thereby protect or solidify their standing simultaneously with members and with employers. In the next two chapters, I turn to industrial relations in Sweden and West Germany to illustrate my arguments about the moral economy of labor, tracing the power and distributional conflicts behind its evolution and identifying how market forces can undermine union control in it. These chapters provide the basis for further elaboration of theory about unions as active agents shaping not only the moral economy but the political economy as well.

[45]Critical leftist views on this are well summarized by Hyman and Gough, *Social Values and Industrial Relations*. Freeman and Medoff give a "liberal" perspective in *What Do Unions Do?*

[46]The phrase is H. A. Turner's, from *Trade Union Growth, Structure and Policy: A Comparative Study of the Cotton Unions* (London: Allen & Unwin, 1962), 364. I share his view, and that of Allan Flanders in "Trade Unions and Politics," in his *Management and Unions*, 26–27, and Hugh Armstrong Clegg in *Trade Unionism under Collective Bargaining: A Theory Based on Comparisons of Six Countries* (London: Social Science Research Council, 1976), 6.

CHAPTER TWO

Centralized Unions:
Shaping the Moral Economy

In shaping the moral economy, unions respond to employer and government constraints from above as well as expectations of fairness from the membership below. Strategic constraints on union activity in markets and politics give form to the moral economy, which membership values and interests alone cannot. In the case of Swedish and German industrial relations, the outcome of past distributional conflicts between capital and labor—and within those classes—has bestowed more or less centralized systems of institutionalized collective bargaining upon the present. The formative events of the first half of the twentieth century shaped not only today's institutions but also the distributive policies of union leaders and, in turn the distributive values of their members.

THE UNIONS AND COLLECTIVE BARGAINING TODAY

In both Sweden and West Germany, the leaders of a relatively small number of centralized national unions, organized primarily by industry or sector rather than craft or occupation, exercise wage policy–making and negotiating authority. The seventeen unions of the German Trade Union Confederation (Deutscher Gewerkschaftsbund, the DGB), fit the vertical, industrial mold more than Swedish unions do, because they include both white-collar and manual workers among their members, although they must compete for white-collar membership with a horizontal or "occupational" union, the German Union of Salaried Workers (Deutsche Angestelltengewerkschaft).

The twenty-four affiliated unions of the Swedish Trade Union Confederation (Landsorganisationen i Sverige, LO), organize only blue-collar workers and compete with the white-collar unions not for members but over the distribution of the wage share. Recently, however, technological changes in manufacturing, especially computerization, have blurred the blue-collar/white-collar distinction, bringing with them the threat that white-collar unions might "raid" technically skilled LO members.[1] The electricians' and painters' unions are the only two craft-based unions that have not yet been absorbed into large industrial unions such as the Metalworkers' Union (Metallindustriarbetareförbundet), the Municipal Workers' Union (Svenska Kommunalarbetareförbundet), and the Building Workers' Union (Byggnadsarbetareförbundet).

Unions in both LO and the DGB, the primary focus of this book, have close ties, if only informal ones in the case of the DGB unions, with social democratic parties. The autonomy of LO union leadership from the Socialdemokratiska Arbetareparti (SAP) was established early in the twentieth century, and socialist unions similarly achieved independence in Imperial and Weimar Germany. In reconstructing the German labor movement after the fall of Nazi Germany, trade union leaders reaffirmed the principle of autonomy and now regularly coopt Christian Democratic union leaders into minor executive posts.

The principle of political autonomy was established during the take-off period for centralized collective bargaining in both countries. In Germany (unlike Sweden) leading industrialists, especially in heavy industry, fiercely resisted contract bargaining and in both countries the law did not yet recognize collective agreements between unions and employers. Under these precarious conditions for union officials, when collective bargaining was not yet institutionalized, unions fought off socialist party attempts to dominate the unions and determine strike strategy and objectives. For union leaders, then as now, "distributionist" objectives in collective bargaining, not political ones in the elec-

---

[1]The Swedish Central Organization of Salaried Employees (Tjänstemännens-centralorganisationen, TCO) has a monopoly on non-professional white-collar workers. About three-quarters of these workers are in eight unions organized on an industry basis, the largest of which is the Union of Salaried Employees in Industry (Svenska Industritjänstemannaförbundet, SIF); the rest are members of twelve white-collar occupational unions. In Germany, the unions in the German Federation of Civil Servants (Der Deutsche Beamtenbund) negotiate pay and working conditions for professional civil servants. Teachers and university faculty, however, have a union in the DGB (Gewerkschaft Erziehung und Wissenschaft). Unions in the Swedish Confederation of Professionals and Civil Servants (SACO/SR) organize higher civil servants, teachers, and professors, as well as professionals such as physicians, jurists, and economists.

toral and parliamentary sphere, dominated the agenda and justified the bifurcation of the labor movement that exists today.[2]

The degree of centralization in bargaining today varies considerably between the two countries and, within them, between industries, between occupational sectors, and over time. In Sweden, for most of the postwar period, LO and the Swedish Employers' Confederation (Svenska Arbetsgivareföreningen, SAF) have negotiatied wage settlements at the "peak" (supraindustrial) level for all manual workers in the private sector. These "central agreements" determined not only the aggregate level of contractually secured wages but also the *distribution* of nominal increases between, and to a considerable extent within, industries. The actual, legally binding, contracts were subsequently negotiated at the industrial level between individual SAF-affiliated employer groups and the LO unions. Negotiators at that level were required to interpret and apply the distributional framework of the LO-SAF agreements for the separate industries in question.[3] In turn, company-level negotiations followed to interpret and apply the industry-level contracts. Since 1982 this highly centralized system has been in decay.

In West Germany, most individual unions of the DGB jealously defend their bargaining "sovereignty" (*Tarifhoheit*) from the confederation and have never delegated administrative control over strike funds or bargaining authority to the DGB, as the Swedish unions in LO did in 1941 and the 1950s. Furthermore, most of the DGB unions conduct wage negotiations regionally, and agreements they sign at the central industrial level tend to set only the procedural and substantive framework for regional bargaining. Nevertheless, ultimate authority over wage policy and control over strike funds reside at the central level. Central coordination of regional negotiations is therefore not unusual.

German unions do not negotiate contractually secured wage increases as the Swedish unions do. For the most part, they negotiate increases in minimum rates, which employers are free to exceed. Instead of one single minimum rate for a whole bargaining region in an

[2]For details see Peter Swenson, "Beyond the Wage Struggle: Politics, Collective Bargaining, and the Egalitarian Dilemmas of Social Democratic Trade Unionism in Germany and Sweden" (diss., Yale University, 1986), 41–74.

[3]If, for example, an LO union wanted to press demands that exceeded or violated the LO-SAF agreement, LO could not support it against an SAF lockout and could conceivably expel it. Likewise, if an SAF association wanted to lock out members from a union that pressed demands consonant with the LO-SAF agreement, LO would be free to grant financial support to the union and its members, and SAF could not intervene. These commitments and powers make the LO-SAF agreements "binding."

industry, unions typically negotiate a scale of rates for different job categories, differentiated according to standard criteria of skill, difficulty, training, and responsibility. Some Swedish unions do the same, but they tend to use much less finely graded scales. Thus Swedish negotiations at the company level are legally restricted to a lesser extent in setting actual differentials. At the company level in both countries, union officials may negotiate even finer gradations than those called for in contracts as long as official minimum rates are honored. In Germany, company rates above the minimum scales are not protected by contract law and can be reduced, unilaterally, by the employer. This is not the case in Sweden.

On the surface, then, institutionalized pay setting looks more or less similar in both countries, differing only in the degree of centralization. In fact the systems differ in important ways. How did the centralized systems come into being? Why did the systems take the shape they did? Why are their differences significant?

INDUSTRY CENTRALIZATION: GERMAN BOOK PRINTERS

What propels the centralization of collective bargaining, why is it arrested in some places and not others, and what sustains it over time? The answers to these questions cannot be brief and all-encompassing. A relatively small number of decisive factors can be isolated, however, by analyzing the centralization of pay setting for German typographers and compositors at the turn of the century. The book printing industry was the first in Germany to experience centralized collective bargaining. It is of interest not only in that regard but also because early events in the industry help explain what happened in many other industries—if not at the national level, then at least over large geographical areas.

In Germany, as elsewhere, the geographic integration of labor and product market competition, and consequently the adaptive strategies of unions and employers with respect to the structuring of wages, set the process of centralization in motion.[4] When centralized bargaining relations finally took root, they were more the product of a cross-class, interfactional coalition of interests than an armistice between classes at war, for there were to be losers in each camp. The losers, and therefore

[4]See Lloyd Ulman, *The Rise of the National Trade Union: The Development and Significance of Its Structure, Governing Institutions, and Economic Policies* (Cambridge: Harvard University Press, 1955).

34

potential opposition, among both workers and capitalists were pacified by the normative as well as the coercive mechanisms of centralized wage policy. Conceptions of equity underlying wage distributional outcomes of collective bargaining "morally disarmed" internal opposition to the centralization of authority within organizations of employers and workers.

Market Integration

The motor driving the evolution toward centralized wage setting on an industry basis was the integration of labor and product markets.[5] For example, expansion of railway networks had made it easier for craftsmen to move where pay and conditions were better and, by flooding local labor markets, to undermine the accomplishments of local unions. In response, printers were among the first to form a national union, the Deutscher Buchdruckerverband, following only the cigarworkers by a year in 1866. Tailors, bakers, and woodworkers followed in 1867 and 1868.[6] Increased labor mobility persuaded union leaders at all levels of the need for centralized authority in setting nationally uniform standards of behavior. It was around this time, too, that unionists began to see the need to amass strike funds and centralize their administration for strategic targeting of action against employers with substandard pay and working conditions. By and large, this centralization of union power on a national scale aimed at and could accomplish no more than a patchwork of enterprise- and local-level union contracts, varying substantially in quality and longevity.

Though labor markets were important, integration of product markets on a regional or national scale proved to be a more powerful stimulus for the centralization of collective bargaining.[7] In the case of printers, the same economic factors that facilitated labor mobility also made the shipment of printed products possible from low-wage firms to regional markets once monopolized by high-wage firms. Sharing interests in a floor on wages (and a ceiling on working hours), and thus a damper on ruinous price competition, employers and printers in

[5]On this process in the United States, see ibid., 49–67.

[6]Georg Fülberth, "Die Entwicklung der deutschen Gewerkschaftsbewegung von den Anfängen bis 1873," in Frank Deppe et al., eds, *Geschichte der deutschen Gewerkschaftsbewegung* ((Cologne: Pahl-Rugenstein, 1977), 24. This was the take-off decade for national unions elsewhere as well; see David Montgomery, *Beyond Equality: Labor and the Radical Republicans, 1862–1872* (Urbana: University of Illinois Press, 1981), 458.

[7]Ulman, *Rise of the National Trade Union*, 175.

1896 signed a landmark agreement initiating a phase of centralized bargaining that was not to be interrupted until the 1930s.

Union and Employer Tactics

Before that phase, the year 1873 had brought the first centralized agreement into force, and centralized relations were maintained until their collapse in 1891. During those years, the spirit of confrontation did not fully dissipate; indeed, it increased over time as general economic conditions deteriorated and centralized relations collapsed. Class warfare had helped leaders forge the centralized organizations required for centralized bargaining. Not until 1896 did advancing market integration and improving economic conditions and the consequent competitive warfare among owners for market shares give a critical mass among them the incentive to treat with the printers' union in a more stable, institutionalized process.

The first national contract in book printing, and in all of Germany as well, had been signed after full-scale confrontation. Up to 1872, printers had been perfecting whip-saw tactics, picking off employers one by one in rolling strikes across wide regions of the country. Centralized control of strike funds gave the union strategic superiority, enabling it to impose leveling trends in wages and working hours on employers in what the latter called "serial slaughter" (*Einzelabschlachtung*). Whether financed by regular dues or by special assessments for a strike campaign, union funds could support a small number of strikers indefinitely and bring a single employer to his knees.[8] However, the tactic did mean a constant drain on union funds, and local successes were always vulnerable to competitive pressure from firms that had not yet been rolled over by a strike.[9] Ultimately, union officials preferred the stability and uniform enforcement of standard conditions that a central agreement would provide.

By 1872 employers had united to retake the strategic advantage and called the first industry-wide lockout (*allgemeine Aussperrung*) of all

[8]On the use of this tactic in Germany and its role in spurring the formation of employers' associations, see Gerhard Kessler, *Die deutschen Arbeitgeberverbände* (Leipzig: Ducker & Humblot, 1907), 40–41, 242–43, 329, and Alexander Wende, *Die Konzentrationsbewegung bei den deutschen Gewerkschaften* (Marburg: Marburg University, 1912), 32–33. On England and Sweden, see Hugh Armstrong Clegg, *The Changing System of Industrial Relations in Great Britain* (Oxford: Blackwell, 1979), 68; Turner, *Trade Union Growth, Structure and Policy,* 371; and Bernt Schiller, *Storstrejken 1909: Förhistoria och orsaker* (Göteborg: Akademiförlaget, 1967), 62–63.

[9]See Peter Ullmann, *Tarifverträge und Tarifpolitik in Deutschland bis 1914* (Frankfurt/M: Peter Lang, 1977), 38.

union workers in response to a single local strike. Their objective was to impose a national contract with more or less uniform standards of wages and working hours far below union demands.[10] Unpopular with the general public, the lockout backfired. Union funds were well stocked. Because of boom conditions, unemployment was low, and firms were operating at full capacity. As a consequence, immediately after the lockout decision, 20 percent of employers defected from the employers' association and most others failed to comply.[11] In the face of this defeat, the employers agreed within two months to negotiate and sign the first national agreement, with substantial compromises on every point.[12]

Between 1873 and 1891, centralized relations between the printers' union and the employers' association suffered considerably from economic crisis, as employers defected *en masse* from their organization or simply refused to honor wage and working-hour agreements. The union had the benefit of neither labor law nor full employment to enforce contract terms on wayward employers. Union weakness in this regard was critical in limiting employers' desire and interest in respecting contracts. In 1891, the union called a massive strike, and almost a third of the work force in the industry responded. But this time the union suffered total defeat within ten weeks, and for over four years printers and compositors were left to their own local defenses against employers. Centralized bargaining, inaugurated by union victory, had been destroyed by union defeat.

Centralized relations were revived five years later. This time they resulted from more than an improved "balance of power" for workers in the printing industry. A new and stable balance of power among employers had developed as well. The time around 1896 was one of intense, low-price competition from what larger, established owners in the industry called "dirty competition" (*Schmutzkonkurrenz*).[13] The established owners had come to miss the benefits of wage and price stabilization that the printers' union had promised thirty years ear-

[10]Ibid., 38–39. German and Swedish employers had a strong penchant to organize and employ the lockout in this manner compared to British employers, who were far harder to organize and more reluctant to use lockouts. See Henry Phelps Brown, *The Origins of Trade Union Power* (Oxford: Clarendon Press, 1983), 112–15, 206–7.

[11]Kessler, *Die deutschen Arbeitgeberverbände,* 240–41.

[12]Ullmann, *Tarifverträge und Tarifpolitik,* 38–40.

[13]Ibid., 49. Employers had the same incentives for centralized pay setting elsewhere. On England, see Friedrich Engels, "The Abdication of the Bourgeoisie," in Karl Marx and Engels, *Articles on Britain* (Moscow: Progress, 1975), 396, and Clegg, *Changing System of Industrial Relations,* 66. On the United States, see John Bowman, "When Workers Organize Capitalists," 289–327.

lier.[14] The union provided a useful enforcement mechanism for larger owners in the industry who wished to stem the market entry of small-scale, low-wage competitors. The leadership of the employers' association first learned this lesson during the bargaining hiatus of the early 1890s and the near-destruction of the union.

Distributional Norms

Union and employer policies with respect to the distribution of wages and uniformity of working conditions across an industry like book printing aided in the institutionalization of centralized bargaining. Institutionalization required that the central leadership of labor market organizations secure the authority to negotiate and sign agreements that would inevitably displease large segments of their membership. For employers, this segment included marginal firms that would find it difficult to compete when forced to pay contract wages and that would naturally prefer aggressive lockouts to achieve more favorable terms. For unions, members expecting to accomplish more by striking tended to be those whose employers enjoyed more favorable cost and demand conditions than their competitors.

Coercion alone helped hold these militants in line. Centrally administered union funds were deployed locally against lone-wolf employers. Strikes by nonunion workers or wildcat unionists demanding wages exceeding the norm could be refused support by the union. Their employers could hold out indefinitely with support from the central association.

Wage policies and their normative foundations also proved indispensable to the leaders of national unions and employers' associations, even before centralized bargaining, in managing opposition and independence. Apparently with few exceptions, statutes of employers' organizations in turn-of-the-century Germany authorized executive officers or ad hoc committees (or occasionally membership assemblies) to judge whether strikes against one or more employers were "justified" (*berechtigt*) or not. Two matters were at stake. First, if the strike were unjustified, the organization would be committed to support—at con-

---

[14]Ullmann, *Tarifverträge und Tarifpolitik,* 34. At their first congress in 1895, Swedish bookbinders called on employers to form their own national association in order to "stem unhealthy competition." Tage Lindbom, *Den svenska fackföreningsrörelsens uppkomst och tidigare historia* (Stockholm: Tiden, 1938), 298–99. German metalworkers in 1905 made a similar appeal. IG Metall, *Fünfundsiebzig Jahre Industriegewerkschaft 1891 bis 1966* (Frankfurt/M: Europäische Verlagsanstalt, 1966), 130. In 1887, for the same reason, the Iron Molders' Union in the United States openly welcomed the formation of a new employers' association. Ulman, *Rise of the National Trade Union,* 502–3.

siderable expense—the employers involved with any strike insurance money available. Second, if the association defended an employer who forced workers to work under "backward" conditions, other employers would pay twice—first out of strike insurance funds and then with the loss of market shares to dirty competition.[15]

The collectivization of resources for defense against workers then set in motion an inevitable process of norm setting among employers. Employers' associations in fact did judge some strikes against their own members as justified and therefore denied help. In some cases the association caused member employers to forfeit money deposits (*Kautionen*) for provoking justified strikes or to surrender managerial control to temporary trustees for negotiation with the union.[16]

With the bilateral establishment of norms, officials in employers' associations and unions empowered themselves with the capacity to disarm internal opposition to official bargaining and strike policies. This "moral disarmament" was especially important for union leaders, who also faced interminable brushfire conflict with union locals that would queue up for aid from very limited strike funds. Among these applicants were groups already enjoying relatively high wages or short hours and who could justifiably be turned away with the argument that limited resources should be used for their less fortunate fellows. In Germany, as elsewhere, this was necessarily a frequent occurrence and a strong incentive for union officials to take tutelary control of the norm-setting process—and therefore, like the printers' union, to seek centralized contracts to help tighten the organizational purse.[17]

Nationwide struggle with employers leading to national contracts probably added to the moral force of distributive norms that union officials used against internal opponents. Nothing could have helped

[15]Employers in printing did not have permanent strike insurance funds. Kessler, *Die deutschen Arbeitgeberverbände*, 290; see also 183–90, 200–206, and 289–307 on "fairness" judgments and strike insurance systems. On strike insurance in England, see Turner, *Trade Union Growth*, 377–78. On the importance of strike insurance for centralization in Sweden, see Göran Skogh, "Employers Associations in Sweden," in John P. Windmuller and Alan Gladstone, eds., *Employers Associations and Industrial Relations: A Comparative Study* (Oxford: Clarendon Press, 1984), 166.

[16]Kessler, *Die deutschen Arbeitgeberverbände*, 183–90, 206–12.

[17]Ibid., 205. German brewery workers anticipated such pressure when they resisted absorption into a union of food and beverage workers, for fear of having to stand aside for the benefit of lower-paid bakers and butchers; stucco workers likewise feared fusion with masons. Both groups suspected they would have to "foot the bill" with their contributions for strikes to close pay differentials. Wende, *Die Konzentrationsbewegung*, 43–44, 46. On the "morally disarming" nature of union policy in the United States and England, see Ulman, *Rise of National Trade Union*, 500, 602, and Turner, *Trade Union Growth*, 378–79. On union leaders' financial motivations, see Ullmann, *Tarifverträge und Tarifpolitik*, 38.

create a sense of belonging and the mutual dependence that fosters egalitarian sentiment better than the nationwide lockout in the printing industry in 1873. Thus the first industry to experience conflict on this scale was also the first to produce a union with the authority to negotiate standards across the entire country, despite considerable regional differences and traditions of local autonomy. Distributive norms written into central contracts helped immeasurably, not only in setting the terms of the moral economy but also in bolstering the authority union officials needed for stable relations with employers.[18]

Impediments to Centralization

Stable relations of centralized bargaining developed early in the printing industry, where the market was well integrated on a national level and where unions and employers were highly centralized. A decisive factor in the stable institutionalization of centralized bargaining was a cross-class coalition of distributional interests between established employers who wanted to restrict market entry by low-pay competitors and union members employed at stabilized if not fully standardized pay rates and working hours. Centralized organizations provided the coercive and moral resources to disarm opposition to the arrangement.

The printing industry was the only major sector in Germany to develop nationally centralized bargaining before World War I. In other industries where collective bargaining developed, centralization was arrested at the provincial (*Land*) level. In 1914, of individuals working under union contracts, about 28 percent were under firm-level contracts, 17 percent under local contracts, 49 percent under regional contracts, and only 6 percent under national contracts.[19] In the construction industry, second only to printing in its reliance on collective bargaining, most contracts were local or regional in nature, no doubt because of the localized and decentralized character of competition. Nevertheless, by 1910, regional- and national-level employers had secured substantial strategic and policy control by prevailing upon local employers to synchronize contract expiration and renegotiation across the whole country, thereby weakening the unions' ability to use the

[18]Among printers, two of the most violently disputed national contracts negotiated from 1896 onward gave inegalitarian and arbitrary pay differentiation that the union accepted under employer pressure—different maximum working hours for printers and mechanics in 1896, and piece rates for typesetters in 1906. The latter gave unstable earnings because of recurrent technical problems in primitively mechanized typesetting. Ibid., 50, 55.

[19]Ibid., 231.

rolling strike.[20] Moreover, the time set for contract expiration and renegotiation was the end of March, which after a long winter's unemployment was a bad time to ask workers to strike.

An impediment to multi-employer bargaining at the regional and national level was the absolutist ideology of German employers. As "lord of the castle" (*Herr im Hause*), German industrial barons resisted the idea of handing over negotiating authority to "outsiders" such as employers' organizations, just as they tried to resist dealing with union officials "on an equal footing."[21] In crafts and light manufacturing, however, this resistance did not prevent local and regional contract bargaining from taking firm hold. The combination of the rolling strike and product competition in expanding (but not yet fully nationalized) markets made the difference.

In heavy industry, mining, textiles, and even many sectors of engineering, however, employer absolutism did not give way to collective bargaining until World War I. Three prominent reasons can be found that relate to market integration and competition. First, some of these sectors, like textiles and unlike book printing, were highly vulnerable to international competition and therefore more resistant to wage concessions that might hurt their competitiveness.[22] Market integration on a national scale seemed to encourage collective bargaining; international integration discouraged it.[23] Second, practically all the heavy industry and mining interests were integrated into price-fixing and quota-setting cartels, making unions superfluous as alternative agencies for stemming domestic competition.[24] Finally, a combination of employer paternalism in steel and coal and wage levels already significantly above those in other industries reduced the ability of unionism to penetrate the ironclad defenses, both brutal and benevolent, that employers used against it.[25] In the absence of a distributional basis for a cross-class coalition such as that characteristic of the printing industry, national unions had little chance to play a significant role in pay setting in those industries—until the revolutionary politics of postwar Germany changed the interests of the employers.

[20]Wende, *Die Konzentrationsbewegung*, 30–32; Ullmann, *Tarifverträge und Tarifpolitik*, 81–91; and Kessler, *Die deutschen Arbeitgeberverbände*, 329–30.
[21]Kessler, *Die deutschen Arbeitgeberverbände*, 195–97.
[22]Ibid., 313–15.
[23]In some textile regions, e.g., Saxony and the Thuringian states, worker militancy pressured employers into unilaterally imposing minimum pay on each other, but without negotiating the rates with the unions. Ibid., 184–85, 316.
[24]Ullmann, *Tarifverträge und Tarifpolitik*, 183.
[25]Elaine Glovka Spencer, *Management and Labor in Imperial Germany: Ruhr Industrialists as Employers, 1896–1914* (New Brunswick: Rutgers University Press, 1984), 71–129.

Book Printers and the Ingham Thesis

The interests of employers and union leaders in regulating the pay structure were critical in motivating the centralization of bargaining power in the German printing industry. This industry does not fit well into Geoffrey Ingham's widely accepted comparative explanation of centralized bargaining. According to Ingham, a high concentration of ownership and technologically integrated mass production produce the most favorable conditions for highly centralized bargaining.[26] The German printing industry, along with other old, small-scale, relatively unconcentrated, crafts-based industries were not the industries that Ingham's theory would predict as sites for the centralization that did in fact develop at the turn of the century. Employers in more concentrated or late-developing industries—like steel and coal mining—fought unions of all kinds and scorned other industrialists who treated with the enemy in centralized bargaining.

The Scandinavian countries enjoyed the conditions that Ingham said should generate highly centralized bargaining, and indeed highly centralized bargaining developed there. But whereas his explanation appears to square with aggregate cross-national comparisons of industrial infrastructure, it fails in a sectoral analysis within countries, as Peter Jackson and Keith Sisson have pointed out.[27] A detailed look at the historical process of advancing centralization in one of Ingham's Scandinavian countries shows why an explanation founded on market integration and pay-distributional coalitions fares better.

PEAK-LEVEL CENTRALIZATION IN SWEDEN

Whereas industry-level centralization in Germany, Sweden, and other countries has been common in the twentieth century, the supraindustrial centralization of collective bargaining has been rare. Businesses not competing with one another over market shares do not have an incentive to use unions to limit market entry by low-pay producers; for workers, the moral call to solidarity for the cross-industrial pay leveling that "peak-level" bargaining makes possible is weak. The

[26]Because centralized unions and employers exercise more successful power over wages and workers' norms about them, Ingham suggests, countries with centralized bargaining institutions experience very low strike levels. Ingham, *Strikes and Industrial Conflict: Britain and Scandinavia* (London: Macmillan, 1974), especially 35–44.

[27]Jackson and Sisson, "Employers' Confederations in Sweden and the U.K and the Significance of Industrial Infrastructure," *British Journal of Industrial Relations* 14 (November 1976).

development of a sense of community across industries is weakened by the segmentation of solidarity that centralized industrial bargaining creates.[28] For these reasons, only extraordinary market and political circumstances can cause peak centralization.

In Sweden, the world economy and parliamentary politics aided unions and employers in crossing the threshhold to a voluntary system of peak-level bargaining. Interindustrial competition in the domestic labor market and intense "wage rivalry" among unions combined with severe competition in international product markets to give employers compelling reasons to seek peak-level bargaining. Before this happened, Swedish employers had already created a centralized peak association with policy-making authority and lockout resources. For workers and unions in LO, the desire to secure the internationally and historically unprecedented Social Democratic control of government from the 1930s onward provided an alternative basis for overarching solidarity. Union, government, and employer collaboration helped further centralize the coercive and normative regulation of a changing moral economy.

As was the case for industry-level centralization in German publishing, peak-level centralization of union authority in Sweden was the outcome of a cross-class distributional coalition. This time, however, the economic and parliamentary interests of a nonindustrial interest group—farmers—joined in. This coalition of interests generated government institutions and policies of a new political economy, what might be called the Swedish "postwar settlement."[29] The institutionalization of peak-level bargaining in Sweden helped not only to shape the moral economy but also to generate the demand for government policies that would stabilize the alignment of interests in the political economy.

Stage 1: Taming the Building Workers

Formation of an encompassing system of peak-level pay determination for private-sector manual workers in LO proceeded in two stages. The first stage began when employer, union, and parliamentary in-

---

[28]In the United States, for example, centralized, industrial-level bargaining committed unions to discourage local units from supporting strikers outside their industry in municipal-level "solidarity strikes." David Montgomery, *Workers' Control in America* (Cambridge: Cambridge University Press, 1979), 53.

[29]See Jonas Pontusson, "Labor Reformism and the Politics of Capital Formation in Sweden" (diss., University of California, Berkeley, 1986), 67–203, and his "Sweden," in Mark Kesselman and Joel Krieger, eds., *European Politics in Transition* (Lexington, Mass.: Heath, 1987), especially 471–92.

terests aligned behind the centralization of union pay setting in at least one major industry where it did not evolve independently.

The wayward unions in this case were in the building trades—the Masons' Union (Murarförbundet), the General Laborers' Union (Grovoch Fabriksarbetareförbundet), and the Carpenters' Union (Byggnadsträarbetareförbundet). For them, centralization of union authority over pay setting and wage policy was far from complete. In 1931, the Masons' Union established, under pressure from below, that no definitive pay agreements could be signed without membership referenda and that the entire membership had to vote even on local settlements of significant size. Such referenda, a severe annoyance to employers in the Swedish Employers' Confederation (SAF), would often result in strikes even when the sum of approving members and nonvoters made up a majority of total union membership.[30]

Employers were also exasperated by the highly decentralized method of negotiating piece-rates. The national piece-rate agreement of 1924 did not list rates for new techniques that were constantly being introduced in the industry. Rates for those procedures still had to be negotiated at the work site. Between 1926 and 1930, therefore, the number of local wildcat strikes by the highly militant workers in the building trades, aiming to force through high rates on new jobs, jumped from eighteen to about ninety-seven.[31] These wildcat "sitdowns" (bodsittningar) were not called by the unions and were not actionable under the landmark labor law passed in 1928.

Militancy and decentralized bargaining in the building trades continued into the early years of the Depression, and relative wages continued to rise in an industry already paying top wage rates. Wages stagnated in other industries exposed, unlike construction, to international competition and dependent on external demand. Wages were particularly depressed for workers organized in the Swedish Metalworkers' Union, which in 1905 had signed the first national pay agreement, including nationwide wage standards, ever reached in Sweden.[32]

In 1931, when SAF began its offensive to reduce wages throughout the economy, the Metalworkers' Union was complimented by SAF chairman Sigfrid Edström (also board chairman at Asea, a major en-

---

[30]Sten Höglund, "Storföretagen, Svenska Arbetsgivareföreningen och beslutsordningen i arbetarnas fackliga organisationer," *Research Reports from the Department of Sociology University of Umeå* 45 (1978).

[31]Hartmut Apitzsch, "Byggnadsbranschen: Produktionsförhållanden och organisationsstruktur," *Arkiv för studier i arbetarrörelsens historia* 2 (1972).

[32]Bernt Schiller, *Storstrejken*, 22–25. Competitive bargaining by unions in the industry motivated both unions and employers to consolidate bargaining so that the unions could not drag one another unwillingly into costly strikes.

gineering firm) for having a leadership that "clearly has a better hold on [its] people" than the leadership in most other unions. In 1932, true to that characterization, union leaders exercised their official right to override a clear membership majority and signed mediated agreements with wage and piece-rate reductions of 4 percent and 6 percent.[33]

By contrast, the building industry was a "constant thorn in export industry's side."[34] High wages for skilled iron workers in the building industry, for example, could make it difficult to attract skilled welders into export firms. Perhaps more important than labor market competition was the dissatisfaction that interindustry differentials aroused among metalworkers, many of whom were not unsympathetic to communist and other opponents of the restrained centralized unionism that employers favored and that seemed better at leveling wages than maximizing them. Wage differentials between sheltered and competing sectors were only increasing.[35]

As early as 1926, high pay in the sheltered domestic construction, printing, and food industries caused the Stockholm local of the Metalworkers' Union to submit a motion at the LO congress calling for "solidarity-based wage policy" to be carried out by "a strongly centralized trade union movement with LO as the real leading central organization and at the head of it a strong and unified leadership."[36] The fact that the wages of construction workers were moving ahead of metalworkers' made it increasingly impossible for the Metalworkers' Union to continue satisfying membership demands in the late 1920s for wage leveling of all kinds—between skill groups, between hourly and piece-rate workers, between age groups, and between the sexes.[37] Continued leveling within the engineering industry would have meant even wider interindustry differentials between skilled metalworkers and building workers.

What the Stockholm metalworkers and, increasingly, their central leadership were asking for was, in effect, superordinate labor move-

[33]Edström quoted in Sven Anders Söderpalm, *Arbetsgivarna och Saltsjöbadspolitiken* (Stockholm: SAF, 1980), 25. See Feiwel Kupferberg, "Byggnadsstrejken 1933–34," *Arkiv för studier i arbetarrörelsens historia* 2 (1972), 15. Steel and foundry workers, unlike engineering workers, voted to accept the cuts. Höglund, "Storföretagen," 40.

[34]Sven Anders Söderpalm, *Direktörsklubben: Storindustrin i svensk politik under 1930- och 40-talet* (Stockholm: Zenit/Rabén & Sjögren, 1976), 21.

[35]See Jörgen Ullenhag, *Den solidariska lönepolitiken i Sverige: Debatt och verklighet* (Stockholm: Läromedelsförlagen, 1971), 32.

[36]Quoted in Axel Hadenius, *Facklig organisationsutveckling: En studie av Landsorganisationen i Sverige* (Stockholm: Rabén & Sjögren, 1976), 36.

[37]See Ulf Olsson, *Lönepolitik och lönestruktur: Göteborgs verkstadsarbetare* (Göteborg: Ekonomisk-Historiska Institutionen vid Göteborgs Universitet, 1970), 36–46.

ment control over construction workers' wages. Interunion leveling had become a precondition for leveling within their own ranks. Within LO as a whole, however, agreement on LO control did not materialize until a strike of the building trades in 1933. This strike threatened to bring on for the minority Social Democratic government a parliamentary crisis that only a settlement externally imposed on the building workers could resolve.

Early in April 1933, less than seven months after the Social Democrats had taken over as a minority government in the Riksdag, the construction strike broke out, bringing the industry to a halt for ten-and-one-half months. This strike helped crystallize a fragile, two-tier coalition of organizations against the building workers. The first tier was political, with the Social Democratic government at the center. On the one side was the LO leadership, representing wage earners and their unions in a radical, deficit-financed, reflationary public works program for pulling Sweden out of the Depression. Newly created jobs were to pay union rates.

Joining the Social Democrats was a recently insurgent and now dominant faction within the Agrarian party (Bondeförbundet). In exchange for support in the Riksdag for the minority government's crisis program, the Agrarians extracted from the Social Democrats a promise to exempt farm products from their traditional free-trade policies.[38] Less widely known, but nevertheless decisive, was their insistence in January 1934 on a satisfactory conclusion to the strike, which had then been going on for about nine months. The new leader of the Agrarian party, Axel Pehrsson, conditioned Riksdag support for crisis measures on the ability of the striking unions "to take account of the economic situation." In a Riksdag committee, Pehrsson's party had extracted a resolution that none of the public building projects would proceed until "unity had been achieved" between unions and employers. Responding to the Agrarian party's threat to withdraw its support for the government, LO's executive leadership itself worried aloud that unless the striking unions accepted a mediated settlement, "we must count on . . . the certain danger that it will no longer be ourselves who master events in the future. If we want to maintain the leadership in our land, we would be wise to contemplate this."[39]

Overlapping this tripartite coalition between LO, the Social Democrats, and the Agrarians was an equally important "economic" coalition

[38]On this aspect of the "crisis agreement" see Stig Hadenius, Björn Molin, and Hans Wieslander, *Sverige efter 1900* (Stockholm: Aldus/Bonniers, 1974), 125–27.
[39]Quotations from Kupferberg, "Byggnadsstrejken," 57, 17.

between unions in the export industry, above all the leaders of the Metalworkers' Union, and employers in SAF. This alliance was predicated on a political cease-fire between business and the socialist government. Gustaf Söderlund, SAF's new executive director, anticipating the possibility that the Social Democrats might hold power for a long time to come, embarked on a policy of political neutrality and partnership with LO. This policy was to some extent supported, some extent undermined, by structural changes in the economy and organizational changes within SAF. The growth and export strategy of large-scale industry had advanced the position of Liberal tendencies among SAF member firms and loosened the late nineteenth-century link between Conservatives and manufacturing industry.[40] Organizational reforms in SAF from 1928 to 1930 increased the centralization of executive authority and redistributed voting strength according to firms' number of employees, which favored such growing engineering firms as Asea, SKF, Electrolux, L. M. Ericsson, and others in the export sector.

On the other hand, the directors of these companies preferred a more militant, partisan political line against the Social Democratic government. Their opposition to Söderlund's "consensus" policies was particularly clear on the question of restrictive labor legislation, which they wanted. Söderlund eventually prevailed; he preferred that "the two sides in the labor market endeavor above all to regulate their affairs with each other on their own." Arguing against both Liberals and Conservatives on this question, he maintained that "one ought not believe that either of the sides could in the long run enjoy the protection of the state and support of its interests while at the same time preserving its freedom in other spheres."[41]

Although Söderlund succeeded in preventing SAF from being used as a political instrument of opposition against the trade unions, he did not differ from the "Directors' Club" faction of big exporters on the lockout question. For him, a lockout of the entire LO membership was a last, but acceptable, resort against the construction workers if the Social Democrats and the other unions could not control them. Thus there was no division within SAF on its hard line against the building trades unions. Should SAF fail with its aggressive lockout threats, however, Söderlund's position on the labor law question would probably

---

[40]Cf. Franklin D. Scott, *Sweden: The Nation's History* (Minneapolis: University of Minnesota Press, 1977), 397. Björn Prytz, director of the multinational ball-bearing manufacturer Svenska Kullagerfabriken, was an important free-trader active in the Riksdag and a strong figure in internal SAF politics. Söderpalm, *Direktörsklubben*, 12.

[41]Quoted in Söderpalm, *Direktörsklubben*, 15.

lose. With the defection of the Agrarian party from the crisis program agreement, moreover, the Social Democrats would no longer be in a position to obstruct the legal emasculation of the unions.

The other important link in the second tier of the coalition was the Metalworkers' Union. Between the union and its employer counterpart in SAF, the Engineering Employers' Association (Verkstadsföreningen), relations had grown heated during the early 1930s on the question of managerial prerogatives over hiring and firing. Recognizing a "strong community of interest" with export industries struggling for survival in the depressed world economy, however, the Metalworkers' Union pursued a consensual and restrained policy on the question of wage levels, to which the 1932 reductions, achieved without strikes and lockouts, bear witness.[42]

For Metalworkers' Union members, the behavior of construction trades workers must have been especially irksome. It was not only that the relative wages of metalworkers were slipping. Building tradesmen, like bakers and butchers, worked in sheltered sectors whose wage and price increases directly affected the basic cost of living of workers whose wages were falling. "Public opinion" and press hostility to the construction workers resonated in the labor movement press and in motions and debate at LO congresses.[43]

LO and its member unions did not officially vent their criticism of construction workers' wages. The LO newspaper *Fackföreningsrörelsen* and its press bureau in fact made some efforts to disprove press publicity against the strikers and their "unreasonably high wages." LO criticism delicately skirted the matter of the wages of the strikers and instead focused on the strike tactics used, especially by Communist firebrands. LO even extended some support from its funds to strikers, though interestingly it refused aid to the large majority of nonstrikers laid off because of the strikes. That work came to a stop was often the result of militants, especially among the unskilled laborers organized by the General Laborers' Union, who struck without prior official sanction. Their union was under pressure from LO to coordinate limited, local actions with the two other unions involved.[44]

Thus the leadership of LO showed deep ambivalence about militancy in the building trades. Ultimately, however, the Social Democrats' crisis program offered a strong justification to take action in line with metalworkers' interests and against the strong tradition of autonomy for individual unions and their internally democratic self-regulation.

[42]Söderpalm, *Arbetsgivarna*, 25.
[43]Kupferberg, "Byggnadsstrejken," 16–18; Ullenhag, *Den solidariska lönepolitiken*, 54.
[44]See Kupferberg, "Byggnadsstrejken," 18–20.

The general climate of disgruntlement if not outright hostility toward construction workers made it possible for LO to intervene, on shaky constitutional grounds, in the internal affairs of the building unions and put an end to the strike.

Motivated by the threats of Draconian lockouts from SAF, the withdrawal of Agrarian party support for the crisis program, and government intervention, LO's representative council (the *representantskap*, an authoritative decision-making body consisting of the leaders of each of LO's forty-one unions) invoked a relatively obscure LO statute that, in a novel interpretation, empowered it to enjoin the unions to call off the strike.[45] The outcome was a two-pronged attack against the status quo. Not only did the construction workers have to accept 12–15 percent piece-rate reductions, far exceeding those the metalworkers had accepted in 1932. They also lost the "free piece-work" clause that allowed decentralized strikes and negotiations on new techniques. Both irritants in construction, wage differentials and upward wage drift, were thus ameliorated. Before the strike, average hourly wages for male construction workers were more than 170 percent of the average for all male industrial workers; immediately afterward that figure dropped to about 130 percent. Engineering workers' wages remained stable at about 106 percent.[46]

LO's extraordinary intervention against the construction unions saved the Social Democratic government and its crisis program. It was the first in a series of moves that increased the Metalworkers' power within a strengthened and centralized LO—at the expense of the higher-pay unions in sheltered domestic industries. The developing political climate helped too, as the political tier of the alliance against the construction unions was strengthened and formalized by the creation of a coalition government in 1936 between the Social Democrats and the Agrarian party.

Equally important for the Metalworkers' Union was the 1935 report of a large Royal Commission appointed by the Social Democrats and in which both LO and SAF participated. The so-called Mammoth Commission (Mammututredningen) had been asked to find ways to improve national economic performance and material welfare. Labor peace was the center of attention. In this "central document for the understanding of consensus politics in Sweden at the end of the

[45]Members of six involved unions conducted separate referenda on a second government-mediated agreement; only four unions accepted the agreement. Aggregation of the results for all six produced a yes majority, and LO invoked its newly interpreted right to step in on that basis. Kupferberg, "Byggnadsstrejken," 29.
[46]See Ullenhag, *Den solidariska lönepolitiken*, 123.

1930s," two major points of agreement were affirmed: first, the critical importance of export industry and the development of its competitiveness for Sweden's economic future and well-being; second, the need to centralize decision making within and between unions and employers.[47]

LO and SAF set about fulfilling the recommendations of the commission and thereby helped consolidate and formalize the economic tier of the cross-class coalition. In 1936, after positive experience with cooperation in the Mammoth Commission, they began constructing the apparatus for pacifying labor market relations. Both declined government offers to participate in these negotiations. The SAF delegation to the negotiations in the pleasant resort town of Saltsjöbaden was dominated by export industrialists. The Metalworkers' Gunnar Andersson, who had (significantly) just become vice-chairman of LO, was accompanied in the delegation by Johan Larsson, from the same union.

Union representatives from outside the export industry included Hilding Molander of the Food Industry Workers' Union, a sector whose sheltered status, associated with craft-based, small-scale production by skilled bakers and butchers, was beginning to erode and whose relative wages were just beginning their long downward slide. The low-pay Wood Industry Workers' Union sent Oscar Karlén. This union would soon become one of the most outspoken advocates of peak-level wage bargaining and nationwide leveling of wages. None of the three major unions in the building trades was represented.

The Saltsjöbaden Agreement of 1938 was the product of a cross-class coalition against high-pay workers in sheltered industries. The "Spirit of Saltsjöbaden," which was to govern LO-SAF relations for three decades, did not, understandably, immediately infect high-pay workers in construction, printing, and a few other industries. This reticence applied in particular to high-pay foundry workers organized in their own craft union, who had been fighting since 1912 against LO plans for their absorption into the Metalworkers' Union.[48]

The Saltsjöbaden Basic Agreement (*Huvudavtal*) was in many respects a codification of existing practices in the labor market outside the building industry. Most important in this context were the restrictions on boycotts and blockades, methods characteristic of strikes in construction more than anywhere else. Peak-level control in the hands of SAF and LO was institutionalized in a Labor Market Commission, with three representatives from each side, for resolution of dis-

---

[47]The characterization is from Söderpalm, *Arbetsgivarna*, 28.

[48]Söderpalm, *Arbetsgivarna*, 33. On the foundry workers see Hadenius, *Facklig organisationsutveckling*, 137–60, and Ullenhag, *Den solidariska lönepolitiken*, 19–21.

putes between constituent units of the two organizations. Furthermore, a Labor Market Committee was established as a permanent negotiating and decision-making body to resolve problems in training and apprenticeship, work safety, and pensions, as well as to work out less conflict-prone and economically destabilizing bargaining practices throughout the economy.[49]

The agreement on such questions was not binding on any LO union wishing to ignore them, and the construction unions, joined by the high-pay Typographers' Union, would not sign.[50] Nevertheless, LO committed itself at Saltsjöbaden to "work toward" the implementation of similar provisions in all centrally negotiated industrial agreements, affirming its general commitment to centralize bargaining authority within its unions and to make union authority more uniform from one union to another.

LO formalized its commitment to centralization in 1941, seven years after the construction strike and two years into a socialist-led national unity coalition of four parties formed to deal with the wartime crisis. At the 1941 LO congress, 320 delegates against 17 opponents and 15 abstainers voted to revise LO's statutes and the conditions to be fulfilled by constituent unions, thereby greatly increasing the central power of the LO's executive and representative councils.[51] Expulsion of unions from LO was made possible for the first time. Most important was the restriction that no union could call a strike involving more than 3 percent of its members without LO approval. The executive board's right to participate in member unions' contract negotiations was established in principle, as was its right to intervene with proposed settlements, which, if not accepted by the union, could lead to the withdrawal of LO strike support. LO could now take the initiative in the offensive use of strikes and offer financial help. Previously, LO could only help unions in their defense against lockouts.

Finally, "standard by-laws" (*normalstadgar*) were drawn up to be adopted by the forty-six constituent unions as their own. The most important feature of the by-laws made the executive leadership of the individual unions the sole authoritative body (below LO) in collective bargaining policy and conflict strategy. This provision would put an end to membership votes on wage agreements—a special source of

[49]Between its establishment and 1972, the Labor Market Committee met sixty-four times, often making decisions "which were of central significance for the development of Swedish society." Interruption in cooperation occurred only once, during the 1945 strike by the Metalworkers' Union, when Communists temporarily held sway within the organization. Söderpalm, *Arbetsgivarna*, 35.
[50]Ibid., 33, and Hadenius, *Facklig organisationsutveckling*, 55.
[51]Hadenius, *Facklig organisationsutveckling*, 62.

exasperation to LO and employers during the building trades strike. From then on, such referenda could be used only as a "consultative" device, and thus fell into disuse by the 1970s.[52]

Clearly, the 1941 reforms conformed to all the trends and interests that had produced an end to the construction trades strike, the crisis program of the Social Democratic and Agrarian parties, the Mammoth Commission report, and the 1938 Basic Agreement at Saltsjöbaden. Most of the small number of individuals voting against the reform were either Communists or delegates from construction unions. Critical debate came from representatives of unions in sheltered industries, all from either high-pay unions or, in the case of the Metalworkers' Union, ideologically radical opponents of the central leadership. Finally, as Axel Hadenius notes, "the strongest support for the proposed reform came—aside from the LO leadership—from the predominantly low-pay unions."[53]

By 1941, the Metalworkers' Union had actually joined the high-pay unions, losing genuine interest in peak coordination and interindustrial leveling—a fact often ignored in the recent past by Metalworkers' officials who give credit to their union for initiating the idea. This reversal came about because the wartime economy had favored metalworkers' wages and hurt wages in construction. Nevertheless, the union, like others, finally supported the reform. The metalworkers recognized that LO needed the power to control unions in a good bargaining position when their independent wage campaigns threatened to set other unions—and strikes—in motion, thereby undermining Social Democratic control in the government, or inviting government management of union affairs on terms set in part by Conservatives sharing power in the wartime coalition.[54] Also, the Metalworkers' Union had secured considerable power within LO's executive board, probably reducing its fears about granting more power to LO.

In sum, the hopes of low-pay unions in the 1930s helped put peak LO coordination on the agenda. By 1941, wartime concerns ensured passage of organizational reforms that gave LO formal powers of central control.[55] This control was used with caution and reluctance, how-

---

[52]In the 1920s and 1930s, LO unions held 170 and 150 referenda respectively. In the 1940s usage dropped to 88; in the 1950s only 48 were held. Two were held in the 1960s, and none in the 1970s. Ibid., 173.

[53]Ibid., 58–63, quotation from 60.

[54]Hadenius, *Facklig organisationsutveckling*, 45–68, and Sten Höglund, "Centralisering och reduktion av medlemsinflytandet i en stor facklig organisation," *Research Reports from the Department of Sociology, University of Umeå* 52 (1979).

[55]Swenson, "Beyond the Wage Struggle," 151–56.

ever, just as Metalworkers' officials expected. Although LO did take over control of pay negotiations during and for a time after the war, it restricted itself to negotiating and managing pay freezes, not pay redistribution in favor of low-wage industries. Full institutionalization of peak-level bargaining did not come until the late 1950s. Between 1949 and 1951, under severe pressure from the Social Democrats and lacking alternative equitable solutions, LO and its unions agreed to accept continued pay freezes to deal with unexpected high levels of employment and the destablizing effects of the booming Korean War economy. Strains among LO unions associated with the freezes produced general agreement that in the future, the unions should conduct their own, industry-level negotiations. What they and employers learned from decentralization under full employment set in motion a new phase of peak-level centralization. A new cross-class alliance secured the stability of this centralization and LO's new leadership in the moral economy.

Stage 2: Institutionalizing Peak-Level Bargaining

By 1951, LO unions and their membership would no longer tolerate pay freezes negotiated at the peak level by LO and SAF. Strong but uneven wage drift—wage increases paid by employers above contractual increases—during the freezes made it appear that both organizations were holding wages back even though individual employers were willing to increase them. In 1951, the LO unions and the LO executive council felt it wise to decentralize. In their separate negotiations, many unions pushed aggressively for high increases, to make up for lost time and to catch up with sectors that had experienced high wage drift in the preceding years. Afraid of losing further ground, officials from different unions nervously pushed, for safety's sake, for high settlements. Thus began the classic inflationary Swedish wage scramble (*huggsexan*).

The following year the unions agreed to the government's plea for pay freezes but insisted on cost-of-living indexing. SAF in turn refused to allow any of its member associations to negotiate wage indexation on their own and thereby forced all but five of the LO unions to hand over the negotiating of wage increases and real-wage protection to LO. The result in 1952 was the first peak-level LO-SAF agreement that involved neither direct government participation nor a simple freeze on existing contracts.

The 1952 agreement was also the first of many to provide for wage leveling across industries. Previously, the pay freeze had been a way of "coordinating" negotiations legitimated in part by the appearance of distributional neutrality. Now, however, high and uneven wage drift after pay freezes had exposed that neutrality as a fiction. In 1953, the LO unions submitted to government pressure to freeze wages by prolonging existing contracts in the separate negotiations of that year. LO encouraged the unions to do so, citing gloomy predictions for the economy. This time, however, LO agreed to support a limited strike by the Food Industry Workers' Union, (Livsmedelsarbetareförbundet), which insisted on pay increases to make up for its recent, exceptionally rapid, downward slippage.[56] The employers locked out a large portion of remaining workers in the industry, and the conflict ended after about two months with a compromise giving the foodworkers' union only slightly more than unions that had held back.

LO, stung by severe internal criticism for agreeing to the foodworkers' strike, stepped out of the ring in the following two rounds, which took place under extremely favorable economic conditions. By the spring of 1955, however, the tide had turned again: the Social Democratic government pressured for restraint, and consensus grew among union leaders about the necessity for central coordination. One probable reason was that the year before, SAF had managed unilaterally to impose its own "incomes policy" on LO unions by refusing to allow any of the sectoral employers' organizations to sign separate agreements until all were finished and reasonably uniform. The historically aggressive and not quite tamed Paper Workers' Union (Pappersindustriarbetareförbundet)—one of the loners in the 1952 wage round[57]—responded to this provocation by calling four thousand members out on strike. In their strong and growing export industry, employment and production volume for paper and pulp workers had grown faster than for workers in any major industry except metals and engineering. Productivity growth was even higher, and relative wages had been growing. The bargaining position of workers here was obviously good. In the pulp industry, wages in the 1950s had even caught up with the recently declining averages for metalworkers, a potential irritant threatening the restraint of the Metalworkers' Union. On behalf of employers in the paper industry, SAF answered by threatening

[56]Despite stable employment levels and decent productivity increases after the war, average hourly wages for food industry workers fell from as much as 110 percent of industry average before the war to 91 percent in 1953 (male, manual workers only), with a big decline between 1951 and 1952. Ullenhag, *Den solidariska lönepolitiken*, 75–76; T. L. Johnston, *Collective Bargaining in Sweden: A Study of the Labour Market and Its Institutions* (Cambridge: Harvard University Press, 1962), 307.

[57]Workers in the paper industries, like construction workers, figure prominently in SAF strategy. On their early obstreperousness, see Höglund, "Storföretagen."

to lock out half a million more workers, a majority of manual workers in *all* industry.[58] The fate of the paper workers' demands would then have rested in the hands of LO had not the government jumped in to mediate, perhaps staving off another massive conflict like the one in 1909.[59]

Whether because of SAF's aggressive and unified action in 1955 or LO's general concern for economic stability and the Social Democrats' economic policy, LO received its unions' unaminous approval to negotiate on their behalf in 1956.[60] From that year until the wage round of 1982–83, a total of twenty-seven years, LO and SAF centrally controlled the overall level and in part the distribution of contract wage increases for practically the entire private blue-collar labor force.

This is not to say that peak-level negotiation was a foregone conclusion after 1956, even in the minds of LO leaders.[61] In 1957, the LO unions once more demanded separate, industry-level negotiations, but again SAF demanded central negotiations, refusing to allow any of its associations even to issue bids to the unions. The separate unions could have called immediate strikes and faced total defeat as a result of SAF lockouts or else submitted to government intervention.[62] Instead, they chose to submit to SAF's demand for centralized negotiations with LO.

SAF's forceful strategy was decisive in the extension of LO authority over wage negotiations in order to bring wage formation under control. Informed observers and participants concur on this point.[63] But why did such an arrangement endure? What could have provided the cement for a potentially unstable balance of power among the LO unions?

---

[58]Hadenius, *Fackling organisationsutveckling*, 86. The taming of the Paper Industry Workers' Union was probably a top item on SAF's agenda. See data in Johnston, *Collective Bargaining in Sweden*, 306, and Ullenhag, *Den solidariska lönepolitiken*, 176.

[59]On the wage-distributional problems setting off the 1909 lockouts and strikes, see Schiller, *Storstrejken*, and Swenson, "Beyond the Wage Struggle," 125–33.

[60]Hadenius emphasizes employers' actions. *Facklig organisationsutveckling*, 86.

[61]Even in the mid-1960s, central "coordination" did not seem to LO chairman Arne Geijer to be taken for granted, if his remarks to the representative council are any indication. See Geijer, "Lönepolitik och förhandlingsformer," in Erik Zander, ed., *Fackliga klassiker: En antologi kring facklig demokrati, ideologi och lönepolitik* (Stockholm: LO/Rabén & Sjögren, 1981), 155, 160–61.

[62]Gösta Edgren, Karl-Olof Faxén, and Clas-Erik Odhner emphasize government threats of tax and forced savings legislation in "speeding up the development toward centralization." *Lönebildning och samhällsekonomi* (Stockholm: Rabén & Sjögren, 1970), 28.

[63]See, for example, SAF's Karl-Olof Faxén, "Wage Policy and Attitudes of Industrial Relations Parties in Sweden," *Labour and Society* 2 (January 1977), 63–65; LO's Rudolf Meidner, *Samordning och solidarisk lönepolitik* (Stockholm: LO/Prisma, 1974), 12, 13, 31, 34, 37 and his "Några funderingar kring den solidariska lönepolitikens framtid," in Landsorganisationen, *Lönepolitik och solidaritet* (Stockholm: LO, 1980), 171; and Gösta Rehn, "Idéutvecklingen," in ibid., 51.

The coercive power of SAF was unlikely to have sufficed by itself in maintaining centralized LO control. In any case it did not need to. Over time LO established its tutelary leadership and a degree of moral authority over its member unions as it outwardly defended the egalitarian justification for the structure of pay increases hammered out in intense struggles for power and autonomy. Those conflicts were at first open and seemingly irresolvable. For example, in 1952, the first postwar year in which LO negotiated wage increases (not freezes) directly with SAF, eight high-pay unions in construction and printing trades and one low-pay union in the paper industry refused to grant proxy bargaining authority to LO.[64] The remaining LO unions united on the question of LO leadership but differed on the structure of pay increases. Clearly in the majority in the representative council, the low-pay unions held firm against standard percentage increases. Experience during the wage freezes in 1949 and 1950 had shown them that they were clear losers from such an arrangement, whereas relatively high-pay workers—for example, in the construction trades and in engineering—actually benefited from substantial wage drift, leaving the low-wage unions further behind. Restrained central agreements of *any* sort, not just freezes, would have similar effects for the low-wage unions, which tended also to be low-wage-drift unions.[65]

In the end, the LO executive council, mediating among LO unions, negotiated a mildly redistributive settlement: women, who benefited little from wage drift, would get increases of 10 percent and men only 8 percent.[66] Everyone would get at least ten öre per hour if the percentage increases did not bring their hourly wages up by at least that amount.[67] SAF hoped not to set a precedent with this "broken-line" increase, and neither did the Metalworkers' Union and other better-off unions.

But the events of 1952 repeated themselves in 1956: the Social Democratic government enjoined restraint; the Metalworkers' Union lead-

[64]Hadenius, *Facklig organisationsutveckling*, 82.

[65]Studies of the period 1952–1961 show that workers in the above-average pay sectors—construction, mining, metallurgy, engineering—also had above-average wage drift, whereas such low-pay sectors as textiles and the food industry received less. Ullenhag, *Den solidariska lönepolitiken*, 100.

[66]Women received generally low hourly wages and were less likely to do piece work, and receive its drift advantages, than men.

[67]This is a simplification of a rather complex multistep procedure for calculating and distributing the wage increases of this and following years. What an individual worker actually received in contract increases was determined in separate, industry-level negotiations, with the "cost framework" or the aggregate increases that could be distributed in those negotiations being based on what that amount *would be* if workers received increases conforming to the formula. In other words, distribution between industries was egalitarian; distribution within industries could still go either way.

ership resisted extra increases for low-income unions; pressure from
the latter unions eventually brought Axel Strand, the LO chairman,
around to their point of view, because the broken-line formula was the
only way to convince all the unions to accept coordinated negotiations
with SAF. As LO chairman Arne Geijer put it in 1958, "the reality is
that LO officials function more or less as arbitrators in the bargaining
delegation"—which included delegates of individual unions. Sum-
marizing the problems of LO in settling its intramural conflicts,
Hadenius says that "finding some wage distribution, which at least to
some degree could satisfy all diverging union interests was, as the leadership saw it, at least as hard as reaching agreement with SAF later on."
SAF strenuously fought the broken-line formula but gave in when LO
announced it could not negotiate for its unions unless such an agreement could be reached. For SAF, centralization was more important
than percentage increases for all. Industry-level negotiations, apparently, were harder to control, as the dynamics of wage rivalry among
the unions made it impossible to keep wage-push inflation in check and
maintain Sweden's export position intact.[68]

The consensus behind egalitarian pay increases as the basis for centralized negotiations was at this time still weak. After all, solidaristic
wage policy at the beginning reflected, as Hadenius says, merely a new
balance of power within LO favoring the low-pay unions. Internal
conflict over the 1956 agreement led the next year to unanimous support among the LO unions for industry-level negotiations. The LO
leadership promised to restrict itself to monitoring negotiations, to
keep demands moderate, and thus to stifle inflation that might be
released by rampant wage rivalry among the unions. But SAF would
have none of the desired industry-level negotiations. The 1957 agreement, reached after LO had received belated authority to step in, was
again a "differentiated" one aimed at reducing wage differences
among the unions.[69]

Within a few years, "solidaristic" agreements laying out the distributional structure of wage increases across and within the various industry-level bargaining units gradually became the norm, and union support for peak-level "coordination" (*samordning*) became a matter of
course. After one interruption in 1959, when SAF successfully forced
through a straight percentage increase for all unions, increasingly
egalitarian agreements were reached. In 1960, SAF began accepting—

[68]Geijer quoted in Hadenius, *Facklig organisationsutveckling*, 92. On SAF see ibid., 84–
86.
[69]See Ibid., 90. The agreement was for a two-year period. The first year's increases
were "broken-line," the second, percentage increases.

and even preferring for easy calculation of their total effects—straight across-the-board increases in absolute öre figures.[70] Agreements containing across-the-board absolute increases for all unions plus special "kitties" (*potter*) for low-wage groups became the norm by 1964. By 1966 special clauses providing for automatic compensation for wage drift were included for the sake of unions, predominantly low-pay ones, with little or no drift.

By the mid-sixties the Metalworkers' former chairman, and now the LO chairman, justified solidaristic wage policy and LO centralization as the only way of dealing with the low-pay problem.[71] Arne Geijer's total conversion to coordination and solidarity gives an idea of the moral force of LO's solidaristic wage policy. By 1969, the Metalworkers' Union was decisive in forcing through special clauses that would appear regularly in the LO-SAF agreements guaranteeing not only egalitarian increases between industries but also within them. Metal employers previously had not been obliged to agree to internally egalitarian increases, which the union wanted, so low-pay workers within the union were being denied the benefits of solidaristic wage policy.[72] In 1973, a delegate to the Metalworkers' congress recalled in floor debate how in the beginning, solidaristic wage policy—and therefore disproportionately low pay increases—unleashed "a lot of racket" (*mycket gny*) at his workplace. However, he said, "today most of the Metalworkers' members accept it." Leveling of wage incomes had by the mid-1960s become an end in itself, legitimating LO's continued authority as the organized representative of all blue-collar wage earners. LO even began justifying the anti-inflationary arguments for wage restraint and economic policy demands by reference to its commitment to egalitarianism: experience had showed that inflation increased wage drift and therefore unions' inability to control pay developments in an egalitarian fashion.[73]

In conclusion, the Metalworkers' initial resistance to peak-level bargaining and the reasons for it illustrate both the pragmatic and the moral bases of the long-term egalitarian consensus. The union's recalcitrance contained an irony: in the 1920s and 1930s, the union had

[70]Until 1966 for time-wage earners only—e.g., 18 öre in 1960 and for piece-rate workers "broken line": 3 percent but at least 16 öre.

[71]See Geijer's speech at a Social Democratic party congress in 1967, reprinted as "Inkomstutjämning och lönepolitik," in Zander, ed., *Fackliga klassiker*, 162–72.

[72]This clause was the so-called *stupstocksregel*, which said that unless the union wanted otherwise, the aggregate allowable increases in the metal industries would be distributed in an egalitarian fashion specified in the LO-SAF agreement.

[73]Delegate quoted from Svenska Metallindustriarbetareförbundet, *Protokoll: Svenska Metallindustriarbetareförbundets Kongress* 26/8–31/8, 1973 (Stockholm: Metall, 1974) 405. See Landsorganisationen, *Lönepolitik: Rapport till LO-kongressen 1971* (Stockholm: LO, 1971), 107.

been a vocal proponent of "socialistic wage policy" and LO centralization for that purpose. Then the context had been Depression-level
demand for export products, wage rivalry with the construction workers, and fear that the latter might sabotage Social Democratic recovery
policies.[74]

The Metalworkers' initial submission to the idea of peak bargaining
and solidaristic wage policy in the 1950s was a pragmatic reaction to the
coalition of interests against the union—similar to the forces operating
against the autonomy of construction trades unions in the 1930s. SAF
was intent on and capable of imposing some kind of control, resorting
to lockouts if necessary. The Social Democratic government's stability
would suffer, motivating government intervention against the union.
Finally, the numerous low-pay unions formed a majority in LO's col-
legial representative council for setting bargaining strategy.

Of particular interest is the employers' position against the Metalworkers' Union, and their willingness to accept egalitarian wage increases to treat intense, inflationary wage rivalry. In the 1950s, the
proportion of all industrial wage earners employed in engineering was
approaching 40 percent. Because of the expansionary momentum, and
despite rapid productivity increases, this "overheated" industry suffered chronic labor shortages. Labor supply bottlenecks, in combination with the increasing use of piece work systems—whose introduction
the Metalworkers' Union gladly accepted during the 1940s' pay freezes, fully in the "spirit of Saltsjöbaden"—kept the union in the high-
wage-drift league it had joined since the 1930s.[75]

In the full employment economy of the 1950s, low-pay unions with
low wage drift remained fully capable of pressing demands independently for "compensation" for metalworkers' wage drift, despite relatively slow growth and even job losses in their industries. Comparative
bargaining aimed at reinstating differentials required the low-pay
unions to demand percentage contractual increases that would exceed
those for metalworkers. Strong productivity growth and generally favorable employment levels made such increases possible.[76] If the low-

[74]The practice of recruiting LO leaders from the Metalworkers' Union is sometimes
said to compensate the union for its disadvantages in central negotiations. It probably
also helps explain LO's forgetfulness about the union's deviation in the 1950s when they
talk about its egalitarianism and advocacy of peak control in the 1920s and 1930s.

[75]Söderpalm, *Arbetsgivarna*, 68, 71; Gösta Rehn, "Finansministrarna, LO-ekonomerna
och arbetsmarknadspolitiken," in Jan Herin and Lars Werin, eds., *Ekonomisk debatt och
ekonomisk politik* (Stockholm: Norstedt, 1977), 217.

[76]In the food, beverage, tobacco, garment, and textile industries, 1945 employment
levels exceeded those of 1958 by 107–111 percent. Increases in productivity per work
hour between 1939 and 1958 in the paper products industries, in the food, beverage, and
tobacco industries, and in the textile and garment industries all *exceeded* productivity
trends in the metal industries. Johnston, *Collective Bargaining in Sweden*, 307.

pay unions were to succeed, crude comparisons of contract increases in percentage terms would appear to put metalworkers behind in the race and therefore generate intense dissatisfaction with leadership in the Metalworkers' Union—hence the "ratchet effect" on pay demands and the inflationary free-for-all.

The LO-SAF formula for differentiated increases in the 1950s eliminated the need for comparative independent wage bargaining and gave concessions by the Metalworkers' Union a moral imprimatur. Export employers, dominant in Verkstadsföreningen (VF) and SAF, in principle opposed leveling but probably benefited, since pay in that sector was relatively high and would be held back somewhat—especially before wage drift, whose distribution could be controlled to a large degree by employers themselves. The fact that LO as a whole, with the Social Democrats' support, imposed the egalitarian formula on the union did not, however, cast a totally unfavorable light on the union's leadership as far as members were concerned. The new reasons for "solidarity" (restraint) appealed to the same principles that the union's leaders themselves applied for *internal* control. As Gösta Rehn writes, "At the beginning of the war, there were already some who thought that the Metalworkers' Union had blundered by becoming the standard bearer for the idea of solidaristic wage policy in 1936. Certainly they had been the underdogs then, but now that they were better off, it gave them the moral obligation to show solidarity even when it was to their disadvantage." Over time, as LO expert Rudolf Meidner emphasizes, the result was a "successive strengthening of LO's moral authority vis-à-vis the unions," including the powerful Metalworkers' Union. This moral authority gave LO officials power exceeding even what was officially conceded in its statutory revision of 1941.[77]

WEIMAR GERMANY: PEAK CENTRALIZATION ABORTED

The Swedish case suggests that the evolution of peak-level centralization is unlikely to be fully autonomous from politics. Politics played a far smaller role in the evolution of centralized bargaining at the industrial level, where the distributional orientations of unions more consistently suited the market-control objectives of established employers. Nevertheless, politics did play a role in Germany, where the formation of strategically well-equipped national employers' associations at the turn of the century resulted in part from a growing recognition that

[77]Rehn, "Idéutvecklingen," 39; on the moral force of the egalitarian wage policy, see 27–28. Meidner, "Några funderingar," 171.

the state was an inadequate and unreliable partner for controlling the growing workers' movement. When it was reliable, the government gave revolutionary meaning to worker demands through statutory repression while only partially containing them.[78]

Some employers' organizations did not accept collective bargaining with unions on any level until the revolutionary politics following World War I forced them to do so. Heavy industry had formed the Verein Deutscher Eisen- und Stahlindustrieller (VDESI) at the turn of the century in order to crush the union movement, not contain it in institutionalized relations. In 1918, however, facing the prospect of a Bolshevik-style revolution, heavy industry hastily recognized national unions and bolstered their political stature and organizational authority by engaging them in centralized bargaining. This action aimed primarily to forestall revolution and restore order by filling the vacuum left by a state in shambles. As Ewald Hilger, coal magnate and bitter opponent of unions and all they stood for, said to his fellows, "Yes, gentlemen, we should be happy that the unions are still prepared to negotiate as they have; for only by negotiation, above all, with the unions, only through agreement with the unions can we avoid anarchy, Bolshevism, Spartacist rule and chaos—call it what you will."[79]

Hilger was defending the so-called Stinnes-Legien agreement, which led to a six-year experiment with the Zentralarbeitsgemeinschaft (ZAG), a pyramid of joint labor-management committees from the peak level down to industrial and regional levels.[80] The ZAG resembled in some ways the peak-level regulative apparatus set up twenty years later at Saltsjöbaden in Sweden.[81] To the extent that politics played a role in Saltsjöbaden, by contrast, reformist unions and private industry there were forestalling encroachment on their autonomy from above by a strong state, not revolutionary destruction from below.

By the mid-1920s in Germany, once government authority had been reestablished in the hands of centrist and conservative parties, bolstered by the virtually intact Imperial bureaucracy, judiciary, and army, it was the coal and steel industrialists who first violated the terms

[78]Kessler, *Die deutschen Arbeitgeberverbände*, 191–92.

[79]From a 14 November 1918 executive board meeting of the VDESI, quoted and translated in Charles Maier, *Recasting Bourgeois Europe: Stabilization in France, Germany, and Italy in the Decade after World War I* (Princeton: Princeton University Press, 1975), 60.

[80]Hugo Stinnes was the owner of a conglomerate of coal mining, iron and steel, electrical power, shipbuilding, and forestry/newspaper enterprises, and was associated with the VDESI; Carl Legien was the head of the Confederation of Free Trade Unions (the ADGB), which was closely but informally associated with the Social Democratic party.

[81]Despite the ZAG's collapse, Swedish employers had studied it with interest. Söderpalm, *Arbetsgivarna*, 35.

and the spirit of their settlement with the unions. Their methods included legal challenge, legislative lobbying, and finally lockout assaults against both the substantive and the institutional compromises of 1918. The major substantive issue was the eight-hour working day. Also under attack were the legal buttresses of regionally centralized industrial bargaining, especially compulsory state arbitration (*Zwangsschlichtung*) and government-decreed imposition of arbitration awards (*Verbindlichkeitserklärung*) for entire bargaining regions.

But politics in revolutionary and postrevolutionary times cannot explain all of the events in Germany from 1918 to 1924. The distributional implications of economic crisis for both unions and employers played a central role, just as they did in Sweden during the world depression of the 1930s. In Sweden, employers' interests in overarching control of the interindustrial wage structure had motivated export-oriented employers to use the lockout capacity of the peak employers' confederation to bring high wages and militancy in sheltered domestic industries under control. One can find analogous circumstances behind the ZAG.

The evolving interindustrial pay structure of Wilhelmine Germany played an important and overlooked role in shaping the organizations whose interests came into play after 1918. Unlike in Sweden, pay in the building trades, the most significant sheltered industry, did not far exceed pay levels in heavy industry, engineering, and mining—where the most successful opponents of collective bargaining in all its forms held sway.[82] In fact, the reverse may be true. Prewar wage and earnings statistics in both countries are not good, and reliable comparisons are hard to make. If the statistics kept by the Imperial workmen's compensation insurance system are to be trusted, however, building workers' yearly earnings for 1908 averaged only 60 percent of earnings in mining, 66 percent of those in engineering, and 72 percent of what iron and steel workers earned. That same year in Sweden, the problems of building workers on strike or locked out aroused little sympathy from officials in many other unions, who noted that wages in the building trades were the highest in the country.[83] However, accurate comparison with Germany is impossible, for high turnover combined with employers' reporting methods meant that the German data seriously underestimated building workers' earnings.[84]

[82]State insurance office figures show that in 1913 there was one worker in construction for every two workers in iron mining and steel, other metals, and engineering. No other sheltered industry with high wages (printing, brewing) was one-tenth the size of the combined mining and metal industries. Calculated from Ashok Desai, *Real Wages in Germany* (Oxford: Oxford University Press, 1968), 114–15.

[83]Percentages from Ibid., 110; on other unions see Schiller, *Storstrejken*, 79.

[84]Desai, *Real Wages in Germany*, 13.

A clearer picture comes from a comparison of contract wages for German building workers in 1913 with average wages of metalworkers and anthracite miners who were not yet covered by collective bargaining. Contractual wages for skilled masons and carpenters in major cities and industrial locations were only incrementally higher than average wages for skilled metalworkers and amounted to only 90 percent of average wages for faceworkers in mining.[85] Because contract rates in construction were often minimum rates, average wages actually paid would have been higher, but probably not by much, since rates in the industry were still fixed at a relatively decentralized level, close to what could be afforded locally. Furthermore, *wage* ratios overestimate the yearly *earnings* of construction workers relative to the earnings of metalworkers and coal miners, whose work, being less seasonal in nature, generated more steady earnings.

Unfortunately, only limited statistics are available for Sweden. In 1913, the only prewar year for which data can be found, the average hourly earnings of adult men in the building trades was 56 öre; in mining and metal manufacturing, 48 öre.[86] Comparisons for the 1920s also support the idea that pay differentials between construction on the one side and mining and industry on the other were significantly greater in Sweden than in Germany. In 1924, Swedish construction workers, skilled and unskilled, earned 156 percent of hourly contract wages in iron-ore mining, iron and steel works, and engineering. Between construction and iron, steel, and copper works the figure was 175 percent.[87] From 1924 to 1928 in Germany, the hourly contract wages of skilled construction workers started at 91 percent and peaked at about 126 percent of skilled metalworkers' wages. For the unskilled, the range was between 120 percent and 150 percent—generally lower than the aggregate Swedish figure. Between skilled construction workers and anthracite miners (faceworkers), the range was 88 percent to about 113 percent. For unskilled building workers and unskilled miners (haulers and surface workers), the range was 123 percent in 1924 to 169 percent in 1925, after which it fell back to about 145 percent in 1928.[88]

---

[85]Computed from Statistisches Reichsamt, *Statistisches Jahrbuch für das Deutsche Reich: Jahrgang 1928* (Berlin, 1928), 371. Similar figures can be found in Gerhard Bry, *Wages in Germany, 1871–1945* (Princeton: Princeton University Press, 1960), 451.

[86]Gösta Bagge, Erik Lundberg, and Ingvar Svennilson, *Wages in Sweden: 1860–1930* (London: King, 1933), 250.

[87]Kungliga Statistiska Centralbyrån, *Statistisk Årsbok för Sverige: Tolvte Årgången 1925* (Stockholm, 1925), 206–7.

[88]Statistisches Reichsamt, *Statistisches Jahrbuch 1928*, 371. In Sweden, between 1924 and the early 1930s, the stated ratios held fairly steady between construction and engineering, while iron-ore mining wages caught up considerably with construction wages. Ullenhag, *Den solidariska lönepolitiken*, 173.

Individual employers, such as the Krupp company, the colossus in steel, engineering, and mining—who dominated in employers' associations—paid wages very close to those received by skilled construction workers, even if many others in engineering did not. For example, Krupp in Essen paid metalworkers on average RM 5.91 a day in 1913, augmenting that sum with significant welfare benefits, especially housing. Carpenters throughout the Reich earned daily wages of about RM 5.74, although the variation was great between cities, reaching RM 7.38 and 8.10 in Berlin and Hamburg.[89] Although Gustav Krupp (von Bohlen und Halbach) kept a low political profile, his executives continuously held leading positions in the powerful organizations that pushed for heavy industry's interests in politics and against collective bargaining. Alfred Hugenberg was the chairman of the Krupp Direktorium in 1909 and from 1911 until the war was a member of the board of the Zentralverband Deutscher Industrieller (ZDI), a national organization representing heavy industry in politics. Earlier, Max Roetger had held Hugenberg's position at Krupp and became chairman of the ZDI in 1909. From 1908 until 1913 he was chairman of the Hauptstelle der Deutschen Arbeitgeberverbände (HDA).[90] The HDA was the more intransigent of the two employers' confederations at the time in its opposition to Social Democracy, unionism, and collective bargaining.[91]

Thus in prewar Germany, unlike in Sweden, dominant steel, engineering, and mining industrialists—especially in the Ruhr district—had little reason to foster unions through collective bargaining. Paternalist practices and relatively high wages paid to attract and keep labor from the East probably weakened the appeal of unionism to many workers.[92] High-level employer collaboration in blacklisting, procurement of strike breakers, strike insurance schemes, and lockouts intimi-

[89]Jürgen Kuczynski, *A Short History of Labour Conditions under Industrial Capitalism*, vol. *3, pt. 1: Germany 1800 to the Present Day* (London: Muller, 1945), 180, 184. On the high wages of the Ruhr, see Spencer, *Management and Labor in Imperial Germany*, 81.

[90]See Hartmut Kaelble, *Industrielle Interressenpolitik in der Wilhelminischen Gesellschaft: Centralverband Deutscher Industrieller, 1895–1914* (Berlin: de Gruyter, 1967), 209–12, and Gerhard Erdmann, *Die deutschen Arbeitgeberverbände im sozialgeschichtlichen Wandel der Zeit* (Nuewied/Berlin: Luchterhand, 1966), 72–73.

[91]The other, the Verein Deutscher Arbeitgeberverbände, tended to include employers in small-scale light manufacturing, and tariff opponents such as those in the chemicals industry.

[92]The strong "iron-rye" political coalition of industrial and agrarian interests brought high tariffs, which allowed relatively high wage costs to be passed on in the form of higher prices. When necessary, German exporters of intermediate goods sold at lower prices to foreigners than to Germans. Finally, technical superiority of products and closer proximity to eastern markets more than made up for higher wages and prices. On the last point, see Desai, *Real Wages in Germany*, 102–4.

dated the rest. Moreover, oligopoly pricing practices in heavy industry probably sufficed to neutralize domestic price competition without the wage floors that unions promoted for other industries such as printing.

Perhaps equally important, the absence of a large differential between coal and steelworkers' wages on the one hand and skilled craftsmen's wages in construction on the other reduced the pressure for overarching, supraindustrial control of wages outside coal and steel that competition for labor and wage rivalry between sectors would have generated, and as construction's sheltered wage leadership did in Sweden. Early on, Swedish employers in metals and engineering had been willing to hand over bargaining authority to representatives within their industries and then beyond, to representatives of peak employers' associations like SAF. There, interindustrial solidarity among some employers was motivated as much by their desire to control and benefit from unions in others' industries as in their own.

It is no surprise, then, to discover that in Germany, in addition to the political motivations behind mining and heavy industry's reversal to support peak-level coordination by the ZAG in 1918, there were motives analogous to the desire of Swedish export employers to control construction wages. In this case, the culprits were not building trades workers but coal miners. According to the workmen's compensation insurance office, miners' yearly earnings had topped all others' by 1900.[93] By 1913, the average hourly and weekly wages of anthracite miners easily cleared average and contract wage levels in all other industries. After collective bargaining was established in the Weimar years, these contract wages remained the highest until sometime in the middle of 1924, when construction wages finally overtook them—only to be brought down below heavy industry's by the Nazi regime.

During World War I, labor shortages, miners' militancy, and the strategic importance of uninterrupted coal output put further upward pressure on miners' wages relative to others. Miners also oriented their demands toward the increasing relative wages of metalworkers in the munitions industry, which faced only inept government efforts to force them to hold down prices and wages. Resulting coal price increases demanded by the industry generated inflationary price increases as well as new wage demands in other industries. The miners themselves would then demand increases, thus closing the vicious inflationary circle.[94]

Problems with militant miners did not end with the war, and the

[93]Ibid., 109–10.
[94]Gerald Feldman, *Army, Industry, and Labor in Germany, 1914–1918* (Princeton: Princeton University Press, 1966), 388–89.

common desire to contain them united employers and unions, including the miners' union, at the peak level in the ZAG. On the one hand,
all sides recognized the need to favor mine workers. At stake in 1918
and 1919 was the necessity of attracting workers back to the mines and
increasing coal production; within the ZAG there was general agreement about maintaining peak wages for miners and giving them priority in food and clothing supply. On the other hand, at the ZAG level
employers wanted to use unions and collective bargaining for the first
time to hold the line against reductions in miners' working time.
Miners, having already obtained seven to seven-and-a-half hour shifts
in April 1919, were demanding six-hour shifts by the end of the year.[95]
As a result, miners had become "fully isolated within the labor movement" due to a widespread feeling that they "had the entire economy
by the throat." Carl Legien, head of the socialist trade union confederation (the ADGB), publicly chastised miners for their lack of solidarity
with the rest of the proletariat and for their potential "ruination" (Ver-
wüstung) of Germany.[96]

Had the miners succeeded in reducing working hours further while
keeping their high wages and special privileges, militants would have
spread similar demands to other industries, especially metalworking.
Bitterly resentful of the unions' collaboration in the ZAG against the
revolutionary workers' council movement, the militant faction of the
Metalworkers' Union (Deutscher Metallarbeiter-Verband) at the 1919
Stuttgart congress, had only months before taken over and pulled the
union out of the ZAG. Miners' successes would have helped pull less
radicalized members in that and other unions under the influence of
the revolutionaries, just as the smaller Catholic and liberal miners'
unions had uncharacteristically fallen in with the militants in support
of the six-hour shift.[97] For all German employers, then, ZAG coordination of centralized collective bargaining provided a collaborative instrument to hold the line against further reductions in coal miners' working hours. For the other unions, consensus in the ZAG provided some
insurance that employers in individual industries would not break
ranks politically and press Reichstag parties for the legal freedom to
increase working time.[98] It would also prevent miners from using their

[95]Erdmann, Die deutschen Arbeitgeberverbände, 136.
[96]Gerald Feldman and Irmgard Steinisch, Industrie und Gewerkschaften 1918–1924: Die
überforderte Zentralarbeitsgemeinschaft (Stuttgart: Deutsche Verlags-Anstalt, 1985), 62, 60.
[97]Ibid., 61. The standard eight-hour day had been the most important substantive and
distributional concession to the unions underlying the 1918 arrangement. The Reichstag
had subsequently established it in law, and miners were now reducing working time
further.
[98]The ZAG, however, had to rely on the government and the threat of military intervention against miners to impose the consensus, since a lockout, by interrupting production, would have been self-defeating.

favorable bargaining position to extract reductions in working time that other unions could not keep up with.

Another distributional basis existed for cross-class collaboration in the ZAG: the interests of large chemical, machine, and electronics manufacturers, as well as iron, steel, and pulp producers, in the centralized setting of export price floors by the ZAG's export control board, which represented both big industry and labor. These industrial sectors wanted to prevent smaller firms from waging the uncontrolled price competition that the undervalued currency and low wages made possible. Such competition would provoke foreign charges of dumping and international punitive action while reducing foreign exchange earnings and exacerbating a trade deficit due to Germany's continued need for high-priced imports of raw materials. The profits earned by commercial exporters would be spent, it was feared, on the import of consumer and luxury goods instead of on investment and raw materials to increase big industry's productivity and capacity. Control of export conditions would benefit big business and secure employment in the new union strongholds, stabilizing newly established but institutionally precarious collective bargaining. Finally, it is reasonable to assume, the unions would have had a keen interest in preventing intense price competition in exports, which would disrupt pay standardization and therefore maintain strong downward pressures on wages.[99]

Clearly, then, the mutual interests of big industry and labor included complex distributional as well as political issues. Overarching control of the labor market, to the extent it was facilitated by peak-level resolution of both political and economic interests, aided both dominant employers and the unions. As soon as economic and political conditions changed, however, the coalition would fall apart. The stabilization and revaluation of the Mark in 1920 and 1921 and the rise of German prices to world levels made the corporatist export control board superfluous in its attempts to maintain price floors. The crisis in coal production had been largely overcome, and even coal magnate Hugo Stinnes, a founder of the ZAG, rebuffed its attempts in 1921 to intervene in order to mediate and prevent strikes over union efforts to renew the overtime pay agreement of 1920. By 1923, galloping inflation brought total disarray to the interindustrial pay structure, with chaotic, rapidly leapfrogging pay adjustments at the industrial and regional level. Most important, rapidly increasing unemployment and catastrophic membership losses for the unions gave coal and heavy industry the bargain-

[99]In 1919, ADGB union official Wilhelm Jansson was even joined in the ZAG by Jakob Reichert from the iron and steel industry in calling for the ZAG to increase German export prices immediately to world market levels. Feldman and Steinisch, *Industrie und Gewerkschaften,* 67.

ing power to do away with the eight-hour day. The fall of the *grosse Koalition* and the Stresemann cabinet over legislative extension of the eight-hour day opened the way, legally and politically, for any industry to attack the substantive and procedural roots of the ZAG consensus.

The consensus had been brittle and could never have been more than temporary. As Gerald Feldman and Irmgard Steinisch argue, it was an "inflationary consensus" between some sectors of industry and the socialist labor movement, supporting a particular structure of increasing wage costs in industry: "When both sides were in agreement that inflationary measures were necessary for the containment of the revolution, or that reparation payments made responsible economic policy impossible anyway, they were able to justify measures whose costs consumers could be saddled with, or measures that could be covered by the printing of money. As soon as the preconditions for stabilization had to be discussed, however, all consensus proved illusory."[100]

Conclusion

A stable moral economy failed to develop in Weimar Germany because parliamentary and economic conditions never stabilized sufficiently to allow union control and "tutelage," especially in heavy industry, to take root at any level of centralization. Centralized industrial relations were founded on inflationary and therefore ultimately destabilizing distributional policy, which in turn helped destroy the grounds for consensus. Foreign demands for reparations, the occupation of the Ruhr, and unstable coalitions in the Reichstag made economic stabilization impossible without ultimately breaking the union and employer consensus. Inflamed economic conflict that the ZAG was incapable of handling inflicted severe social damage and set the stage for the tragedies of the Nazi period.

The egalitarian distributional policies supporting peak-level centralization in Sweden also had economically destabilizing and potentially self-destructive effects. Nevertheless, the balance of political power in favor of the Social Democratic party was stable enough to enable LO to use its political influence over economic policy that could help neutralize the destabilizing forces. Over time, with the help of peak-level control over wage policy and Social Democratic economic policy, LO succeeded in establishing strong ideological leadership in

[100]Ibid., 128.

Swedish society and politics, setting the ideological terms of debate at an unusually egalitarian level.

In Germany, a more or less stable, institutionalized moral economy did develop (at a less centralized level than in Sweden) after World War II. The exceptional political stability and economic growth of postwar Germany allowed partially centralized collective bargaining to stabilize as it had never done before. Starting from scratch gave the postwar union makers the opportunity to combine blue- and white-collar workers, both socialists and Catholics, into a small number of relatively encompassing industrial and officially nonpartisan or "unitary" organizations (*Einheitsgewerkschaften*). Experiences of division during Weimar and collaboration in exile during the war made organizational unity desirable. However, both unions and employers were prevented from reconstructing their organizations with encompassing peak-level authority by the Allied occupying forces.[101] The relative regional autonomy retained by West German employers' associations that was attributable in part to Allied intervention ensured that bargaining was institutionalized largely at the regional level within industries.

The distributional terms of bargaining at this level in the Bonn Republic were set during the Nazi period. As regards interindustrial pay structure, wages in the construction industry were brought down to the level of steel and engineering workers to a degree not possible even in Sweden. Destruction of the unions in the building industry as in all industries, in combination with the Nazi rearmament drive, had pulled metalworking wages back up to, if not beyond, the level of construction wages, after the latter had enjoyed exceptional upward drift during the latter half of Weimar.[102] Again, construction wages crept up slowly relative to others after the war, yet in 1960, gross weekly wages for male building workers at all skill levels were still considerably below those of workers in iron and steel and incrementally below wages in engineering.[103] This pattern would have important consequences for

[101]Union leaders who had spent time in exile in Sweden were among the most enthusiastic supporters of peak centralization. Eberhard Schmidt, *Die verhinderte Neuordnung 1945–1952: Zur Auseinandersetzung um die Demokratisierung der Wirtschaft in den westlichen Besatzungszonen und in der Bundesrepublik Deutschland* (Frankfurt: Europäische Verlagsanstalt, 1970), and Wilhelm Vorwerk, "Wie entstand die Bundesvereinigung der Deutschen Arbeitgeberverbände?" *Der Arbeitgeber* 13 (January 1961).

[102]By 1938, average hourly contract wages for skilled construction workers were Rpf 81.7 and for metalworkers in manufacturing, Rpf 79.0. *Wirtschaft und Statistik* 19 (January 1939), 24. In Silesia, hourly earnings for skilled metalworkers were about Rpf 85. Masons and carpenters were earning only Rpf 71.2 and 74.6. *Wirtschaft und Statistik* 19:20 (October 1939), 690. See also Jürgen Kuczynski, *Darstellung der Lage der Arbeiter in Deutschland von 1933 bis 1945* (Berlin: Akademie-Verlag, 1964), 169–74.

[103]See trend data in Jürgen Kuczynski, *Darstellung der Lage der Arbeiter in Westdeutschland seit 1945* (Berlin: Akademie-Verlag, 1963), 388. Average gross weekly earn-

the internal politics of the German labor movement in the 1960s and 1970s.

Nazi policy regarding interoccupational distribution also survived, largely unaffected by occupation and reconstruction, most strikingly in piece-rate methods and job evaluation schemes for differentiating pay in the metal industries. For example, the system of job evaluation and pay ranking now in use was introduced in 1942 in the armaments industries and carried over into other industries.[104] Much of the internal distributional conflict within IG Metall, the postwar metalworkers' union, crystallized around problems with the high degree of pay differentiation this system established.

Centralized union control in the moral economy depends on a political and economic environment in which stable power relations within and between unions and employers' organizations can evolve around distributional issues. How union control in the postwar moral economy is strained and maintained in the very different distributional and organizational systems of West Germany and Sweden is the subject of the next chapter.

---

ings in construction were DM 133.28 for construction workers, DM 161.17 for iron and steel workers, and DM 139.19 for workers in engineering. Statistisches Bundesamt Wiesbaden, *Fachserie 16 Löhne und Gehälter, Reihe 2.1 Arbeiterverdienste in der Industrie* (Wiesbaden, November 1960).

[104]Schmiede and Schudlich, *Die Entwicklung der Leistungsentlohnung*, 301–14.

Chapter Three

Rank-and-File Rebels:
Enforcing the Moral Economy

Governing the moral economy of the labor market is no easy task. In collective bargaining, officials in centralized unions can easily fail by the very standards they help set in the minds of members in general and of lower-level leaders in particular. Such standards may be those that helped legitimize centralized authority in the first place. Failure to enforce norms can set two interdependent processes in motion. First, members and local leaders may take matters into their own hands and with wildcat strikes try to enforce the terms of the moral economy as they perceive them. Second, and perhaps worse from the standpoint of central union officials, latent power conflicts within the union hierarchy can become inflamed as lower-level leaders gain support in their efforts to undermine the power of central leaders. Top leaders fight back, claiming with considerable justification that decentralization of authority will undermine the union's ability to maintain the distributional foundations of union solidarity and political influence.

This chapter illuminates these ideas by looking at the events of the late 1960s and the 1970s in Germany and Sweden. For the first time in the postwar period, both countries were startled by explosions of working-class militancy. At the time, it may have been reasonable to think that a revival of militant class consciousness was under way. In retrospect, we see this interpretation is wrong. Workers' demands were inspired in substantial measure by the unions' traditional principles of distributional equity. But at the same time, union officials faced credible ideological challenges to their authority from below. Demands for decentralization of control shared causes with the strikes themselves. At the root of the problem were the effects of centralized wage restraint in response to government pressures and the desire to maintain high employment levels. Restraint gave free play to the powerful distributional shocks of high profits and wage drift, upsetting the relative distributional equilibrium once associated with centralized bargaining. Unions in the two countries took varying approaches to maintain and recover authority. For Germany, the behavior of the massive Metalworkers' Union (Industriegewerkschaft Metall, IG Metall) will be the focus. For Sweden, I illustrate the point by looking at LO, the peak confederation of blue-collar workers.

Wildcat Strikes in Germany, 1969–1973

As in many other European countries, thousands of workers in West Germany broke through the institutional bonds of collective bargaining in the late 1960s and, with waves of unofficial strikes and organized internal opposition to union hierarchies, threatened to dismantle the centralized system so well stabilized since the war. As strikes in the metal industries showed, the threat emerged more from the system's failure to perform according to its own standards than from new, militant demands pressed from below.

Powerful structural and conjunctural changes in the world economy interfered with the smooth operation of centralized bargaining by Germany's—and the world's—largest union, IG Metall. As late as 1980, industries covered by IG Metall's contracts still accounted for about half of the nation's total manufacturing employment and sales.[1] Although, as David Soskice explains, the same international factors helped set off strikes in different European countries, domestic political and institutional factors explain their peculiar character and timing from country to country and industry to industry.[2] In Germany, centralized bargaining in the metal industries, and the moral economy it gave form to, patterned the strikes themselves.

The Septemberstreiks of 1969

Considering the highly charged political atmosphere of the time, marked by the collapse of the SPD-CDU/CSU coalition government and the upcoming general elections, and considering the alarmist national debate, it is intriguing that the work stoppages were essentially

[1]In 1980, the figures were 60 percent and 48 percent respectively. Andrei S. Markovits, *The Politics of the West German Trade Unions: Strategies of Class and Interest Representation in Growth and Crisis* (Cambridge: Cambridge University Press, 1986), 159.

[2]David Soskice, "Strike Waves and Wage Explosions, 1968–1970: An Economic Interpretation," in Colin Crouch and Alessandro Pizzorno, eds., *The Resurgence of Class Conflict in Western Europe since 1968*, vol. 2 (New York: Holmes & Meier, 1978), 221–46.

local and apolitical in nature. An estimated 140,000 workers from about 70 different plants and workplaces went out on strike for an average of about 3.8 days each during the short period of 2–18 September 1969.[3] By and large, the strikes were restricted to the steel industry and coal mining, whose contracts were negotiated by IG Metall and IG Bergbau und Energie (the Union of Mining and Energy Industry Workers). Both steel and coal mining had in the 1960s begun a long-term structural decline and were shedding labor. Union-sanctioned rationalization brought rapid productivity increases in exchange for job security and favorable severance and early pensioning arrangements.[4] Anger at changes in traditional work practices no doubt contributed to the strike mood.

What seems actually to have set the strikes in motion, however, was anger at wage disparities combined with high profits. A survey of workers in the Huckingen works of Mannesmann Steel and AEG's Winnenden electronics plant, which both experienced wildcat strikes, demonstrates as much. In the steel works, 86 percent of the workers interviewed responded that "unfair pay in relation to company profits" was one of the causes of the strike, and 39 percent said that either "unfair pay in comparison to other workplaces" or "unequal pay for equal work" played a role (more than one cause could be chosen). At the electronics firm, the response was the other way around: 86 percent cited wage disparities or unequal pay as the causes, whereas only 55 percent said that excessively high profits in comparison to wages were responsible.[5] Another study comparing two steel works with two coal mines produced similar results: in the steel sector, the main reason for the strikes was, in the minds of steelworkers, low pay in comparison to profit levels; low pay in comparison to other firms and low pay in comparison to recently increased wages in manufacturing were chosen as second and third reasons. In the coal mines, the rank order was reversed.[6]

Eberhard Schmidt confirms the special importance of pay disparities

---

[3]On the alarmist debate see Eberhard Schmidt, *Ordnungsfaktor oder Gegenmacht: Die politische Rolle der Gewerkschaften* (Frankfurt: Suhrkamp, 1971), 146, 152. For data and background documentation on the strikes see Heinz Jung, Josef Schleifstein, and Kurt Steinhaus, eds., *Die Septemberstreiks 1969: Darstellung, Analyse, Dokumente* (Cologne: Pahl-Rugenstein, 1969); Michael Schumann, Frank Gerlach, Albert Gschlössl, and Petra Milhoffer, *Am Beispiel der Septemberstreiks: Anfang der Rekonstruktionsperiode der Arbeiterklasse?* (Frankfurt: Europäische Verlagsanstalt, 1971); and Institut für angewandte Sozialwissenschaft, *Spontane Arbeitsniederlegungen im September 1969* (Bad Godesberg, 1970).

[4]These arrangements were worked out through the system of parity codetermination (*Montanmitbestimmung*) in the coal and steel industries, in which the unions chose half of all board representatives and the executive director in charge of labor relations.

[5]Schumann et al., *Am Beispiel der Septemberstreiks*, 229.

[6]Institut für angewandte Sozialwissenschaft, *Spontane Arbeitsniederlegungen*.

in precipitating the strikes. Striking miners in the Saarland wanted Ruhr miners' wages. Steelworkers in Bavaria and Oberpfalz struck for wages paid in North Rhein–Westfalia. Some workers justified demands on the basis of disparities within single concerns. For example, the very first strike of the September wave started at Hoesch Steel's Westfalen works, where three thousand workers took matters into their own hands after management's three-year delay in fulfilling a promise to equalize wages with two other Hoesch mills. The Kiel shipyard workers of the Howaldt yards wanted parity with Howaldt workers in Hamburg according to a similar unfulfilled promise; the strike at Rheinstahl's pressed-steel works in Brackwede was in part based on demands for parity with Rheinstahl's branches in Mulheim and Meiderich. At the Reisholz tube works in Düsseldorf, workers struck immediately when they heard that workers across the street at another firm had just received twenty pfennig more per hour for their strike efforts.[7]

High profits alone probably did not induce workers to strike. This, anyway, is how the highest officials in IG Metall saw matters. Otto Brenner, chairman of IG Metall, put it this way: "The high profits in the steel industry . . . certainly had an effect on the attitudes of the members, but could not have been decisive, for in the past twenty years high profits have often been recorded—without leading to spontaneous strike actions. Even in September, enormous profits were being made in manufacturing, but there were no strikes there." In fact, there were strikes in manufacturing, but far fewer than in steel.[8] And interestingly, employers in that sector tended to share IG Metall's view that wage differentials, not profits, caused the strikes.

In their July 1970 "Action guidelines for firms during wildcat strikes," the Confederation of Metal Industry Employers (Gesamtverband der metallindustriellen Arbeitgeberverbände, or Gesamtmetall) declared that "wildcat strikes arise mostly due to dissatisfaction with local conditions," and that of five "precipitating factors," three directly concerned wage disparities: "genuine or alleged discrepancies in the wage structure of the shop or firm," "wage increases in comparable firms," and disruption of wage relations following from "adjustments in the firm's wage-setting practices due to new contracts." Moreover, in the first two of five specific measures recommended for preventing wildcats, Gesamtmetall advocated improved communications about the

---

[7]Schmidt, *Ordnungsfaktor oder Gegenmacht,* 114–16.

[8]Quoted by Schmidt, *Ordnungsfaktor oder Gegenmacht,* 322. Brenner must have known that at least 21,000 of the September strikers were employed in metal processing. Jung, Schleifstein, and Steinhaus, *Die Septemberstreiks 1969,* 39–44.

grounds for wage differences and avoidance of wage differentials that could not be justified.[9]

But union officials did recognize the disconcerting effect of high profits. In reaction to a letter from Hoesch Steel to stockholders triumphantly announcing high dividends for 1968–69, Willi Michels, local secretary of IG Metall in Düsseldorf, said, "When I saw this letter from Hoesch, I said how can they be so stupid! Psychologically it was all wrong."[10] The "psychological" problem lay in workers' perceptions that industries earning high profits can *afford* to be fair. Steelworkers generally, more than other workers in IG Metall, had clearly identifiable reasons to be aroused by feelings of inequity. In 1969, average gross weekly earnings of steelworkers, after a decade of relative decline, had just fallen below those of auto workers. Previously high contract minima negotiated by IG Metall for skilled workers in steel also fell relative to those for workers in mechanical engineering and automobiles.[11]

Leveling of wages between steel and metal processing had not been an explicitly legitimated, morally grounded distributional policy of IG Metall. Instead, it had been a pragmatic response to structural decline in the steel industry and resultant employer pressure. No official policy existed to address the question. In effect, however, through past "pattern bargaining," IG Metall had openly committed itself to rough parity in pay trends between sectors, as negotiating results after September 1969 suggest. Pay in auto manufacturing accelerated relative to steel between 1963 and 1969; by the late 1970s pay trends in the two sectors were running closely parallel, despite worsening crisis in the steel industry.[12]

Although structural economic factors led to the relative decline in steel wages, the structure of employers' associations and bargaining inhibited IG Metall from recovering differentials quickly when a favorable opportunity presented itself. Just as in Weimar Germany, so today

[9]Schmidt, *Ordnungsfaktor oder Gegenmacht*, 333–34.

[10]Quoted in *Der Spiegel*, 15 September 1969, p. 33.

[11]In 1958, auto wages for men were 92 percent of wages in steel; after 1969, steel wages stayed consistently below auto wages. Statistisches Bundesamt Wiesbaden, *Statistisches Jahrbuch*, years 1959 through 1974; see also Industriegewerkschaft Metall, *Daten, Fakten, Informationen* 13(1982), 18–20.

[12]In official documents, IG Metall carefully avoids rigid formulations about desirable pay ratios, especially interregional and intersectoral. On the other hand, through pattern bargaining—enforcing the terms of pay settlements reached in one bargaining district on others—and by promoting the results of pattern bargaining as fair, IG Metall in effect promotes the norms of trend parity. This happens even in years when local demands and economic conditions vary considerably among IG Metall's bargaining regions. Projektgruppe Gewerkschaftsforschung, *Tarifpolitik 1977* (Frankfurt: Campus, 1978), 71–116. On effective pay trends, see Statistisches Bundesamt Wiesbaden, *Statistisches Jahrbuch*, years 1963 through 1980 (average gross weekly earnings for men).

iron and steel employers organize their affairs separately from employers in metal processing (mechanical engineering, automobiles, shipbuilding, aerospace, electronics, etc.).[13] Coordinated by the center, regional branches of the Iron and Steel Industry Employers' Association (Arbeitgeberverband Eisen- und Stahlindustrie, AGVESI) bargain with IG Metall with full formal autonomy from the peak employers' confederation (Bundesvereinigung der Deutschen Arbeitgeberverbände, the BDA) and from metal-processing employers in Gesamtmetall.

For steelworkers, insult had followed injury in August, at the beginning of a steep upward climb in production and profits for German industry, when Gesamtmetall granted IG Metall early contractual increases of 8 percent for workers in metal processing. Consumer prices were rising rapidly, and due to the undervalued Mark and price increases of up to 40 percent for steel in 1968, steel profits seemed to know no limits. Despite early warning signs, in the form of short work stoppages in steel that summer and pressure from IG Metall officials, the AGVESI adamantly refused to follow suit and renegotiate wages before the late-November expiration of the current 18-month agreement signed in 1968. In Otto Brenner's view, "the date alone of the first spontaneous work stoppages shows what worsened the situation: right in the midst of an extremely tense election campaign, manufacturing got money and steel did not. This divergence of contract expiration dates, the one before, the other after election day, in combination with the accumulated grievances, was the precipitating factor, especially since the Bundestag election campaign was fought almost exclusively over economic arguments: the price surge, profits explosion, revaluation, etc."[14]

Seeing the problem in these terms, IG Metall officials were eager to pass the blame on to the steel employers for their rigidity and manipulation of the union's outspoken desire to observe the legally enforceable "no-strike clause" (Friedenspflicht). The union then made quick amends in later years, and by 1975, contract minima for steelworkers were brought back above those for the manufacturing sector, thus stabilizing relative gross earnings at rough parity.[15]

---

[13]In the fluid postwar situation, both unions and employers were prevented from creating centralized cross-industry organizations by the Allies. The extension of the immediate postwar "Montan" codetermination law giving steel and coal unions parity board representation and labor directors on executive committees also inhibited formal association and coordination of steel and engineering employers. Markovits, *Politics of the West German Trade Unions*, 166.

[14]Quoted in Schmidt, *Ordnungsfaktor oder Gegenmacht*, 326.

[15]See IG Metall press releases (*Metall Pressedienst*) from September and October 1969, reprinted in Jung, Schleifstein, and Steinhaus, *Die Septemberstreiks 1969*, documents ap-

In sum, what happened in the steel industry in September 1969 was largely the consequence of IG Metall's insufficient coordination of sectoral negotiations. Government economic policy, employer division and obstinacy, and a steep inflationary boom in the international economy combined to make it practically impossible for the union to honor a more or less explicit distributional policy commitment to keep relative wages in steel and manufacturing in line. This particular failure explains why many of the September strikers took matters into their own hands to enforce at least some of the moral terms of their subordination as wage laborers. These terms had been institutionally violated, just as they had been institutionally secured. The militant reaction of workers was essentially conservative, whether it was led by communists or not.[16]

The Wildcats of 1973

The strike wave of 1973 revealed even more fundamental problems in IG Metall's bargaining policies and results. Some of the 1969 strikes, seen in retrospect, warned of problems that arose four years later. Again the causes lay in employers' violation of the distributional principles written into IG Metall contracts and in the mixture of incapacity and seeming indifference of the union leadership with respect to the the need for correction.

The new wave of strikes resembled the previous one in significant aspects. Aggravated by steeply climbing profits and inflation, workers' frustration began building shortly after IG Metall settled for relatively moderate pay increases in early January. Within two months, a handful of strikes in steel and manufacturing broke out. In the period from February through April, there were eight strikes; May brought at least forty-six more. Having learned from their mistake four years earlier, employers in the steel industry tried to calm things down by granting a modest one-time pay supplement of DM 280 (about 75 percent of a week's wages) at the end of May, before contract expiration. This time, however, it was Gesamtmetall that refused to follow suit, thus helping ensure that metal processing would bear the brunt of strikes. In June, the number of strikes continued to climb. July brought a temporary decline before the biggest surge in August, when over eighty thousand

---

pendix, 73–75. On post-1969 contract wage ratios between steel and engineering, see Industriegewerkschaft Metall, *Daten, Fakten, Informationen* 13(1982), 18–20.

[16]Communists and radicals of varying ideological persuasions did in fact play important organizational and communicative roles, explaining some of the rigid and oppressive—and potentially self-defeating—responses of both employers and unions.

workers struck at least one-hundred-seven firms. By November, the number of strikes had steadily declined to two. Overall, about 335 firms were affected, and over 275,000 workers struck without official sanction during 1973.[17]

A prelude to both waves of strikes was IG Metall's willing compliance with government pressure for wage restraint at the early stages of an inflationary boom. Neglecting in the winter to organize strikes against the employers' hard line when the legal opportunity to do so arose, the union abdicated considerable power over wage distribution to the market, individual employers, and finally a hot summer of spontaneous worker action.

Inflation, of course, and workers' desire to protect the purchasing power of their wages, was one of the most obvious causes of anger. In the minds of strikers, high profits afforded employers the ability and duty to fulfill what for unions in general is an elementary condition of fair play: maintain the status quo before letting one side benefit at the expense of another. High profits and the reduction of real wages did not fulfill that condition. In correcting for this in 1973, wildcat strikers, though not all successful, managed to force through a tiny rise in average real wages, something that the official wage increases would not have done.[18]

The effects of inflation and boom conditions on employers' strategies in the labor market, and therefore on income distribution, were not limited simply to disturbances in wage and profit shares. Between 1972 and 1973, as between 1968 and 1969, actual earnings rose rapidly in relation to increases in contract wages.[19] In other words, high wage drift created a growing "wage gap" between effective wages and contract minima in both steel and metal processing. In 1973, as in 1969, high wage drift seems to have contributed to rapid and uneven rates of

---

[17]Dates and figures from Walther Müller-Jentsch, "Die spontane Streikbewegung 1973," in Otto Jacobi, Müller-Jentsch, and Eberhard Schmidt, eds., *Gewerkschaften und Klassenkampf: Kritisches Jahrbuch '74* (Frankfurt: Fischer, 1974), 45–47.

[18]Aike Blechschmidt, "Abrisse der wirtschaftlichen Lage 1973/74," in Jacobi, Müller-Jentsch, and Schmidt, *Gewerkschaften und Klassenkampf '74*, 13–14.

[19]This can be only crudely established from figures in statistical yearbooks, by paired comparisons of index increases in contract wages (base years 1962 and 1970) with computed indexes for nominal wages. Comparisons of average contract increases for raw materials/production goods with effective pay increases in steel, and comparisons of average contract increases for the capital goods sector with effective increases in iron and steel production, mechanical engineering, and auto manufacturing, all show high wage drift before the strikes. Statistisches Bundesamt Wiesbaden, *Statistisches Jahrbuch*, years 1963 through 1976. See also crude aggregate measures in Jung, Schleifstein, and Steinhaus, *Die Septemberstreiks 1969*, 28–30. On German wage drift and its measurement, see Harald Gerfin, "Ausmass und Wirkung der Lohndrift," in Helmut Arndt, ed., *Lohnpolitik und Einkommensverteilung* (Berlin: Duncker & Humblot, 1969), 473–79.

wage growth between firms, thereby imparting momentum to wildcat strikes. Furthermore, in 1973—though apparently not in 1969—the structure of growing wage gaps violated intrafirm or *interoccupational* differentials as well.

In the manufacturing sector, a couple of mechanisms were probably at work.[20] First, earnings tended to drift upward for piece-rate workers concentrated in middle and upper wage groups, partly due to increased output, partly due to employers' delay in reducing piece rates in tempo with productivity increases resulting from rationalization. These earnings thus exceeded the earnings of hourly workers classified in the same or even higher categories in IG Metall contracts, who could then demand compensation from the employer on "equal pay for equal work" grounds. Because of the intensified competition for skilled labor associated with boom conditions, employers were inclined to concede. To the extent, then, that this process favored higher-pay groups and low-pay workers were left behind, the interoccupational differentials sanctioned by IG Metall's regional wage scales (*Lohnschlüssel*) of minimum rates were violated. In the metal industries, these differentials had been systematically violated anyway; now the situation was getting worse.[21]

From the mid-1960s to the early 1970s, IG Metall had been pursuing a steady policy of wage leveling in the attempt to bring up wages of women, who tended to be grouped in the lowest contract categories. For example, in North Rhein–Westfalia, the ratio of contract minima between the lowest job category and the lowest classification for skilled workers (*Ecklohngruppe*) was increased from 70 percent to 80 percent between 1967 and 1973.[22] As Figure 1 shows, this increase followed a period of noncontractual slippage in rates and appears to have had the desired effect.

Figure 1 also shows a sudden fall in the earnings ratio of unskilled women to skilled men in 1973, despite a mildly opposing trend in *contractual* ratios for that year. The relative fall of unskilled workers' wages, and women's and foreigners' in particular, can probably be attributed to the uneven spread of wage drift across skill levels, favor-

[20]For a fuller discussion, see Eckart Teschner, *Lohnpolitik im Betrieb: Eine empirische Untersuchung in der Metall-, Chemie-, Textil- und Tabakindustrie* (Frankfurt: Campus, 1977), 21–35.

[21]Within firms, the gap between actual and contractually protected wage rates increases both absolutely and proportionately with skill and wage level. See Teschner's data on seven individual firms, *Lohnpolitik im Betrieb*, 27, 189–201, where the wage gap ranges from 6 percent to 40 percent in the metal industries.

[22]Statistisches Bundesamt Wiesbaden, *Fachserie 16 Löhne und Gehälter, Reihe 4.1 Tariflöhne* (Wiesbaden, October 1981), 40.

79

Figure 1. Average earnings for unskilled women as a percentage of the average for skilled men in automobile and electronics manufacturing in West Germany

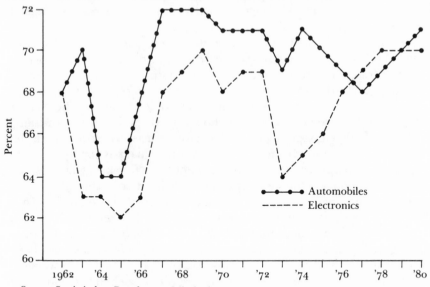

Source: Statistisches Bundesamt Wiesbaden, *Fachserie 16 Löhne und Gehälter, Reihe 2.1 Arbeiterverdienste in der Industrie,* for years 1962–80. For 1962–66 and 1972–80, the data are for average gross weekly earnings; for 1967–72, for average gross hourly earnings. Data for 1962 and 1963 include wages in aircraft manufacturing. The months were November for 1962–63; October for 1965–76; July for 1977; and October for 1978–80. Wages for West Berlin not included.

ing high-pay workers most. Why this happened in 1973 and not 1969 is not clear.

What is clear, however, is that a prominent feature of the 1973 strikes—absent in the 1969 strikes—was the militant activation of women and foreign "guest workers." These badly paid workers, least integrated into union life, took an active and often leading part in local revolts against pay and working conditions. Their demands revealed impatience with slippage not only in real earnings but also in relative earnings. In practically every case, strikers demanded "linear" as opposed to percentage wage increases, either as equal, one-time supplements for all or as hourly wage increases in absolute pfennig or Mark figures. In a number of cases, women workers demanded that the lowest-pay categories be abolished as well, which would give those who moved into higher categories extra pay increases.[23]

[23]See Godula Kosack and Stephen Castles, "Gewerkschaften und ausländische Arbeiter," in Jacobi, Müller-Jentsch, and Schmidt, *Gewerkschaften und Klassenkampf '74,* 176; Müller-Jentsch, "Die spontane Streikbewegung 1973," 48; and Horst Kern, "Die Bedeutung der Arbeitsbedingungen in den Streiks 1973," in Jacobi, Müller-Jentsch, and Schmidt, *Gewerkschaften und Klassenkampf '74,* 34.

Pierburg-Neuss, for example, a large auto parts manufacturer employing about three thousand workers, came to a halt over twelve concrete demands raised by low-pay workers. Two of the most important demands and five of the rest dealt directly with questions of pay structure bothering the largely female and foreign work force. Most important were demands for the elimination of the lowest pay group and reclassification into the next of IG Metall's wage groups and for a unitary one-Mark-per-hour increase for all. Other equity demands were for equal pay for women who like men performed heavy work; for a dirty-work bonus (*Schmutzzulage*) for everyone, "since there are no clean jobs in this factory"; and for fairer distribution of overtime work.[24]

High wage drift and widening wage gaps created a further problem both times IG Metall accepted low general increases, in 1969 and 1973, letting profits and inflation run away with workers' distributional entitlements. As by law employers are obligated to pay only contract minima, extra-contractual pay (*übertarifliche Lohnbestandteile*) is a matter about which employers alone have final say. In practice, works councils frequently haggle with employers about extra-contractual changes, patterning their increases and structure generally after contractual changes (thus maintaining the wage gap). On the other hand, employers frequently exercise their right unilaterally to reduce and restructure extra-contractual pay. Employers also pressure works councils to exchange improvements in this area for concessions in other areas where they do have statutory power of codetermination. Shop-floor representatives often find both practices infuriating.

In 1973, industries such as steel and shipbuilding were experiencing a combination of high wage gaps and structural decline (due to low-wage international competition). Employers were thus strongly tempted both to reduce pay, at least with respect to other industries, and to increase internal differentials in order to save costs and enhance productivity. The wage gap had become, as union officials put it, a "playground" (*Spielwiese*) for employers, an area where unions had no legal right to tread and where workers' distributional norms could be violated with impunity.

High wage gaps—frequently up to 30 percent of contract wages—created union troubles that became noticeable in 1969 and acute in 1973. In 1969, as mentioned above, differentials between extra-contractual pay levels at several of Hoesch Steel's mills set off the first of the September strikes at Westfalen, and the same problem brought strikes to the Brackwede works of Rheinstahl, which paid its workers at

---

[24]Kolleginnen und Kollegen von Pierburg Autogerätebau Neuss, "Streik bei Pierburg, Neuss," in Jacobi, Müller-Jentsch, and Schmidt, *Gewerkschaften und Klassenkampf '74*, 72.

Mulheim and Meiderich better. Workers struck at Howaldt's shipyard in Kiel to achieve parity with Howaldt's workers in Hamburg. High profits meanwhile erased the impression that those firms could not afford fairness, bringing on unofficial strikes.

In the large, relatively militant workplaces in steel and shipbuilding, union authority suffered worst when employers, because of long-term structural problems, began exploiting their full maneuverability within the wage gap. In 1973, events at Mannesmann Steel in Duisburg, for example, demonstrated that IG Metall's loss of control over internal and external pay differentials had reached crisis levels. Indeed, as IG Metall officials insisted in self-defense, workers at Mannesmann struck over internal wage reforms. Earlier, their wages had been high, but since the recessionary and stagnant conditions of the mid-1960s, their earnings had become extremely unstable because of an incentive pay system that was highly sensitive to fluctuations in production levels.

In the attempt to remedy this instability, the works council had negotiated a new job evaluation system with twenty pay groups and a different performance pay system to ameliorate the "murderous" effects the earlier system had on workers as they tried to maintain steady earnings. As a result, workers got their steady pay but were reclassified so as to bring their earnings down considerably. In 1973, real wages at Mannesmann-Duisburg had declined below the levels of five years earlier.[25] Over the same period, a combination of technological improvements and labor shedding reportedly increased the intensity of work. The workers wanted reclassification of their jobs for higher pay, but Mannesmann dug in its heels and even high-handedly refused to consider a unanimous compromise worked out by a joint worker-management task force that management had sponsored.

Not surprisingly, Mannesmann workers vented their anger with a wildcat strike. IG Metall openly disapproved of the strike and admonished the strikers to return to work. Because other Mannesmann plants were dependent on rolling-mill production at Duisburg, however, the strikers were able to force through a compromise despite the company's intense resistance, complete with threats of firing and legal retaliation.

The compromise that strikers attained showed that the distributional norm-setting process at Mannesmann had become fully autonomous from IG Metall leadership. Years of employer manipulation and union impotence or indifference had encouraged the formation of demands

[25]Kollegen von Mannesmann-Huckingen, "Streiks bei Mannesmann, Duisburg," in Jacobi, Müller-Jentsch, and Schmidt, *Gewerkschaften und Klassenkampf '74*, 57.

beyond the tutelage of the centralized union. The local agreement retained very little resemblance to the standard union pay scale and the way it regulated internal differentials. For example, in addition to substantial pay increases, the Mannesmann agreement abandoned IG Metall's "analytic job evaluation system." This system—used in many firms of the metal industries—superimposed dozens of indexed and ranked job categories onto the less finely graded minimum pay scale used throughout the sector. Instead, the new pay system ranked *groups* of jobs, instead of individual ones, whereby all workers performing a set of interdependent production tasks would receive the same pay based on the highest skill level required for any single task performed by any member of the group. This unusual system departed radically from IG Metall's traditional principle of individual pay differentiation according to the job performed, and even from the core idea of equal pay for equal work within a workplace.

It is hardly puzzling that high wage drift and large wage gaps caused worker militancy to break out when and where it did in Germany. The ability of employers to violate union norms of wage distribution within and between industries and firms set waves of strikes in motion as workers tried either to enforce old norms or, in some cases, to institute new ones. Neither a widespread renewal of radical working-class consciousness nor a rejection of centralized, reformist unionism was fully under way, as many on the Left wished or expected. Had IG Metall acted *only* rigidly, indifferently, and unsympathetically—as it did at times—the process of ideological radicalization may have gone further, spreading from Communist shop stewards to normally inactive union members.[26]

In fact, IG Metall did not respond with complete indifference or impotence to the disruptive consequences of its failures. After 1969 and 1973, the leadership adopted militant postures, organized strikes, and recovered lost ground.[27] The union actively forced through higher wages in steel to restore differentials with metal processing in the 1970s. After 1973, low-pay groups in the pay scale in practically every bargaining region for metal processing were eliminated in the attempt to bring women's wages closer to men's. In North Rhein–Westfalia, for example, the union acted immediately, increasing the lowest minimum rate for unskilled workers from 75 percent to 80 percent of the rate for

[26]For discussions, see Schumann et al., *Am Beispiel der Septemberstreiks;* Schmidt, *Ordnungsfaktor oder Gegenmacht;* Horst Kern, "Die Bedeutung der Arbeitsbedingungen"; and Markovits, *Politics of the West German Trade Unions,* 202–36.

[27]Konrad Schacht and Lutz Unterseher, "Spontane Arbeitsniederlegungen—Krise des Tarifverhandlungssytems?" *Gewerkschaftliche Monatshefte* 25 (1974), 99.

the lowest category of skilled workers.[28] Other contract regions followed suit in the following years.

In this necessarily short discussion of the spontaneous strikes in Germany, I have neglected many of the factors contributing to the strikes and many of the issues on the minds of workers. Rationalization and work intensification, in particular, contributed to the angry mood of the strikers and figured in their demands. On the other hand, no single factor so well explains the timing and pattern of strikes as the violation of the same distributional norms that underlay official wage policy and that were written into IG Metall's contracts. Indeed, both the strikers and the union responded in largely the same direction to right the distributional wrongs that resulted from structural and conjunctural economic disturbances. The similarity of response reveals both the existence of a moral economy of wage labor and the way one union and its members helped enforce it.

WILDCAT STRIKES IN SWEDEN

In Sweden, as the previous chapter showed, the formative circumstances of peak-level wage bargaining gave the blue-collar trade union confederation an unusual degree of progressive, egalitarian leadership in the Swedish labor market. LO control did not provide complete immunization against rank-and-file militancy, even though, as elsewhere in Europe, centralization since the 1930s had clearly reduced strike levels. In fact, centralized governance of the moral economy helped shape the character of militancy when it did break out. Though wildcat strikes in Sweden often appeared to go against the grain of official distributional policy, in fact LO's explicit egalitarian appeals in aggressive pursuit of wage leveling helped fuel the spontaneous strike waves. Not only did LO fail at critical points to meet its own standards when short-term economic conditions made this both possible and compelling from various members' standpoints. LO also tangled itself in the inevitably acute dilemmas of radical egalitarianism, by generating inequalities of one kind while remedying others. For these reasons, the Swedish strikes give us reason to refine and modify, though not fully depart from, the notion that worker militancy in well-institutionalized centralized systems tends to be largely "legitimist"—either conservative, in the sense of restorative of traditional pay structures, or progressive, in attempts to carry out principles of leadership policy that

---

[28]Statistisches Bundesamt Wiesbaden, *Fachserie 16 Tariflöhne, Reihe 4.1 Löhne und Gehälter* (Wiesbaden, October 1981), 38–43.

remain unfulfilled.[29] In either case, "rank-and-file revolt" is in a real sense, and despite appearances, usually with rather than against union leadership.

The LKAB Miners' Strike

The strike at the state-owned iron-ore mining company, Luossa-vaara-Kiirunavaara AB (LKAB), and the following year's wave of wild-cats throughout the country, especially in the metal, construction, and forest-products industries, were to Sweden what the September strikes of 1969 were to Germany. Starting at the Leveäniemi mine in Svap-pavaara on 9 December 1969, the strike spread within two days to other LKAB mines in neighboring Kiruna and Malmberget. The strike lasted 57 days, and about 4,800 workers participated. Independent strike committees led by Communists formed to conduct the strike. Extremely long and tense negotiations, involving both unofficial strike leaders and Miners' Union officials, were finally brought to a successful conclusion with LO mediation. Ten months after the strike broke out, and eight months after they had returned to work, the miners made substantial gains.

Although the strikers' demands were exclusively "local" and "economic" in nature, the unofficial and illegal character of the strike was widely interpreted by outsiders and many of the strikers themselves as a repudiation of the LO-affiliated Miners' Union (Gruvindustriar-betareförbundet) and, perhaps just as much, of centralized LO control in peak-level bargaining. Miners' demands for decentralization of the legal right to call strikes and abolition of no-strike clauses indicated as much.

The character of strike demands, however, recommends more subtle conclusions. Pay equity with respect to white-collar groups figured prominently. Strikers called for overtime, emergency-duty, and shift-work pay comparable to what white-collar employees enjoyed. Only white-collar workers received recreation allowances, paid training leave, and compensation for the use of private autos to and from work, and miners wanted comparable benefits. Guaranteed monthly earnings, characteristic of what white-collar workers enjoyed, were also demanded.[30]

[29]This usage of the term legitimism is suggested by but only analogous to its usage in E. J. Hobsbawm, *Primitive Rebels: Studies in Archaic Forms of Social Movement in the 19th and 20th Centuries* (New York: Norton, 1959), 118–21, and Reinhard Bendix, *Nation-Building and Citizenship: Studies of Our Changing Social Order* (Berkeley: University of California Press, 1977), 54–57.

[30]Anders Leion, *Solidarisk lönepolitik eller löntagarfonder? Den svenska modellens sammanbrott* (Stockholm: Rabén & Sjögren, 1979), 53–56.

Equally important, the strikers called for large general pay increases secured by guaranteed minimum hourly wages. The final settlement brought overall payroll costs up at least 18 percent, far above the contract increases won for them by LO. These demands reflected the fact that, for a long time, miners had been losing ground—and high ground at that. In 1960, miners were earning 134 percent of average industrial blue-collar wages. By 1970, their wages had fallen to 120 percent of the average for industry, while food and beverage industry workers had moved up from 89 percent to about 95 percent, and textile and garment workers had moved up from 79 percent and 74 percent to 85 percent and 89 percent respectively.[31] Within the mining industry, too, miners—virtually all male—saw women in other jobs, but under the same contracts, make phenomenal progress from 48 percent to 83 percent of men's wages during the same time. In 1960, in fact, blue-collar women employed by the mining industry were by far the most disadvantaged relative to their male counterparts in any industry; in 1970, women in mining were the fifth-best situated in eleven major industries.[32]

The general trend was in part the result of a 1960 agreement between LO and SAF to abolish wage categories for women, which resulted in an upgrading of traditional women's work into higher-paid categories. The miners' relative position was also considerably damaged by a two-year LO-SAF settlement concluded in the early summer of 1969. This agreement had markedly favored low-paid manual workers. As LO president Arne Geijer reported to the 1971 LO congress, efforts on behalf of the low-paid had become the top priority in the last two wage rounds. The 1969 agreement was the "best ever" in this regard. Hence miners had been forced to accept some of the smallest contract pay increases of any union in LO as a direct result of LO's success with its solidaristic wage policy. In line with the agreement, miners in Norrland were to receive hourly increases of roughly 20 öre for 1969, whereas members of the Metalworkers' Union would receive on average 28 öre and typically low-pay groups—workers in the textile, garment, and food industries and hotel and restaurant workers—were to receive approximately 60 öre, the maximum. Furthermore, the agreement reduced official regional differentials in contract pay based on living costs, to the detriment of LKAB miners, who worked north of the Arctic Circle.[33]

[31]Ingvar Ohlsson, "Den solidariska lönepolitikens resultat," in Landsorganisationen, *Lönepolitik och solidaritet*, 239.
[32]Meidner, *Samordning och solidarisk lönepolitik*, 51.
[33]Landsorganisationen, *De centrala överenskommelserna mellan LO och SAF, 1952–1982* (Stockholm: LO, 1981), 64–73. LKAB, though not in SAF, usually matched its policies.

The erosion of miners' differentials with respect to other blue-collar groups does not appear to have been the strongest incitement to rebellion.[34] Most explosive at LKAB was the fact that white-collar earnings in mining were then, and remained into the 1980s, the highest in all industry.[35] Organized outside LO, salaried workers received pay increases that tended to follow average blue-collar increases, not simply those received by high-pay wage earners such as miners. In other words, salaried workers tended to receive higher wage increases, both in absolute and in percentage figures, than the skilled or otherwise fortunate LO member whose wage development was being held back for the sake of others.

Two factors help account for the delay between the decline of miners' wages and the LKAB strike. First, the moral force of LO's egalitarian wage policy had a disarming effect on internal opposition. At the 1971 LO congress, in motions and speeches, miners' representatives pulled no punches in blaming LO centralization, bureaucratization, and restraint for alienating the membership. For example, a motion submitted by the Malmberget local asserted that the Miners' Union executive veto over strikes had "castrated" (snöpt) the trade union movement.[36] The egalitarian objectives and successes of LO's wage policy, by contrast, went unchallenged.

Net profits as a percentage of equity in iron-ore mining had steadily sunk from 24 percent in 1949–50 to 7 percent in 1969, and the related economic difficulties, including unemployment, also help explain earlier quiescence.[37] The associated crisis mentality no doubt helped the company buy time for reducing relative wages as well as break down workers' autonomy with increasingly centralized decision making, authoritarian supervision, intensification of work, and an inflexible, bureaucratically administered, piecework system. Explicit worker dissatisfaction and demands reflected worsening working conditions, just as they did in German mining and manufacturing. Nevertheless, pay equity demands dominated in late 1969, when profits had for a short time been improving and unemployment had finally begun to ease.[38]

The feeling that fairness was now not only more affordable but also

[34]They had asked for holiday pay similar to what metalworkers were getting under their contracts, and "cold-region" differentials like those received by construction workers. Edmund Dahlström et al., *LKAB och demokratin: Rapport om en strejk och ett forskningsprojekt* (Stockholm: Walhstrom & Widstrand, 1971), 134–43.

[35]Statistiska Centralbyrån, *Löner 1981, Del 1: Industritjänstemän, handelsanställda m.fl.* (Stockholm, 1982).

[36]Motion 8, Local no. 4 of Gruvindustriarbetareförbundet, in Landsorganisationen *Protokoll: 18:e ordinarie kongress 1971* (Stockholm: LO, 1972), 104.

[37]Leion, *Solidarisk lönepolitik eller löntagarfonder*, 47.

[38]Dahlström et al., *LKAB och demokratin*, 205.

imperative was considerably strengthened by LO's new and openly aggressive posture toward white-collar pay since 1967. In that year, LO's Arne Geijer had delivered a speech to the Social Democratic party congress openly criticizing the white-collar unions (whose members and leaders were well represented) for demanding full "compensation" for LO wage increases. White-collar groups, he implied, should keep their demands and increases in line with the limited increases that skilled blue-collar workers got out of the LO-SAF agreements. Instead, they had oriented their demands to average increases for all blue-collar workers. In 1966, they had gone even further, in LO's view.[39]

The LKAB strike was therefore less restorative than progressive and was given steam by contradictory signals in LO's official policy. The view that LO had lent miners the moral steam for their demands is substantiated by Social Democratic prime minister Olof Palme's public portrayal of the LKAB strike in light of the conflict between manual and nonmanual workers. "The significance of the conflict at the ore-fields is that it confronted many people with the conditions of manual labor in today's working life. It has opened many eyes to the shortcomings and problems that still prevail in Swedish working life and in Swedish society and thereby heightened the demand for equality."[40] If this is the way LO and the Social Democrats were seeing things, then it is not surprising that the miners took matters into their own hands. They worked, after all, in a company that was under Social Democratic government control and therefore especially accountable to union and Social Democratic standards.

Ironically, though, in bringing about a mediated settlement to the strike, LO had to beat a retreat from its egalitarian pay policy. The settlement enabled miners to recover some loss in their high-pay status with respect to other blue-collar workers. Within LO, then, the leadership dodged predictable criticism for favoring a privileged group, not the underdogs Palme had portrayed. Reporting on a high-level official discussion of the strike, LO's Report of the Executive for 1970 stated in self-consciously unapologetic but implicitly defensive tones that "LO's participation in the mine conflict . . . did not imply any acceptance of a one-sided and egoistic [skråmässigt] wage-relativities argument. . . . The agreement could be regarded as a good one and . . . defensible in every regard. Considering the difficult and stressful

[39]Geijer's speech is reprinted as "Inkomstutjämning och lönepolitik," in Zander, ed., *Fackliga klassiker*, 162–72.
[40]From *Dagens Nyheter*, 23 January 1970, quoted in P. O. Johansson and Ann-Britt Hellmark, *Från LKAB till ASAB: Strejker och lockouter på den svenska arbetsmarknaden 1970–1974* (Stockholm: Arbetslivscentrum, 1981), 14.

work, its geographic location, and the necessity of meeting recruitment needs of the mines, the miners must receive acceptable earnings."[41]

In the past, for the most part, LO had been spared such embarrassment over the distributional contradictions of its policy of restrained but egalitarian pay increases when white-collar unions had refused to adjust their behavior accordingly. (This contradiction is described in analytic depth in the next chapter as one between internal and external leveling, what I call the "horizontal trilemma".) In few cases had the contradictions become so acute as at LKAB, because most high-pay workers in LO had over the years benefited from substantial wage drift in their favor. A combination of years of slack markets for miners and the centralization of piece rate setting at LKAB had eliminated two of the most important causes of wage drift there.[42] Structural change and management changes in mining had eliminated the safety valve that usually operated on behalf of skilled workers elsewhere and simultaneously took the internal pressure off LO.

The Volvo Strike

Within months of the LKAB strike in 1970, and again in 1974, great waves of unofficial and therefore illegal strikes swept over Swedish industry. In 1970, not counting LKAB, there were over 250 wildcat strikes, involving over 25,000 workers and resulting in about 155,000 days of lost working time. In 1974, there were almost as many wildcat strikes involving about 21,000 workers and a loss of about 22,000 working days due to wildcats. The number of strikes fell off slightly in 1975 and then precipitously in 1976.[43]

The strike at Volvo in Göteborg in the middle of January 1970, before the LKAB miners had returned to work, intensified the public debate and, because of its apparently quick payoff for Volvo workers, incited further strikes. LO's moderate and egalitarian settlement had been followed by an unexpectedly rapid upswing in production and profits. The auto industry was favored by both events: low-cost wage increases for the relatively highly paid auto workers and a surge in orders. The drawback for auto makers, however, was a serious shortage of labor for unpleasant factory work and difficulty in attracting

[41]Landsorganisationen, *Landssekretariatets berättelse for år 1970* (Stockholm: LO, 1971), 10.
[42]In 1968, for example, more than half of the total 6.5 percent increase in manual workers' wages in industry was made up of wage drift.
[43]On 1974 see Johansson and Hellmark, *Från LKAB till ASAB,* 37, 56. In 1974 and 1975 together, there were at least 410 wildcat strikes. Bo Ohlström, *Vilda strejker inom LO-området 1974 och 1975* (Stockholm: LO, 1977), 20–22.

workers at wages restrained by a combination of LO moderation and egalitarianism.

High profits and demand gave Volvo the desire and ability to appease the strikers and, in the minds of strikers, robbed the company of any excuse not to right "local" injustices. With the Metalworkers' Union leader on location in Göteborg and the strikers back to work, Volvo managers and local union leaders negotiated a 1.5 kronor (11 percent) increase instead of the 46 öre negotiated by the union and engineering employers, which corresponded to the LO-SAF agreement. Furthermore, to cool off assembly-line workers, fair payment was finally guaranteed for down time not caused by workers themselves. Also, the highly resented six-minute down-time minimum for such payment was eliminated. The number of line substitutes was tripled, and "service" workers were now obligated to help out on the line when needed. On the distributional front, eighteen-year-olds were now to get equal pay for equal work, raising their wages by 37 percent. Furthermore, Volvo committed itself to experiments with guaranteed monthly pay, from which only white-collar workers had previously benefited.[44]

The strike at Volvo revealed some additional dangers in LO's system of peak bargaining and egalitarian policies. At high-pay firms, which benefited from very low pay increases, superhigh profits could suddenly appear when external "disturbances," such as an unexpected upswing in demand, followed centralized negotiations. High profits magnified feelings of injustice at local conditions. Having signed contracts, LO unions were legally restricted from conducting and paying for strikes at the very moment when workers felt most inclined to act.

The great danger for the unions was that workers would conclude they could get quick and good results for any objective by acting on their own. In fact, as LO officials realized, such a lesson would be erroneous, for in 1970 it was unions' egalitarian successes in centralized bargaining under accidental circumstances—high profits and tight labor markets—that helped create the conditions for localized success. In the case of Volvo, management was only too willing to give in to the strikers in order to get on with business and keep workers from drifting away to more pleasant and perhaps even better-paying jobs. Chairmen of both Volvo and the Metalworkers' Union were eager to point this out. It was therefore not so much LO's failure to live up to its own wage-distributional principles that caused the strikes as the very effects of its success in leveling wages across and within industries. That success allowed profits to boom at firms where, as is inevitable in centralized if not all systems, local injustices had been neglected. Leveling

[44] "Fackbasen: Strejken pådrivande," *Dagens Nyheter,* 20 January 1970.

within the blue-collar working class not only increased inequality with respect to white-collar workers, as LKAB showed; blue-collar leveling also increased the inequalities between capital and labor. To the extent that a local, militant culture existed and took notice, as in Göteborg, problems resulted.

The Volvo strike thus establishes two points about the moral economy of pay distribution and the role of parochial or local norms with regard to profits and work rules within a system of highly centralized and institutionalized collective bargaining. First, there is the matter of the distribution of wage and profit shares. At most, centralized unions like those in Sweden and West Germany assert in principle the need to protect or advance labor's aggregate share, but they studiously avoid saying much about the proper size and stability of this share *in any particular enterprise.* Explicit norms about profits would necessarily clash with pay distributional norms when regulation of interfirm and inter-industry wage differentials entails irregularities and disturbances in factor income distribution from one firm to the next and over time. Second, and largely as a result of employer conditions for centralized bargaining, centralized unions typically limit their efforts to regulate by official and uniform policy the particulars of production design and work rules.

Two consequences follow. First, union unwillingness and inability to generate norms about profits and production give free play to autonomous local forces, including ideologically motivated union activists as well as local collaborative institutions, in generating expectations and values. Centralized unions tend not to intervene in the process by propagating clear, competing notions—and even encourage local expectations by paying lip service to ideas about worker control. Second, to the extent that centralized unions zealously and successfully pursue wage-leveling policies, and to the extent that expectations with regard to profits and working conditions are well rooted at the local level, contradictions will necessarily arise and occasionally generate a militant response. That seems to have been the case at Volvo, where an active and militant membership chose a moment when extraordinarily high profits, caused in part by egalitarian wage policy, provided an opportunity and a justification to demand the righting of some locally perceived wrongs on grounds of income distribution and working conditions.

It may also be true that LO's extraordinary emphasis on egalitarianism helped sensitize workers to distributional injustices and legitimized demands for leveling beyond what had already been achieved. At Volvo in 1970, workers in the lowest of the three wage categories wanted to be moved up into the middle category, eliminating the lowest. Failure to achieve this demand in the local negotiation threatened momentarily to set off a new strike.[45] At Volvo, the highest group's rate was only 6 percent higher than that of the lowest.[46] The German auto industry, by comparison, had up to eight standard wage categories in 1970, and the highest category was 47 percent higher than the lowest.[47] LO's egalitarianism, then, deserves some credit for generating high and refined expectations of pay equity which inspired wildcats in LKAB as well as in engineering. "Justice to the millimeter" (*millimeterrättvisa*), to use the wry expression of the time, had come to characterize workers' as well as union demands.

The 1974–1975 Strike Wave

The wildcats that rolled across Sweden once again in 1974 and 1975 were in many respects similar to the earlier wave that had followed the LKAB and Volvo strikes, as well as to the German wildcats of 1969 and 1973. In anticipation that high inflation and industrial recession would result from the Arab oil embargo, LO settled in 1974 for low, albeit egalitarian, increases with SAF. This turned out to be another mistake. The three-year agreement for 1971–73 had already contributed to a profits boom by keeping relative unit labor costs down while wages and prices in other OECD countries, especially Germany, had risen rapidly in the 1973 boom. The European boom contributed further to the Swedish profits explosion in 1973 by driving up the prices of Swedish exports, especially of raw materials and capital goods. The Swedish government contributed to the problem with a small devaluation of the krona early in 1973, although many economists had recommended the opposite. The restrained agreement for 1974, combined with badly timed demand stimulation by the Swedish government, prolonged the explosion in profits. A chain reaction of increased hiring and production, tight labor markets, and wage drift unleashed a frenzy of strikes against widespread violations of distributive norms that had been established under calmer economic conditions.[48]

---

[45]"Storstrejk avvärjd vid Volvo: Avtalet godtogs ej utan gnissel," *Göteborgs Posten*, 20 January 1970. Wildcat strikers at Göteborg's shipyard were also calling for upward leveling. "Efter Volvo-strejken: Verkstadsindustrin oroad—ska strejkerna sprida sig?" *Aftonbladet*, 20 January 1970.

[46]"Fackbasen: Strejken pådrivande," *Dagens Nyheter*, 20 January 1970.

[47]These figures are for contract region North Rhein–Westfalia. In Nordwürttemberg-Nordbaden, there were five categories, but the spread was the same. Statistisches Bundesamt Wiesbaden, *Fachserie 16 Löhne und Gehälter, Reihe 4.1 Tariflöhne* (Wiesbaden, October 1981), 40–41.

[48]On these and following events, see Andrew Martin, "Trade Unions in Sweden: Strategic Responses to Change and Crisis," in Peter Gourevitch et al., *Unions and Economic Crisis: Britain, West Germany and Sweden* (London: Allen & Unwin, 1984), 288–92.

The uneven spread of profits ensured that initial wage drift would also be uneven from industry to industry. As in Germany, wage drift favored the higher-paid within industries and enterprises. On both dimensions, then, the timing of restrained egalitarian increases with the exogenous disturbances in factor income distribution produced systematic violation of LO's wage-distributional policy. Wildcat militancy inspired by these violations spread wage drift across the Swedish economy, resulting in an explosion of wages and prices in 1975 and 1976. Reinstatement of wage-distributional equilibrium with inflationary wage drift and militancy then contributed to a fall in profits, a disequilibrium in external payments, and a long-term recession that plagued the country for the rest of the decade.

Evidence that the wave of militancy in 1974 and 1975 represented in part the attempts of workers to enforce the moral economy can be found in a study commissioned by LO of fifty-two firms that experienced wildcats.[49] According to researchers, the matter of high profits seldom arose in interviews with local unionists and strikers, thus confirming that, by and large, pay distribution is more important than factor income distribution in motivating militancy. LO leaders had no compelling reason to conceal the problem of high profits in this study, because officials at all levels had, in the wake of the 1969 and 1970 strikes, begun openly and intensely debating how to deal with the "excess profits" left behind by egalitarian wage policy.

What stood out most prominently in the study was the importance of wage differentials in motivating the strikes. In twenty-seven of the fifty-two cases, one or more of the following were regarded by those interviewed as the main causes of the strikes: (1) wages in the firm or department were too low in relationship to wages in other firms or departments; (2) workers with fixed hourly wages were receiving too little compared to those on piece rates; (3) unskilled workers' wages were too low compared with those of skilled workers; (4) women's wages were unfairly exceeded by men's. These factors easily outweighed all others. For instance, in only one strike were "technical changes or rationalization" regarded as a main cause. In this case, firm/department wage disparities and other dissatisfaction with wages or wage forms were also main causes. A similar pattern showed up regarding working conditions and personnel policies.[50] In the remaining twenty-five cases, no single factor played such a systematic and prominent role.

Wage drift associated with high profits and a tight labor market

[49]The results were reported in Ohlström, *Vilda strejker.*
[50]Computed from Table 6 in Ohlström, *Vilda strejker*, 25–32.

helped create all the perceived imbalances described above. Some firms would have experienced it early whereas others followed only later, voluntarily, because they competed for labor, or not at all. Workers on piece rates enjoyed more drift. They also tended to be higher-paid than those on time wages. Men received higher wages and more often did piecework. Furthermore, skilled workers, always in short supply, were often favored by employers who granted extra pay above contract increases.[51] In firms where wages did not drift upward, strikes helped transmit drift, creating further imbalances and encouraging other workers to take matters into their own hands.

After both the 1969 and the 1974–75 strike waves, LO's response, like that of IG Metall, was to reassert its dominant role in the moral economy. In 1970, LO pushed for and achieved a high-cost wage agreement and initially gave priority to the reduction of fringe-benefit differentials between LO contracts and those negotiated by unions in the Central Organization of Salaried Employees (TCO). These demands directly addressed the problems of white-collar privileges experienced by workers at LKAB and Volvo, for example. In 1975, LO abandoned its traditional restraint and forced through high contract increases for 1975 and 1976 in order to bring profits and wage drift under control.[52] By 1977, high contractual increases of the two earlier years had combined with the severe structural crisis in Sweden's raw materials, producer, and capital goods industries and the generally stagnant condition of international demand to bring distributional relations back into line. Wildcat activity diminished drastically, now replaced by more threatening unemployment problems.

The pattern of strike waves in Sweden revealed, as it did in West Germany, the existence of a moral economy of industrial wage labor whose implicit and explicit norms are sanctioned and, if the inferences of this chapter are correct, to a significant extent *created* by centralized bargaining institutions. To the extent, then, that centralized unionism

[51]On Swedish wage drift, see Sture Eskilsson, *Löneutveckling under kontroll* (Stockholm: SAF, 1966); Kjell-Åke Dahlström, *Horndalseffekt och löneglidning: Några studier av produktivitets- och löneutveckling i verkstads- och processföretag* (Stockholm: SAF, 1971); Hans T:son Söderström and Eva Uddén-Jondal, "Does Egalitarian Wage Policy Cause Wage Drift? An Empirical Study of Sweden, 1960–1979," Seminar Paper no. 203, Institute for International Economic Studies, University of Stockholm (Stockholm: 1982); Landsorganisationen, "Vem behöver ackorden?" (Stockholm: LO, 1980[?]); and Sveriges Verkstadsförening, "Löneglidning och ackordsättning" (Stockholm: VF, n.d.).

[52]In 1970 LO dropped the benefits issue in order to prioritize low-pay adjustments for LO workers with respect to skilled workers, because in separate negotiations public-sector unions in LO succeeded in making substantial progress along those lines before LO had settled with SAF. LO leaders felt compelled to follow suit. Martin, "Trade Unions in Sweden," 265, 293–94.

helped create a measure of unity behind consensual values, it did not simply deactivate workers and replace the power of solidarity with bureaucratic and juridified control. Instead, we can just as well argue that centralized unionism *empowered* workers to enforce the distributional norms that underlie strong, centralized trade unionism. These norms tend to be the same ones that the slow and rigid bargaining practices of centralized unionism can realize in the long run but cannot always enforce in the short run.

INTERNAL POWER STRUGGLES

Wildcat strikes were more a cause than a symptom of a crisis of authority within the centralized reformist unions of Germany and Sweden in the 1970s. Many local union activists found in them an opportunity, as well as a genuine justification, to cultivate rank-and-file support and press for internal reforms that would give them more control at the expense of the authority of top union officials. For ideologically motivated local activists, with limited influence and upward mobility in the unions, centralized collective bargaining obstructed the struggle against neglected local problems. Law and centralized strike financing limited their ability to harness local bargaining power for these local objectives, whether they were distributional, and therefore fully within the realm of union strategy, or related to job control, about which centralized unionism can and will do little.

In attacking union centralization, local militants rode a wave of discontent and confusion during and after the wildcat strikes. This temporary disequilibrium in the moral economy intensified the power struggles that always occur in some form within centralized unionism. In the 1970s, rancorous conflict broke out openly for the first time in postwar Germany and Sweden, and central officials, shaken into action, managed only with some effort to prevail.

IG Metall in the Wake of the Strikes

From the beginning, IG Metall's leadership posed the problem as one of protecting distributional equity against the divisive effects of the decentralization that many dissenters wanted. Chairman Otto Brenner regarded the 1969 strikes as symptoms of tight labor markets and low and badly coordinated wage settlements for steel and manufacturing. Opposing calls for greater local autonomy over strikes and bargaining, Brenner reasoned before a September 1969 meeting of officials from

95

all over the country that "If it were true . . . that the leadership should only make larger social policy and try to bring about change in the system . . . and let the rank-and-file realize their interests themselves to the extent that the market situation allows, then that is the death sentence for all future wage policy. . . . The principle of solidarity that is inherent in [central] wage contracts would simply no longer exist."[53]

Brenner's efforts did not prevent a November conference of works council members and union shop stewards from passing resolutions criticizing the centralization of authority in collective bargaining and demanding decentralized "plant-level bargaining policy" (*betriebsnahe Tarifpolitik*). The concerns motivating such reforms had already been voiced at the 1968 IG Metall congress, especially in connection with IG Metall's cooperation in the voluntary tripartite incomes policy of wage restraint (*konzertierte Aktion*). Now they had been given new urgency by the strikes.[54]

At the next IG Metall congress, in 1971, radical shop stewards and works council members seized the opportunity to force open debate on their grievances and demands. During the congress, a challenger to Eugen Loderer, the executive council's candidate for IG Metall's chairmanship, was announced, and he won 97 out of a total of 466 votes recorded—an unusual sign of disunity. (A similar challenge would be mounted in 1974.) Debate at the congress was then dominated by demands for more support, protection, and autonomy for shop stewards, who are elected by union members at the shop level. Shop stewards wanted to strengthen their representation in decision-making bodies, especially by gaining direct control over elections to bargaining councils (*Tarifkommissionen*), which deliberate about bargaining demands and settlements and counsel negotiators chosen by the executive leadership. They sought to secure rights to control activities of union representatives in works councils and to strengthen supraplant and regional committees of shop stewards. Finally, their demand for codification of the duties and powers of stop stewards in the IG Metall constitution received a majority of congress votes, against the recommendation of the executive leadership. But as a two-thirds' majority was required to pass constitutional change, this recommendation was "buried" with the others as *Material* for consideration by the executive in its preparation of new "Guidelines for Shop Steward Activity."[55]

[53] "Info-tagung für Mitglieder des Beirates und Bevollmächtigten der IGM" (Stuttgart, September 1969), cited in Schmidt, *Ordnungsfaktor oder Gegenmacht,* 307.
[54] Eberhard Schmidt, "Die Auseinandersetzung um die Rolle der Vertrauensleute in der IG Metall," in Jacobi, Müller-Jentsch, and Schmidt, *Gewerkschaften und Klassenkampf '74,* 133–37.
[55] Ibid., 137.

In 1973, shortly before that year's unofficial strike wave reached its spring peak, IG Metall finally issued its new "Guidelines for Shop Stewards", and in the autumn, after the second peak, presented a final draft of "IG Metall Principles for Shop Stewards' Union Activity." On practically every count, shop stewards *lost* ground. Their independence, duties, and powers were circumscribed in the "Principles" in order to keep them under the control of works councils (which, as critics pointed out, are not even formal organs of the union hierarchy, but rather legally independent bodies) and under the direction of the local, regional, and central executive organs. Possibilities for lateral communication and strategic consultation among shop stewards at the supraplant and local levels were if anything reduced by new limitations on the size and frequency of regular conferences. The new version of the "Guidelines" dropped the previous version's clause outlining the duty of shop stewards to consult with members about contract demands. Election of collective bargaining commissions no longer *required* active consultation with members in the formulation of demands—except when the executive found it useful.[56]

The leadership's actions conformed with Otto Brenner's and Eugen Loderer's statements since 1969. Worried by the increasing dependence of elected secretaries of IG Metall's city locals (*Verwaltungsstellen*) on "transitory vote swings and local intrigues," which "creates an incentive to pass the blame onto Frankfurt" (IG Metall headquarters), Brenner emphasized the need in a 1970 memorandum to increase the "executive discipline" that ran from the center, through the coopted regional leaders (*Bezirksleiter*), down to elected leaders in the city locals where executive decisions often "ran aground."

In calling for a more participatory process of opinion formation and decision making, Brenner suggested that the links from top to bottom had to be strengthened, for example with more shop steward and works council conferences on selected issues. Nevertheless, the "advisory character" of these conferences had to be emphasized: "The hierarchical, that is to say the executive lines should on the other hand be more strongly centralized."[57] During the 1973 strikes, Loderer, Brenner's successor, bewailed the worsening "shop-floor jungle" (*innerbetrieblicher Wildwuchs*) of conflicts among shop stewards, members of works councils, and union officials, caused in part by legal restrictions (until 1972) on access behind factory gates for full-time IG Metall officials. Loderer also addressed the problem of large wage gaps, which gave too much independent responsibility to works councils in deter-

[56]Ibid., 138–42.
[57]Schmidt, *Ordnungsfaktor oder Gegenmacht*, 327–28.

mining actual wage policy and made the union itself appear ineffectual and superfluous.[58]

Evidence of executive moves to deal with the union's problems by securing more discipline at the shop-floor level was the dramatic rise in expulsions from IG Metall, as well as from other major unions, in the mid-1970s. Probably the single largest category of reasons for expulsion during the period was candidacy on "oppositional" lists in works council elections—that is, in opposition to official IG Metall lists, nomination to which was controlled by the head of the works council and the local union secretary, who in many important cases were the same person.[59] After initial purges of Communists in the 1950s, expulsions had been rare during the 1960s. In the 1970s the leadership revived the procedure to tame the shop-floor jungle and inhibit the formation of oppositions with an institutional foothold in works councils.[60]

The demands raised by opposition groups in works council elections demonstrated that the union simultaneously inspired and suffered oppositional reactions. At Opel in Bochum, as at many other large workplaces with a mobilized union membership, an Oppositional Unionist Group attacked entrenched union officials on distributional issues raised in the strikes in 1969 and 1973. Equalization of pay for men and women, Germans and foreigners, compression of the pay scale, and elimination of the "point system" (a highly articulated system of job

[58]Loderer is reported to have blamed works council officials, who dominate in collective bargaining commissions, for conceding too easily to low wage demands and contracts and thereafter taking credit for the extra-contractual pay increases determined by local labor market conditions. Kollegen bei Mannesmann-Huckingen, "Streiks bei Mannesman, Duisburg," 56. Limited evidence suggests that bargaining commission members sent from works councils representing larger enterprises (where, significantly, extra-contractual pay is high), were biased in favor of low contract increases. Hermann Kotthoff, "Zum Verhältnis von Betriebsrat und Gewerkschaft: Ergebnisse einer empirischen Untersuchung," in Joachim Bergmann, ed., *Beiträge zur Soziologie der Gewerkschaften* (Frankfurt: Suhrkamp, 1979), 302–5. See also Joachim Bergmann, Otto Jacobi, and Walther Müller-Jentsch, *Gewerkschaften in der Bundesrepublik, Band 1: Gewerkschaftliche Lohnpolitik zwischen Mitgliederinteressen und ökonomischen Systemzwängen* (Frankfurt: Campus, 1979), 372–73.

[59]Rainer Erd, "Gewerkschaftsausschlüsse in den 70er Jahren," in Otto Jacobi, Walther Müller-Jentsch, and Eberhard Schmidt, eds., *Gewerkschaftspolitik in der Krise: Kritisches Gewerkschaftsjahrbuch 1977–78* (Berlin: Rotbuch, 1978).

[60]On expulsions see Rainer Kalbitz, "Gewerkschaftsausschlüsse in den 50er Jahren," in ibid., 159–65. On some of the celebrated cases of alternative lists and their successes, see Markovits, *Politics of the West German Trade Unions*, 221–24; "Betriebsratswahlen 1972," in Otto Jacobi, Walther Müller-Jentsch, and Eberhard Schmidt, *Gewerkschaften und Klassenkampf: Kritisches Jahrbuch '73* (Frankfurt: Fischer, 1973), 43–64; "Betriebsratswahlen 1975," in Otto Jacobi, Walther Müller-Jentsch, and Eberhard Schmidt, eds., *Gewerkschaften und Klassenkampf: Kritisches Jahrbuch 1975* (Frankfurt: Fischer, 1975), 47–85; and "Betriebsrats- und Personalratswahlen," in Otto Jacobi, Walther Müller-Jentsch, and Eberhard Schmidt, eds., *Arbeiterinteressen gegen Sozialpartnerschaft: Kritisches Gewerkschaftsjahrbuch 1978/79* (Berlin: Rotbuch, 1979), 92–149.

evaluation and ranking for pay differentiation) were prominent demands and generated strong support.[61] At Opel, as in other major firms, the large gap between contract and actual pay levels made it possible for the company to manipulate the actual internal pay structure in arbitrary and inegalitarian ways inconsistent with the rate structure of IG Metall's own contracts.[62]

At the 1977 IG Metall congress, delegates from Opel, including Günter Perschke, the works council chairman at the Bochum plant, energetically pleaded on behalf of a motion for plant-level collective bargaining and contracts.[63] Implicitly, they called for the right to strike to achieve or protect pay and conditions over and above the contract minima. For one thing, they said, employers had repeatedly threatened unilateral cutbacks in extra-contractual pay in order to extort concessions from the works council on matters where it had the legal right of codetermination—such as increases in overtime work. Without contractual protection of Opel wages and the right to strike, the works council was powerless to obstruct the company's tactics. For another, one Opel delegate asserted that what the works council had accomplished recently, in the way of internal pay leveling for example, set off divisive and demoralizing debate at the local level about the superfluousness of IG Metall's centralized bargaining strategies when other works councils could not match those results.

For IG Metall to accept, even in principle, the idea of bargaining, strikes, and contracts at the firm level would, in the future, throw the responsibility for preventing unilateral pay cuts and other injurious management decisions into the lap of the central leadership. Were the leadership to provide selective strike support in defense of auto workers, they would arouse a powerful backlash from others against the use of scarce union resources to protect relatively privileged auto workers. Failure to provide support would alienate auto workers further. Hence, the leadership, backed by other delegates, defended with equal

[61]In 1975 the opposition list received about 36 percent of the vote, the official IG Metall list 53 percent. In 1978, both fell, to 25 percent and 44 percent respectively, while other lists increased from 11 percent to 31 percent. For the official list, these were terrible showings, because DGB unions on average take about 80 percent of works council seats. Kollegen der Gruppe oppositioneller Gewerkschafter in der IG Metall, "Listenvielfalt bei Opel, Bochum," in Jacobi, Müller-Jentsch, and Schmidt, *Arbeiterinteressen gegen Sozialpartnerschaft*, 111–12.

[62]In 1982, when recessionary conditions of the late 1970s and early 1980s had brought the wage-gap problem under control, gaps between contract and actual wages still ranged from 20 percent at the low end (wage group 2) to 30 percent at the high end (group 11). Computed from "Lohntafel [Wage table], Werk Bochum," Adam Opel A.G., made available by a works council representative.

[63]Industriegewerkschaft Metall, *Protokoll: 12. ordentlicher Gewerkschaftstag 18-24 September 1977* (Frankfurt: IG Metall, 1978), 303–4 and 311–12.

energy IG Metall's policy of negotiating standard minimum rates, even if the policy meant that pay in some sectors might exceed the mimina by 30 percent or more. At stake was a basic level of solidarity without which the union could not survive.[64]

On everyone's mind was the specter of a breakaway auto workers' union, or its de facto equivalent, especially under the conditions of 1977. In the auto industry, infuriatingly high profits were being recorded, whereas in other sectors, most notably steel, structural decline prevailed. Debaters reminded the auto delegates of earlier situations, like the one in 1971–72 when the auto industry had been doing miserably yet auto workers had gotten raises they would not have gotten on their own. Then, other sectors had led the way. As one speaker put it, "Colleagues, in the past it was not at all unusual for employers, time and again, to lay a stinking cadaver on the table for us to start amputating." When that happened, "the colleagues from a plant that was doing badly were jolly glad that they were part of a collective with regional contracts." Applause followed.[65]

Parrying motions for decentralization, the leadership repeatedly conjured up fears of an erosion of solidarity (*Entsolidarisierung*) in a union increasingly divided by economic conditions diverging between regions and sectors. The need to maintain some level of equity within an immense and heterogeneous organization effectively disarmed those discontented with centralization. Only "a few" votes were cast in favor of plant-level bargaining according to congress minutes.[66] That there was widespread criticism of the leadership with regard to the substance of central policy, and hence potential support for decentralization, was clear, however. Large numbers of votes were soon to be cast against the leadership on the question of shop stewards' rights to elect bargaining commissions and to convene them at will. A motion requiring elimination of IG Metall's job-evaluation scale for differentiating and ranking job categories (the *Lohnschlüssel*), for which the minimum rates in the regional contracts are negotiated, was actually passed against the leadership's wishes, as was a resolution committing the union to the thirty-five hour workweek as a job-creating measure.[67]

[64]Ibid., 304.

[65]Ibid., 305.

[66]Applause followed this final statement before the vote: "If we . . . for example concluded general agreements for 8 percent, but then with supplementary contracts after the fact were to give Opel 5 percent, Ford 6 percent and Daimler 7 percent . . . then that would bring this organization to the breaking point [*dann wäre das die Zerreissprobe für diese Organisation*]." Ibid., 313. See also 286, 301.

[67]Manfred Thomas of Opel-Bochum spoke out vehemently in favor of this motion. Ibid., 299.

The IG Metall congress of 1977 showed how precarious the central leadership's control of wage policy making had become. What saved the leadership may have been the voting clout of delegates from the steel industry, whose support would have been crucial for decentralization. Recently, steel workers had become fully dependent on other sectors to hold up their wages. Steel delegates from North Rhein–Westfalia, though interested for tactical reasons in breaking up their large, dense, and heterogeneous bargaining region into several more autonomous parts, were not ready to support company-level decentralization. Decentralization of the kind they called for would strengthen not weaken them against the centralized power of employers, because West German labor law prohibited lockouts across several bargaining regions in response to a strike in only one.[68]

The steel sector of the union, where unemployment was high, could gain by protecting centralized policy control in the hands of the Frankfurt officials. In fact, representatives of steel workers wished to use centralized leadership for objectives impossible to achieve without centralized control. At the 1977 congress they succeeded in committing the leadership against its will to a policy of reducing the workweek to thirty-five hours. The leadership had not wanted to be committed to any inflexible conception of how to create jobs by reducing working time, especially because of pressure from the Baden-Württemberg area. There, unemployment was less of a problem than was the power of employers to exploit both the high wage gap and IG Metall's pay differentiation principles to intensify work and dequalify workers whose jobs were rationalized, thus reducing individuals' earnings and squeezing more work out of them. Reflecting "humanization" more than employment concerns, "the 'Stuttgart line' favored longer breaks, a slower work pace and other micro-level approaches to weekly work-time reduction," according to Andrei Markovits. "The activists from Stuttgart believed that increased control by labor of work time at the shop level was more effective in securing these improvements than the introduction of the 35-hour work week."[69]

IG Metall's leadership fought hard to preserve its central authority and maneuverability despite—and because of—the regional and sectoral heterogeneity of the membership. Decentralization would have quickly caused widening disparities within the union, in turn setting off even more intense internal disputes about structure and policy. The cost of centralization was a permanent if manageable level of discontent among workers in healthy, highly profitable industries and re-

[68]Markovits, *Politics of the West German Trade Unions*, 243.
[69]Ibid., 242–44.

gions, where local bargaining power based on tighter labor markets could not be fully exploited. High and differential wage gaps were the result. Earnings differentials across regions resulted, despite fairly uniform contract wages, but at least these differentials were not "policy." With decentralized bargaining and a selective targeting of strike resources benefiting privileged groups, such differentials would be rooted in policy and hence bitterly divisive.

High profits, high wage gaps, and the greater maneuverability of employers at the shop level in some sectors, which resulted from centralized wage policy, contributed on the other hand to waves of wildcat strikes, localized opposition movements, and formal challenges to centralization at union congresses. The leadership managed these problems with appeals to solidarity for the sake of equity and equity for the sake of solidarity. Flexible and responsive yet centralized remedies to distributional disturbances worked reasonably well, and IG Metall's leaders fought hard against all internal efforts to reduce their flexibility and autonomy to govern the moral economy.

In the Wake of the Swedish Strikes

Despite the higher degree of centralization in Sweden, the challenge there to centralized union authority in the 1970s appears to have been weaker than in Germany. Even in the Swedish Metalworkers' Union, calls for decentralization did not generate the same intensity characterizing the debates at IG Metall congresses. In only one case did an LO union seriously challenge LO's central control. Why should this be so?

The absence of a works constitution law in Sweden is one explanation. In Germany, works council elections gave dissenting groups the chance to establish an institutional foothold not available to Swedish workers. With proportional representation, opposition lists can gain representation even without majorities. Internal opponents in Sweden had no such easy rewards, and their presence and influence remained less visible and institutionalized in plant- and company-level union bodies.

Perhaps a more important reason is the fact that in Sweden, effective wages are *legally* secure. The Metalworkers' Union, for example, negotiates changes in a three-tier minimum wage structure for whole industries, in principle much like IG Metall's five to ten tiers (depending on the region). But the Swedish union, like the rest in LO, also negotiates pay increases for *individuals*, in line with LO-SAF guidelines, to be added on to whatever their existing pay was at the time of the agreement. There may be "wage gaps," as in Germany, between minimum and effective rates, but employers have no legal right to bring an individual's effective wages down. To put it another way, German employers may unilaterally close the wage gap over the course of a contract period, which at the firm level would register as negative wage drift. In Sweden, there can only be positive or upward drift.

Because individual employers in Sweden cannot unilaterally cut back wages for individual workers (without redeploying them in jobs assigned lower pay), centralized bargaining, even at the peak level, does not come under the fierce criticism it often gets in less centralized Germany. There, the unions must hide behind their no-strike agreements whenever employers cut back or restructure extra-contractual pay, or when they threaten cutbacks to extract concessions on other matters at the shop level. If, in doing so, employers in Germany violate distributional norms explicitly or implicitly underlying union policy, the union becomes both the instigator and the object of rebellion.

This is not to say that employer violation of union norms is uncommon in Sweden. In fact, Swedish wage drift systematically undermines the leveling between and within firms and industries that peak bargaining accomplishes. On the other hand, the drift is always positive: it tends to benefit the better-paid without reducing the pay of other workers. Such is not the case in Germany.

Equally important is the fact that since the beginning of peak bargaining, and increasingly over the years, LO has demonstrated an unbending commitment to yearly correction of the inegalitarian effects of wage drift. By the mid-1960s, "earnings-development guarantees" (*förtjänstutvecklingsgarantier*) for workers with little or no wage drift had become a permanent addition to the vocabulary of centralized bargaining. These guarantees resulted in the substantial reinstatement of distributional relations between and within union units at the beginning of each new contract period, so that the base for new egalitarian pay increases would not simply be the eroded egalitarian structure that resulted from the previous increases. In the wake of the strikes, LO even managed to improve these guarantees with reforms in 1975 and 1977.[70]

When wage drift exploded in periods of high profits and tight labor markets in Sweden, wildcat strikes erupted, largely to bring compensation for distributional disturbances. This result was fully in line with

[70]In 1975, the LO-SAF agreement strengthened the power of the unions in industry and plant-level negotiations to ensure that wage-drift compensation was actually distributed to those individuals who merited it. In 1977, the usual absolute ceilings on wage drift compensation were removed, so that compensation could amount to 80 percent of average industrial wage drift no matter how high it went.

official policy but in advance of officially negotiated correctives. Centralized contracts came under attack, under these circumstances, not so much for fundamental reasons as for bad timing or for being too low and therefore not capturing enough of the profits that were causing wage drift and distributive inequities.

At the LO congress in 1971, for example, only a handful of motions from individual locals of three different LO unions challenged centralized bargaining practices. Not surprisingly, the Malmberget local of the Mineworkers' Union called for a return to membership votes to decide on strikes and contract acceptance. Two locals from the Metalworkers' Union and the Construction Workers' Union agreed and called for abolition of the right of the central leadership of individual LO unions to veto the decision to strike by advisory referenda or bargaining councils. Another Metalworkers' local specifically demanded that elected bargaining councils have the final decision. All of these motions challenged LO's standard by-laws established in the 1941 reform for its constituent unions.[71]

Similar motions from isolated locals of some LO unions reappeared at the 1976 congress, but little supportive debate followed. Also notable is the rather laconic self-confidence in the undetailed response from LO leaders. In part, this can be attributed to the fact that such motions periodically appear at individual union congresses and run aground at that stage on the opposition of the leadership at the sub-LO level. As the Metalworkers' Union leadership put it rather more passionately to the 1973 congress, in response to motions against central control of strikes without binding membership referenda, "How it would be more democratic to let a small and perhaps highly paid group decide is hard to understand. Where is the democracy in giving the right to such a group to eat away at the membership's common funds? In addition, the group could have such a key position that their strike would bring unemployment to thousands of the union's members, who perhaps had already approved their contract and whose wages perhaps were considerably lower than the strikers'." The Metalworkers' leadership therefore did most of the work in defense of LO, finding it necessary to repeat this kind of reasoning in information to members before the next few congresses.[72]

<hr />

[71]Landsorganisationen, *Protokoll: 18:e ordinarie kongress 1971* (Stockholm: LO, 1972), 103–5.

[72]Quotation from Svenska Metallindustriarbetareförbundet, *Protokoll: Svenska Metallindustriarbetareförbundets Kongress 1973* (Stockholm: Metall, 1974), 145. See also Svenska Metallindustriarbetareförbundet, *Protokoll, Svenska Metallindustriarbetareförbundets Kongress 1977* (Stockholm: Metall, 1978), 184–88, and *Kongressprotokoll, Del 1: Svenska Metallindustriarbetareförbundets Kongress 1981* (Stockholm: Metall, 1982), 181–82.

Such reasoning no doubt helps achieve the desired effect of disarming internal discontent that might lead to a breakdown of central control. Practically identical arguments had been used in Germany. Centralized control prevents raids on strike resources. At the same time, it prevents well-placed groups from dragging the entire organization into costly lockouts and enabling employers to exploit division and the weaknesses of more vulnerable groups.

Within LO, it is not surprising that the strongest defense of centralized power and egalitarian wage policy came from low-pay unions that lack much bargaining power of their own, such as the Agricultural Workers' Union, the Textile and Garment Workers' Union, and the Wood Industry Workers' Union. An interesting exception was the Transport Workers, which in the mid-1970s was the only union that openly challenged LO and wished to reassert bargaining autonomy. Representing a relatively low-pay work force and a relatively large number of members who supported very egalitarian pay settlements, the union as a whole had lost interest in LO's protection.[73]

This stance can be attributed to three things: low wage drift, strong bargaining power associated with the union's ability to paralyze much of the economy, and the industry's ability, sheltered from international competition, to pass on increased wage costs with price increases. No other low-pay union shared all of these characteristics. The transportation sector experienced the third-highest number of wildcat strikes among LO unions in the 1970s, though it was only the tenth-largest union.[74] Furthermore, a significant number of longshoremen in Norrland and Göteborg had been expelled and others bolted to form their own union, independent of the Transport Workers' and LO, in 1972.[75]

Hasse Ericson, the controversial boss of the Transport Workers' Union, horrified other LO leaders in 1974 by openly criticizing peak bargaining. Ericson admitted that independent, industry-level bargaining would prevent the solidaristic wage policy from functioning. "But it doesn't do that now anyway," he added.[76] Ericson explained that transportation workers were among those in LO who did not share in the high wage drift paid out in export sectors blessed at the time with

[73]According to a 1974 LO study, 33 percent of the union's members wanted pay increases only for the low-paid, and roughly 30 percent wished to go it alone in bargaining. Only three other unions (like the low-pay Agricultural Workers' and Garment Workers' unions) had as many or more members favoring highly egalitarian increases, and only four others (like the high-pay Miners' and Painters' unions) had as many or more members favoring independence from LO. *Fackföreningsrörelsen* 22 (1974), 4.

[74]Johansson and Hellmark, *Från LKAB till ASAB*, 64.

[75]See Erik Nyhlén and Nils Viktorsson, *Stuvat: Spelet om hamnarna* (Stockholm: Tiden, 1975).

[76]Quoted in *Fackföreningsrörelsen* 19 (1974), 12.

windfall profits or in sectors where wages automatically drifted upward because of productivity increases and a tight labor market. Furthermore, he was a frequent critic of LO coordination, largely because other LO unions tended to exceed the agreed-upon "cost framework" in implementing the distributional guidelines of LO-SAF agreements in the following industrial agreements (by means of improvements in benefits, for example). These excess increases were not counted as wage drift, and so transport workers did not get compensation for them with the "earnings-development guarantees."

As he had done in 1971, Ericson obtained agreement from LO and SAF to waive the no-strike clause for his own independent negotiations for the stevedore branch in 1974, but he failed to obtain a waiver for all of the union's bargaining sectors in 1975 despite his disputed claim that the LO executive had actually promised it.[77] LO had agreed in 1974, having sympathized with the union's problems with the dockworkers. The renegade union was threatening a strike for its own contracts and therefore recognition from employers. Success would draw members away from the LO union. Ericson was countering with efforts to achieve what turned out to be a popular uniform national contract for longshoremen, which eliminated differences in earning levels from port to port, did away with the earnings instability associated with the old piecework system, and ensured guaranteed monthly pay for idle periods. This agreement was going to be expensive, and one that would exceed the bounds of the LO-SAF guidelines.

Following the 1974 success, however, the union failed to get LO and SAF consent to a waiver of the no-strike agreement in 1975, largely because it was responding to membership pressure to demand special compensation for wage drift in manufacturing. This demand would have meant disproportionately high increases, exceeding the rigid cost framework for sector-specific increases allowed in the LO-SAF formula.

The LO leadership was clearly unwilling to resort to a general strike and trigger lockouts in defense of Ericson's ambitions against SAF, which was protecting the interests of its employers' association in the transportation industry from strikes by transport workers. Here we see a cross-class coalition of interests at work protecting the peak-level bargaining system against power and distributional conflicts within the labor movement. The equity considerations motivating Ericson and the Transport Workers' Union to break away from LO control were, if at all, motivated by LO's own distributional principles. Ericson felt justified in his demands by rampant wage drift for which he could not

<hr>

[77]Hans Ericson, *Facket mot folket* (Nacka: Förlags AB Lansering, 1981), 113–14.

obtain adequate compensation without the authority to strike independently. In this case, the "moral disarmanent" applied against high-pay opponents to centralization was of no use. Instead, power relations within LO and SAF, and between the two, did the job of maintaining LO's centralized control. Just as it had done in the creation of peak bargaining, the interplay of interests and values helped enforce the centralized moral economy of the labor market in Sweden. It would continue to do so until the 1980s.

CONCLUSION

Analysis of unions and the moral economy helps explain why rank-and-file militancy in both countries did not turn into the full-fledged revival of a radicalized working-class movement for which many on the Left hoped. In the moral economy of wage labor, German and Swedish labor leaders defined to a substantial degree the terms of willing obedience and revolt. Workers' demands in the 1970s were by and large conservative—either restorative of previous pay structures or consonant with elements of the leadership's own internally contradictory egalitarian principles. Had the unions responded with only rigidity and indifference to the demands of strikers, they might have stimulated a revival of transformative demands. Only if the unions had fully abandoned their own principles—the same principles that moved the strikers—would a widespread and durable revival of militant ideology have been likely.

The argument and evidence presented here, some of it more speculative than conclusive, should not give the impression that a centrally governed moral economy is or can be tidy and uniform. Central control is self-limiting in its scope and penetration, especially with regard to norms about job design, personnel management, and factor income distribution. Local norms about pay differentials will also evolve to complement and often contradict official principles in their operational form, especially when employer autonomy over extra-contractual pay setting is retained. Even within particular workplaces, there will never be perfect agreement about the fairness of existing pay relations.[78] Hence officials in centralized unions confront a system of labor

[78]IG Metall's defense of interindustrial leveling and active pursuit of upward interoccupational leveling of low wages in the mid-1960s probably generated some of the egalitarian sentiment in 1969 and 1973 against short-term inegalitarian trends. But in the two metal industry firms whose workers Teschner interviewed in late 1970, 49 percent and 57 percent wanted reductions in pay differentials, whereas 46 percent and 37 percent preferred they stay the same. Only 4 percent and 6 percent wanted increases in differentials. *Lohnpolitik im Betrieb,* 183.

relations with no guaranteed equilibrium in power and income distribution. When latent conflicts become overt, pressure builds for democratization and decentralization of control, especially when uncontrolled market events put wind in the sails of militant activists.

Although both IG Metall and LO would not give way to pressures for democratization and decentralization of union authority, they showed considerable flexibility in response to the distributional grievances of the early 1970s. Leaders zealously guarded their centralized control against internal and external pressures generated by the difficulties of controlling pay structures while at the same time protecting employment and keeping high profits under control. As Part II of this book shows, their efforts to protect centralized control in the moral economy extended into the political sphere as well. The next chapter provides the analysis upon which we can build an explanation of their evolving strategies in the political economy.

UNIONS IN THE POLITICAL ECONOMY

Chapter Four

The Wage Policy Trilemma

Of what consequence are the pay leveling objectives of unions for the politics of reform and transformation in capitalism? Just as the literature on unions tends to neglect wage-distributional issues in attempts to explain the evolution and behavior of centralized unions in the labor market, so it also neglects the ramifications of leveling in the sphere of politics. The need for integrated analysis of the moral economy of pay and the political economy of centralized unionism emerges when one examines the universal problem of unions in politics: the trade-off between wages, on the one hand, and price stability, employment, and growth, on the other.

WAGE RESTRAINT AND PAY STRUCTURE

The analysis of union wage policy and political economy usually draws attention to the trade-off between employment and wage levels, making little reference to their structure. If unions force wages up too fast, it is said, prices may rise, production and investment fall, and unemployment result. Unemployment then undermines the future bargaining power of unions and their political and governmental support. If unions succeed in influencing government policy to protect full employment, labor supply bottlenecks tighten, bringing localized pay raises. These increases are transmitted throughout the economy by unions strengthened by full employment and intent on reinstating earlier patterns of distribution. Generalized inflation then brings medium-term threats to employment from consumer reactions (declining domestic and foreign demand), business reactions (declining investment

111

and capital flight), and government reactions (deflationary policies in response to balance of payments disturbances and shrinking foreign currency reserves).

The old idea of an "uneasy triangle" in the relationship between full employment, price stability, and free trade unionism describes in a tidy way some of these causal processes. Free trade unionism, accordingly, is compatible with either full employment or price stability but not both at the same time.[1] This belief inspires ideological and legal assaults against unions.[2] Union officials understandably fear both unemployment and state regulation associated with their power to generate inflation, and often they readily accept the need for self-restraint. Stopping half way between free, aggressive collective bargaining and statutory control over union wage setting, unions in many countries bend under pressure to cooperate in the voluntary, "concertative" design of incomes policy in which wage restraint is everybody's goal.[3] Unions frequently try in this context to extract something from employers and government in exchange for restraint. Because of the autonomous pricing and investment behavior of capitalist enterprise, unions and their members enjoy no guarantees that their wage restraint will automatically pay off in employment effects.[4] Hence they often demand full-employment policies from government in exchange for restraint.

But as events in Sweden and Germany showed, official wage restraint, when combined with government demand stimulation or rising external demand, gives free play to the distributional shocks of high and uneven profits and wage drift, which in turn trigger rank-and-file

[1] A similar model holds that full employment, price stability, and external surplus cannot be held in stable equilibrium, except in the absence of market clearance, especially in the labor market. For this reason, "cost-conscious" German unions in the past may have cooperated in opening borders to immigrant labor. See Robert J. Flanagan, David W. Soskice, and Lloyd Ulman, *Unionism, Economic Stabilization and Incomes Policies: European Experience* (Washington, D.C.: Brookings, 1983), 216–17.

[2] See for example Peter Wiles, "Are Trade Unions Necessary?" *Encounter* 7 (September 1956), 5–11. Even economists not ideologically antagonistic to unions have asserted the incompatibility of unions with economic stability and full employment. A notable example is Charles E. Lindblom, *Unions and Capitalism* (New Haven: Yale University Press, 1949); recently, Martin L. Weitzman, *The Share Economy: Conquering Stagflation* (Cambridge: Harvard University Press, 1984). For a general discussion of various viewpoints, see Hans-Adam Pfromm, "Einkommenspolitik und Verteilungskonflikt" (diss., Johann Wolfgang Goethe University, 1974), 23–32, 62–73.

[3] The most comprehensive study of unions and incomes policies is Flanagan, Soskice, and Ulman, *Unionism.*

[4] On the uncertain employment payoffs of pay restraint or "responsible wage policy" ("the fiction of the wage-employment bargain"), see Arthur M. Ross, *Trade Union Wage Policy* (Berkeley: University of California Press, 1948), 80–94, and Colin Crouch, "Varieties of Trade Union Weakness: Organised Labour and Capital Formation in Britain, Federal Germany and Sweden," in Jack Hayward, ed., *Trade Unions and Politics in Western Europe* (London: Cass, 1980), 89–91.

rebellion. Disturbances in pay structures set off wildcat strikes and challenges to centralized union authority over wage and strike policy. From the standpoint of union objectives in the moral economy, in other words, wage restraint imperils past accomplishments—especially when demand and employment enjoy simultaneous protection.

Wage restraint does not always work against unions' objectives in controlling pay structures. To complicate the picture, we must remember that unions often exercise a restraining force on wages for the purposes of wage leveling. Arthur Ross has pointed out that unions, by insisting on uniformity of wage rates within industries, voluntarily forego the higher average wages or total wage income for members they could achieve according to the "ability to pay" criterion.[5] In the Swedish case, the unions generally came to embrace supra-industrial bargaining, which created the opportunity for broad-scale leveling while neutralizing the inflationary wage rivalry and wage scrambles whose resulting high pay increases endangered the small, open economy.

To make sense of these phenomena, we can distill yet another "uneasy triangle" of relationships. In this chapter, I argue that unions' objectives in (1) *internal leveling* (structuring pay within a union or confederation), (2) *external leveling* (either by increasing the wage share with respect to profits or by compressing interunion or interconfederation pay differentials), and (3) *full employment* stand in a systematic relationship of conflict. With wage regulation in collective bargaining, union leaders simply cannot achieve improvements in all three areas at once. At any one time, the best they can do is make progress toward two out of the three—at the expense of the third.

The analysis of this "wage policy trilemma" describes a set of powerful market and power constraints that unions face as agents in the moral economy. From the trilemma we can derive a fuller picture of union interests in shaping the political economy as a way of strengthening their position in the moral economy. A political economy is a pattern of state-society interaction in which interest groups and coalitions obtain government market-shaping policies that help those organizations maintain both internal authority and coalitional unity. As seen earlier, wage distribution figures prominently in the development of centralized unions and their cross-class coalitions with employers for

[5]Ross, *Trade Union Wage Policy*, p. 48. Sidney and Beatrice Webb cite the case of the flint-glass makers in Yorkshire who in 1895 negotiated cutbacks in piece rates in exchange for rate standardization. *Industrial Democracy* (London: Longman's, Green, 1902), 280–81. H. A. Turner cites the British wallpaper workers' union, which once chose a lower overall settlement but more egalitarian wages over an employer offer of extra increases at the high end of the pay scale. "Trade unions, differentials and the levelling of wages," *Manchester School of Economic and Social Studies* 20:3 (1952), 239.

governance of the moral economy. In the political economy, centralized unions seek government action to structure the market environment of wage bargaining in ways that secure the distributional foundations of centralization.

Egalitarian Unionism

Let us consider a "model" egalitarian union and its distributive goals in wage bargaining in centralized, multiemployer agreements (as in West Germany and Sweden). The fundamental problem for leaders of our model union is this: How can a larger share of income be distributed as wages, to more people, and with greater equality? The question concerns how unions should choose wage bargaining objectives to meet their commitments to (1) an increase in the wage share at the expense of profits (regardless of its distribution), (2) the leveling of wages (whether upward or downward), and (3) wider and more secure access to wage income for the entire labor force, employed and unemployed.

A number of interesting propositions can be made about the objectives of egalitarian unionism. First, moving toward any one of the three objectives cannot easily be accomplished in a way that is neutral with respect to the other two. Out of this emerges another, more interesting proposition: simultaneous movement in all three directions is impossible. In other words, *with wage regulation alone,* a union can make progress on no more than two of the objectives at any one time—at the necessary expense of the third. Finally, when real unions consistently try to pursue any pair of these three egalitarian policies in collective bargaining, the market effects of the policies generate punitive reactions from members and activists, employers and the state, thereby forcing a retreat. The trilemma and its consequences for union policy making suggest that unions will try to harness state power over markets in order to preempt or neutralize the costs of their egalitarian objectives in wage bargaining.

Non-neutrality

Contractual regulation of pay levels and structure to achieve any one of the three egalitarian objectives—wage share maximization, wage leveling, job supply—cannot be achieved, I have suggested, without severe risk to previous egalitarian accomplishments on at least one of the other two dimensions. A few illustrations suffice to show the point. No wage increases or reductions are neutral from a wage-distributional standpoint, for instance (excepting the trivial case where all wages were equal before and after the change).[6] Percentage increases necessarily change absolute differences and vice versa. Compression of wages may alter the costs of various production techniques using more or less skilled labor and affect productivity, with corresponding effects on employment levels for different classes of labor. Wage share increases, cutting into profits, are likely to affect employment levels adversely.

To increase the supply of jobs (redistribute access to wage income), unions have several possible though not always reliable options in wage bargaining. First, they can accept real wage increases below productivity increases, or even wage reductions, in the hope that cost and therefore price reductions will increase demand and employment. Alternatively, profit increases may spur expansionary investment. A potential loss in labor's share of value added relative to profits is implied here. Alternatively, unions may attempt to restructure wages to create productivity incentives, improve the performance of labor markets, or even increase investment levels through other mechanisms discussed below. In all cases, attempts to move toward full employment with wage policy are unlikely to be neutral with respect either to wage-share growth or to pay leveling. Those objectives must be adjusted or neglected altogether.

THE VERTICAL TRILEMMA

In fact, no pair of egalitarian objectives can be pursued simultaneously without sacrificing the third. There are three such combinations, or three distributional policy "fronts" depicted in Figure 2— leveling plus employment growth (Front I), profit squeeze and employment growth (Front II), and profit squeeze plus leveling (Front III). Analysis of short- and medium-term effects of action on these three policy fronts reveals the complex but systematic clash of union interests in redistributive bargaining policy. I call this the vertical trilemma, in reference to unions' objectives in the vertical conflict between capital and labor over the distribution of income from profit-making enterprise.[7]

---

[6]"It has never . . . been true that normative systems governing employment relations had the effect of determining only the distribution of rewards and privileges as between capital and labour. Whether intentionally or as a by-product, the comparative fortunes of different groups of employees were also determined." Allan Flanders, *Management and Unions* (London: Faber & Faber, 1970), 257.

[7]This usage is suggested by Hans-Adam Pfromm, *Solidarische Lohnpolitik: Zur wirtschaftlichen und sozialen Problematik tariflicher Lohnstrukturnivellierung* (Cologne: Europäische Verlagsanstalt, 1978), 7, 20.

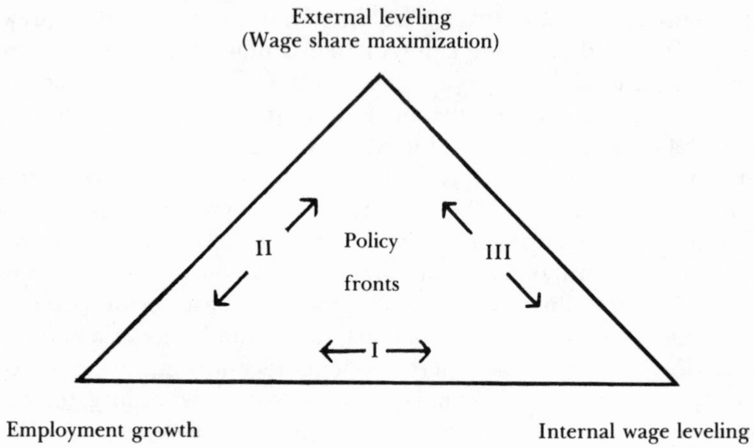

External leveling
(Wage share maximization)

Figure 2. The vertical trilemma

Employment growth · Internal wage leveling

Front I

Achieving some degree of wage leveling while increasing employment levels generally requires "restrained" leveling: either downward leveling (in the sense of wage reductions at the higher end of the wage structure) or upward leveling (extra-slow growth of higher wages) at a time of growth in productivity. In both cases, productivity growth must exceed average wage growth. Both of these options aim to reduce unit labor costs relative to those of other industries or of other national economies, depending on the scope of bargaining in question. Both point toward an increase in the profit share and therefore the sacrifice of one of the egalitarian objectives.

Increased profits may induce employers to expand output and hire more labor. When centralized pay setting brings an industry-wide increase in profits, more capital may gravitate to the industry, expanding capacity and employment. Relative or absolute price reductions due to easing of labor costs may also help or be necessary to increase demand and employment,[8] but price reductions will not necessarily negate the

[8]Price elasticity of demand and labor market mobility faced by the firm or industry in question are important conditions that will affect the actual outcome of a Front I policy. In the case of *industry-wide* downward leveling of wages, for example, leveling might create problems for employers in hiring extra skilled workers when expanding production (while current employees might leave for better pay elsewhere). Employment benefits of downward leveling require some price elasticity of demand for the industry's products, since at this level relative price reductions and increased demand will be necessary for employment expansion—unless reductions in wages lead to the replacement of machines with labor, which is not very likely. At the *economy-wide* level, downward wage leveling will be less problematic in its consequences for skilled labor supply, at least in the short run.

116

profit-share increase.[9] On the other hand, profits from a Front I policy may not be invested to the benefit of the union members in question. Employers may prefer to distribute them as dividends, lend them out, or invest them in other industries or countries or in nonproductive assets. Hence negotiating a wage share decline does not *guarantee* job creation. On the other hand, it is the only wage-regulative tool that unions have for that purpose if they want at the same time to level wages. Potentially, they can increase both the wage share and employment, but only if they are willing to restructure wages in an inegalitarian direction—the Front II option.

Front II

Most discussions of unions and wage policy suppose that encroachment on profits by wages can only hurt employment, or in other words, that a Front II policy is technically impossible. This is a mistaken premise.[10] The combination of an aggressive policy of wage increases with changes in the structuring of wages might allow for simultaneous increases in the wage share and employment. Company-level "productivity bargains," often entailing both hefty pay increases in exchange for relaxation of work rules and rigid pay practices, may produce that result. Success on Front II is predicated in this case on productivity increases large enough to increase profits along with wages, with the latter getting the disproportionate increase. The same effect might be possible through industry-wide or economy-wide negotiation of payment-by-results schemes, especially in combination with sophisticated time-study and job evaluation procedures, thereby potentially increasing productivity, profits, and the spread of wage earnings within firms.

A Front II policy might also succeed by reducing investment risks and improving "investor confidence." If unions agree to allow a good deal of upward and downward flexibility in wages over time, from firm to firm and industry to industry, so that returns to investment absorb less of the shock in demand fluctuations and thereby make investments less risky, they *might* increase the supply of capital despite concurrent

[9]In competitive industries facing highly elastic demand, the risk of increased profit shares will be small and the likelihood of strong employment growth will be high. Price reductions will capture the increase in profits, and increased demand as a result of the price reductions will spur job creation.

[10]By calling for increased wages as a source of demand stimulation to prime the economy and reduce unemployment, unions may defy this premise. They cannot argue, however, that the success of such a policy would necessarily result in a gain for the wage share at the expense of profits, for the consequences of wage increases vary widely. "It is . . . entirely possible for a union simultaneously to raise the relative wages of its members and to reduce their aggregate share of income arising in their industry." Albert Rees, *The Economics of Trade Unions* (Chicago: University of Chicago Press, 1977), 96.

decline in the profit share. By absorbing more of the shocks, labor has the potential to reduce the profitability levels that risk-averse investors demand in order to increase investment levels. As a consequence, within and across industries, the increasingly unevenly distributed wage share might grow and investment might increase, even though the profit share stagnates. The efficiency effects of wage differentiation on the mobility of labor might also be mentioned here, along with some skepticism about their real significance.[11]

Profit sharing suits the Front II strategy. Profit sharing combines the productivity and shock-absorbing properties of other pay systems that allow relative pay to fluctuate from firm to firm. In his recent call for the replacement of the "wage system" with a "share system," American economist Martin Weitzman suggests that the chronic tendency of modern capitalism to underutilize labor, and the incompatibility of full employment and price stability, can be remedied in this way.[12] The German Council of Economic Experts, appealing to a German audience more concerned than the American one about factor income distribution, suggests that company profit sharing could achieve exactly what Front II calls for—not only better macroeconomic performance but also an increase in the wage share. A combination of company profit sharing plus more widespread use of performance and merit pay would greatly enhance the likelihood of meeting two egalitarian objectives of labor: a higher wage share plus increased employment.[13] Pay leveling, on the other hand, must suffer.

Front III

The most militant of all possible egalitarian union policies is the maximization of the wage share along with wage leveling. The direct

[11]Workers, according to many economists, are highly unresponsive to differentials in their location decisions. See for example OECD, *Wages and Labour Mobility* (Paris, 1975), and Gordon F. Bloom and Herbert R. Northrup, *Economics of Labor Relations* (Homewood, Ill.: Irwin, 1969), 232–44. On the origins and costs of wage rigidity, see Wilfred Beckerman, ed., *Wage Rigidity and Unemployment* (London: Duckworth, 1986), and James E. Annable, *The Price of Industrial Labor* (Lexington, Mass.: Lexington Books, 1984).

[12]Weitzman argues that any "share system" creates an incentive for employers to hire more labor by making the marginal cost of labor less than average cost. He does not suggest however that the wage share can or will increase. *The Share Economy*, especially 82–95. See also his "The Simple Macroeconomics of Profit-sharing," in Beckerman, *Wage Rigidity and Unemployment*, 171–200.

[13]See Sachverständigenrat, *Zeit zum Investieren: Jahresgutachten 1976–77* (Stuttgart: Kohlhammer, 1977), 144–48, especially 146–47. The effect of performance pay techniques in reducing fixed labor costs can be augmented by strengthening the prerogatives of employers to lay off workers when supplies and orders are low. This also tends to increase dispersion in wages or, more precisely, wage earnings.

cost is unemployment. This combination of egalitarian objectives calls not only for the upward leveling of occupational differentials but also the insensitivity of wages to productivity and profitability at the enterprise and sectoral levels. It also entails a reduction in performance pay components because of their characteristic differentiation of wage income.

Such a radical policy would have immediately deleterious effects, as labor costs and prices rise, productivity declines, labor markets function worse than usual, profits decline, and capitalists respond with their own form of strike: they stop investing. The decline of business activity does not immediately threaten labor's objective of increasing the wage share of income, even though the number of wage earners declines, for typically wages' share of income during recessions *increases*—profits simply decline at a faster pace than wages.[14]

Implications

Even union leaders genuinely motivated by radical egalitarian objectives will tend to respond to motives of self-maintenance and thus steer clear of the extremes of any of the three policy fronts. In other words, they will be strongly inclined to pursue a moderate course of action, as most unions do, at least in the long run. Membership, employer, and even government reactions will play a deciding role, if not in bringing moderation then in forcing egalitarian leaders along an erratic policy path toward one policy front and then another.

If, for example, a union's leadership pursues a Front I policy, localized windfall profits and obscure payoffs may add ideological fuel to the latent opposition among relatively high-pay workers with a potentially strong independent bargaining position. The intensity of members' reactions will probably bear some relationship to their concentration in high-wage and high-profit firms or sectors, because the extra restraint they are called upon to exercise for the sake of leveling disproportionately favors their already prosperous employers. The resulting threat of wildcat strikes, development of autonomous, informal bargaining arrangements, or even breakaway unions naturally tends to drive unions away from Front I, even when employers are amenable.[15]

---

[14]Rees, *Economics of Trade Unions*, 95.

[15]The evolution of plant-level bargaining conducted by powerful stop stewards in some sectors of postwar British industry (which helped erode the authority of national unions) can in part be attributed to the rigidity of unions and especially nationally organized employers with respect to the regional equalization of wages. Hugh Clegg blames the egalitarian settlement of 1943 in engineering for the ensuing rash of wildcats and the ten-year decline in the regulatory force of centralized collective bargaining. *The*

Leaders may then retreat to Front II, still intent on facilitating growth in employment but now intent on recovering the wage share at "hot spots" where opposition arises. By doing so they relax pressure for pay equity across firms, and resulting pay disparities may only fuel oppositional groups that invoke the leadership's own egalitarian principles or even set in motion wildcat strikes where wages have lagged behind. Latent conflict between various member groups, and especially between union leaders and functionaries in different levels and in different sectors of the union, may be aggravated, and the generation of consensus for future wage rounds becomes more difficult. If sensitive to these concerns, leaders are unlikely to push toward Front II, and if they do, not for long.

If a union then adopts a Front III policy to improve its performance with regard both to internal equity (wage leveling) and external equity (wage share maximization), the costs will be borne by firms with low profitability and their employees. Unemployment potentially brings political and union-busting assaults, while guaranteeing deterioration of long-term bargaining strength. One or all will sooner or later punish unions for pursuing the militant strategy.[16]

In sum, market forces render the three distributional objectives of egalitarian unions systematically incompatible, while power struggles within and against unions militate against a rigid offensive on any of the three policy fronts over time. In effect, in collective bargaining, egalitarian unions are "boxed in" by their own objectives and those of member and employer groups whose support is required for organizational maintenance. The cross-fire of external and internal politics is likely to keep unions with egalitarian leadership in disequilibrium, making them erratic if not conservative in their policy choices.

The Business Cycle, Structural Decline, and Distributional Strategies

Even if a union is less than radical in its egalitarian ambitions, the leadership is likely to waver in the face of cyclical economic events, which chase union leaders from one policy front to another. The most striking instance is what happens during strong upturns, which tend to

---

Changing System of Industrial Relations in Great Britain (Oxford: Blackwell, 1979), 67–71. In the United States, the United Auto Workers Union in particular has felt the anger of craftsmen at its leveling policies in the past and has even had to negotiate special increases for them to undo the damage and prevent the formation of a breakaway union. See Rees, *Economics of Trade Unions*, 64.

[16]Ross, in *Trade Union Wage Policy*, 28, points out that the "employment effect" of high wage bargains *may* move in the opposite direction to the "membership effect": "An upward wage adjustment may bring in new members, even though the employer is reducing personnel."

bring high profits, tighter labor markets, and highly inegalitarian upward movement in wages (wage drift).[17] Pressured by members whose wages failed to drift in step with those of others and by members whose employers bring in higher-than-normal profits, a union leader is likely to respond by trying to recover lost ground on leveling and the profit squeeze (Front III). At the top of the boom, considering the prospective downturn, businesses often find that unions have pushed too hard in these directions. Unions that fail to abandon Front III as recessionary conditions set in may well meet with attempts by employers, with the active support or indifference of governments, to exhaust union strike funds in strikes and lockouts or even to break unions by hiring nonunion workers.[18] Unions rarely antagonize employers and government so sorely before they retreat.

Whereas external threats guard Front III, it is the powerful fear of *internal* discord and the breakdown of solidarity that scares unions away from combining a full employment strategy with either leveling or a profit squeeze (Fronts I or II). In response to business-cycle downturns and balance of payments problems, unions may try to pursue "restrained leveling" (Front I) at the risk of angering higher-wage union members or members whose firms are still turning good profits. The restraint imposed on such members for the sake of wage leveling and employment means neglecting opportunities to remedy the distributional wrongs they perceive with respect to other wage, salary, or profit earners, whose incomes may at the same time be growing apace. Windfall effects—in relative pay for workers outside the union's bargaining jurisdiction and in absolute terms for company profits within— inspire intraunion dissent and wildcat job actions whose independent success discredits the union leadership.

If in response to sagging employment a union pushes for increased wage flexibility while trying to maintain or even increase the wage share (a Front II strategy), it may jeopardize its moral claim to leadership over conflicting groups within the membership and ultimately lose support and membership levels. Subordination to employers' interests in greater wage differentiation may involve unions actively in

---

[17]*Wage drift* is the noncontractual change, usually upward, in wage rates—measured as the difference between the percentage increase in effective wages and that in the officially negotiated increase. On the inegalitarian structure of wage drift in Sweden and Germany, see Horst Hart and Casten von Otter, *Lönebildningen på arbetsplatsen* (Stockholm: Prisma, 1973), and Eckhart Teschner, *Lohnpolitik im Betrieb* (Frankfurt: Campus, 1977).

[18]"The real significance of . . . economic influences . . . is to be found elsewhere than in a continuous functional relationship between the wage rate and the employment level in the bargaining unit. . . . [The] economic environment is important to the unions at the second remove: because it generates political pressures which have to be reckoned with by the union leader." Ross, *Trade Union Wage Policy*, 14.

the administration of productivity-based and profit-sensitive wage adjustments. Application of efficiency principles means repeated repudiation of fairness principles, at great potential cost to internal support.

Structural decline in any industry suffering from a long-term slump in demand usually brings pressure from employers for differentiated and across-the-board wage reductions. Union leaders, who naturally fear what long-term unemployment brings in the way of employer and government action against them, will be hard put to defend the existing wage structure and wage levels or the wage share simultaneously, and in acute circumstances they may feel pressure to sacrifice both of them indefinitely. By confining themselves to defense against unemployment, leaders undermine the long-run vitality of centralized unionism. Rigid Front II policies, by violating established norms of equity or avoiding the further propagation of any such norms, may sap the basis for solidarity that had contributed to the formation of centralized unionism in the first place. Long-term Front I policies, by letting profits loose in some sectors where there is (1) a militant subculture, (2) relatively high wages held back by leveling, and (3) a strong bargaining position for local units, can set in motion powerful tendencies for defection and internal discord.

THE VERTICAL TRILEMMA AND POLITICS

To the extent union leaders are committed or pressured to pursue egalitarian policies (or, as in the case of structural decline, to defend existing accomplishments), they are likely to seek state action to help them cope with the trilemma. In fact, market-shaping economic and social policies that practically all union movements demand from government are fully consistent with, if not rigorously derivable from, the trilemma. These policies can be classified into three general categories: "decommodification" of labor (welfare state and redistributive measures), macroeconomic demand management, and industrial policies.

Decommodification of Labor

Decommodification of labor involves establishing conditions for the reproduction of labor power outside the labor market.[19] It describes a

[19]This notion is closely related to that of Claus Offe in *Contradictions of the Welfare State* (Cambridge: MIT Press, 1984), 61, 197. See also Gøsta Esping-Andersen, *Politics against Markets: The Social Democratic Road to Power* (Princeton: Princeton University Press, 1985), 31–36, and 148.

wide variety of state actions behind which trade unions have historically been a powerful force: unemployment insurance, labor market training and mobilization programs, health and housing provision, retirement and disability income maintenance schemes, child support, other redistributive tax and transfer programs, and public employment for administration of the welfare state and for maintenance of employment for its own sake. Strong union support for decommodification might well be explained by union dilemmas in wage bargaining.

Decommodification loosens the binds of the wage policy trilemma in collective bargaining in two important ways. First, nonmarket provision of workers' basic needs reduces the severity of competition between the unemployed and the employed in the work force, thereby weakening the punitive mechanisms against wage policies that jeopardize employment. Second, welfare state measures help reduce the load and urgency of membership demands on unions in collective bargaining. For example, the costs to union leadership of neglect or regress with regard to wage leveling are mitigated when existing or increasing earnings differentials do not significantly divide wage earners by their ability to secure "life chances." The universalistic welfare state, redistributing resources largely within the working class, helps destratify that class, solidifying it both organizationally and politically.[20] Progressive personal and corporate income taxation, helping finance the welfare state in a redistributive manner, can also "take the heat off" union leaders unable to eliminate the irritants of sectoral high profits and high wage differentials.[21]

Demand Management

Demand management policies for full employment maintain bargaining power for unions and at the same time—to the extent they are successful in encouraging growth—loosen the binds of the trilemma. Growth affords unions some "slack" for the intermittent neglect of their objectives, for three reasons. First, and most obviously, demand-side stimulation of employment relieves unions of the task of independently inducing hiring by lowering their claims on profits. Second, growth in workers' purchasing power may forestall membership pressure on union leaders to squeeze profits. Because of efficiencies of

[20]Esping-Andersen develops this argument in detail in *Politics against Markets*, esp. 30–36 and 145–90.

[21]Offe argues that welfare state decommodification is both functional and dysfunctional for modern capitalism; in other words, "capitalism can't live with it and can't live without it." Unions experience another facet of the contradiction: decommodification reduces the load while at the same time reducing the "bargaining space" (*Spielraum*) in collective bargaining, since to the extent that the welfare state taxes productive income, it reduces what is left to allocate in the wage bargain.

capacity utilization, growth in demand and output loosens the equation between real wage increases and the profit squeeze, especially when firms are operating far below full capacity.[22] Third, economic growth and attendant labor market pressures leave the "safety valve" of wage drift open, relieving pressure on the leadership from groups disaffected by efforts to reduce wage differentials, especially when the drift helps cancel localized profit-share gains that result from leveling.[23] (Too much drift, as we saw earlier, creates other problems.)

Unions may also call for aggregate demand management in the hope that it will even out the business cycle, which tends to force rapid turnabouts in policy. A demand-managed economy promises the stable medium in which wage policy can achieve reasonably predictable results. Keynesian activism may also guarantee the uncertain employment payoffs associated with wage restraint. The deals struck between unions and governments in collaborative incomes policy making provide an illustration. Here, unions promise to restrain wages and governments promise to maintain demand and employment. Wage restraint without demand stimulation may not lead to expansion of production and productive investment, whereas demand stimulation without wage restraint may generate inflation, balance of payments problems, and then deflationary responses.

A common element in this brand of incomes policy is some kind of *differentiated* restraint of wages, whereby lower wages are allowed to rise disproportionately, thus giving some moral purpose to the restraint of other, better paid workers for whom national employment priorities are perhaps not important or not understood. Government demand stimulation thus increases the chances of payoff in the wage-employment bargain, helping assure that letting profits loose will cause growth to take place.[24] Unions can therefore approach one policy front (Front I) with less hesitation.

[22]It might be asserted that the trilemma loses general validity or even in a sense is "resolved" by growth. First, during expansionary phases when excess capacity is being soaked up, and as labor productivity increases, the wage share could increase, along with wage leveling, without threatening further hiring. As the "economies of expansion" vanish with full capacity utilization, the trilemma will reappear. Second, growth-related changes in technology and the labor process may render long-run relations between the wage share and employment indeterminate.

[23]Growth may also contribute to the leveling of intrafirm, interoccupational wages, as demand for unskilled workers increases along with production levels.

[24]The earlier discussion of the wage policy fronts implicitly assumed that union policy can have a determinate as well as an independent effect on economic events. There is of course much indeterminacy in all economic reactions. Government policy can help wage policy be effective, just as wage policy can help government policy. For example, restrained leveling alone might have a *depressive* effect on employment due to its effect on the demand side, since it is the prospect of profits from future demand that affects hiring decisions, and demand may be maintained only by government intervention.

Industrial Policy

Broadly conceived, industrial policy (sectoral and regional) is another common domain of union pressure on the state. From the standpoint of leveling and the trilemma, the union motivation is fairly clear. The export focus of industrial policies promises, though may not always deliver, demand stimulus and growth levels beyond what unregulated capital markets and domestic demand can provide. Such policies can counteract forces of structural decline, which tighten the binds of the trilemma. They also promise to ameliorate balance of payments problems, which reduce the leeway for domestic demand management. Industrial policies, as unions conceive them, often aim at regional and sectoral aid in order to reduce *uneven* growth and development. The less the dispersion across and within industries in profits, employment, and so on, the less difficult it is to pursue egalitarian pay policy. Even protectionism, which unions often seek for sectors vulnerable to import competition, can relax the trilemma for unions, for similar reasons.

THE HORIZONTAL TRILEMMA

The vertical trilemma describes an interplay of constraints that complicates union efforts to gain higher wages at the expense of the profit share without sacrificing other egalitarian objectives. Implications for union behavior in the political economy also arise from another, very similar set of constraints associated with the contradictions between external and internal leveling.[25]

If the "profit squeeze" is a trade union's egalitarian objective in "vertical" distributional relations between capital and labor, then wage leveling between unions represents the egalitarian bargaining objective of a union in "horizontal" relations within the working class. The horizontal trilemma, which replaces the profit squeeze with "wage leveling between unions" at the external leveling apex, describes the interplay of constraints on low-pay unions or those whose members' wages are sliding with respect to others. In fact, those unions face horizontal and vertical trilemmas simultaneously.

Union leaders generally have an interest in regulating the ratio of their own members' pay to the pay earned by wage- and salary-earners in other sectors. This interest arises by and large from the way union members "measure" the value and success of their leaders, as well as

[25]This usage of "external" and "internal" to describe leveling was suggested by Erik Åsard, *LO och löntagarfondsfrågan: En studie i facklig politik och strategi* (Stockholm: Rabén & Sjögren, 1978).

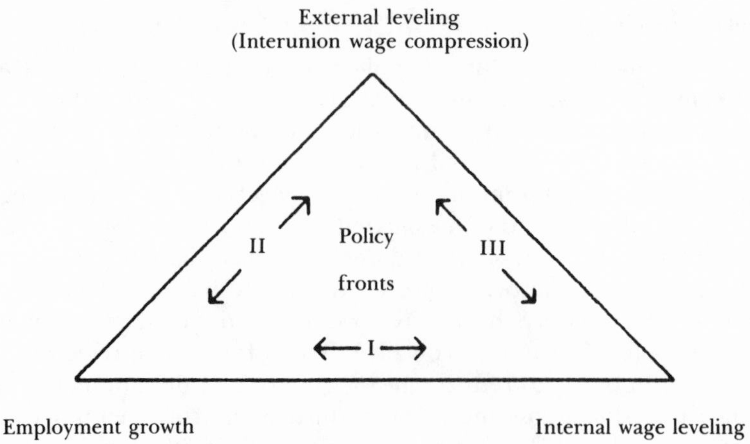

Figure 3. The horizontal trilemma

the way union leaders measure their own sense of professional worth. Leaders try at least to maintain existing external differentials over time by patterning their own results after results in other jurisdictions. Interest in closing differentials will depend on ideology, prevailing norms, and the objective job similarity and skill overlap between unions. Large differentials within the same skill and occupational groups organized by different unions can undermine a low-pay union's tutelary leadership in the norm-setting process, thus legitimating and empowering internal opponents who hold competing norms.

The analysis of the horizontal variant of the trilemma (see Figure 3) proceeds similarly to that of the vertical trilemma and therefore needs less lengthy treatment. A relatively low-pay union seeking to close the gap between its own members and wage earners outside its bargaining sphere must choose between one of two other objectives. It may choose to abandon employment maintenance while leveling wages within the union (the militant Front III strategy), or it may try to improve job prospects by letting wage differentials increase within the union (Front II). In the latter case, only the wages of some of the unions' members—the higher-paid—can be allowed to rise with respect to wages outside the union. Upward movement of higher wages and downward movement of lower wages will have offsetting effects on total wage costs, while productivity and investment prospects might improve, thereby benefiting employment. The remaining Front I strategy, internal leveling plus job creation, will only increase the distance between high-pay groups in the union and groups outside.[26]

[26]To the extent that interindustry mobility of skilled labor is strong, this strategy is unlikely to produce growth and will meet employer resistance.

126

The implications of the horizontal trilemma for union strategy regarding wage policy in collective bargaining are much like those of the vertical trilemma—erratic policy shifts if not conservatism despite egalitarian impulses, incoherence in the face of cyclical disturbances, and organizational division, demoralization, and decline in the face of structural crisis. The implications differ largely in the *political* responses of unions to the vertical and horizontal variants of the trilemma. Most important, the horizontal trilemma primarily motivates union leaders to protect the union's collective bargaining autonomy from other unions, or else to delegate official bargaining power to superordinate units such as peak confederations. In other words, internal power struggles of the entire union movement will be decisively affected by the workings of the horizontal trilemma. In contrast, the vertical trilemma primarily shapes union motivations in government social and economic policy.

In short, the horizontal trilemma should predispose low-pay unions to hand over some of their bargaining autonomy to higher authorities—peak confederations, to be precise—when supraindustrial coordination of industry wage policies promises to moderate the wage developments of high-pay unions, thereby reducing interunion differentials and divergent pay trends. It should also render them more favorable to government intervention in other sectors against wage developments they are structurally incapable of matching. By the same logic, the horizontal trilemma should motivate high-pay unions to defend their autonomy, to the extent that a loss of autonomy threatens their high-pay status and thus exposes them to the horizontal trilemma. Furthermore, the *vertical* trilemma complements the horizontal variant's effects on high-pay unions by predisposing them to protect their bargaining autonomy and hence their flexibility to adjust wage strategy in order to meet fluctuations in membership demands and the business cycle. For example, a high-pay union forced to restrain wages by peak-level control will likely face a long-term problem of latent or overt internal dissatisfaction about its neglect of the squeeze on profits.

The behavior of Swedish unions described earlier illustrates the argument. In the 1930s and 1950s, it was primarily the low-pay unions that stood to gain from centralization, and indeed they advocated peak-level control by LO, the central confederation. Furthermore, the policy reversals of the Metalworkers' Union on the centralization question from the 1920s and 1930s to the 1940s and 1950s corresponded closely to its changing status over time. Initially, it was a relatively low-pay union "competing" with high-pay unions in domestic, sheltered industries such as construction; later, as a relatively high-pay union, it became less concerned about keeping up with construction workers and

more bedeviled by internal conflicts associated with the vertical trilemma and the need for flexibility and autonomy from LO. More recent
experiences of both the Swedish and the German unions, whose analysis follows, further validate this interpretation of earlier Swedish experiences with the trilemma.

CONCLUSION

The general tendency of unions to support decommodification, demand management, and industrial policies gives preliminary support
to the idea that the trilemma, in its vertical version, can be useful for
our understanding of union behavior in the political economy. The
horizontal variant of the trilemma predicts that unions will seek relief
from the dilemmas of wage bargaining by restructuring control in the
entire labor movement, in particular by changing the degree of centralization. As the next chapters show, the level of centralization in a
country's labor movement, influenced in part by these interests, affects
the character of labor politics in the country as a whole.

The trilemma thus offers a motivational connection between unions'
strategies and problems in the moral economy and their political objectives both within the labor movement and with respect to government
economic policy. The following chapters show that the trilemma can
help explain *changes* in political strategy over time, as well as *differences*
between unions within and across national borders.

CHAPTER FIVE

Resolving the Trilemma: Unions in Sweden

As a radically egalitarian movement, successful at least in its commitment to full employment and wage leveling, Swedish labor should exhibit most clearly how the wage policy trilemma affects unions and their political objectives. In light of the unique nature of peak-level pay bargaining in Sweden, one would also expect the political objectives of the unions arising from the trilemma to be distinctive.

The appearance of two prominent issues in postwar Swedish politics fulfills these expectations. The Swedish Labor Confederation's strenuous efforts on behalf of active labor market policy in the 1950s and 1960s, and on behalf of wage-earner funds in the 1970s and early 1980s—both of which have given the "corporatism" and later "fund socialism" of Swedish unions a degree of international prominence surprising for the size of the country—are direct consequences of the trilemma. Central to both are LO's determined pursuit of wage leveling and the play of constraints on peak-level bargaining described by the trilemma.

WAGE LEVELING AND ACTIVE LABOR MARKET POLICY

By the 1980s, roughly 8 percent of the Swedish government budget, and between 2 percent and 3 percent of the country's gross domestic product, was being spent on labor market measures, the largest share going into "active" policies of retraining and relocation. No country came close in terms of active labor market policy, most others spending larger shares of smaller manpower policy budgets on passive measures for income maintenance such as unemployment insurance.[1] From the beginning, LO has been the moving force behind Sweden's active labor market policy, and its full-time staff economists have been the leading architects of that policy. With employers in SAF, LO also wields statutory power in the publicly funded Labor Market Board, where its experts help administer the policy on a corporatist basis.

The central role of LO economists and their ideas in shaping labor market policy has given rise to a common misunderstanding about why LO and Social Democratic governments committed themselves to an expensive policy of mobilizing manpower and investing in "human capital." In particular, it is widely believed that LO adopted its "solidaristic wage policy" in the 1950s because it was called for, along with the labor market policy, in the Rehn-Meidner model of stabilization and growth. Indeed, LO economists Gösta Rehn and Rudolf Meidner did call for wage leveling in conjunction with manpower mobilization. The truth is, however, that LO's leveling policy emerged independently of the economists' ideas and that the adoption of active labor market policy occurred later, resulting more from the experience of leveling and the trilemma than from persuasive economic theory.

The Rehn-Meidner Policy and Peak Centralization

In the late 1940s, before peak-level centralization and LO's pursuit of interindustrial leveling, Rehn and Meidner had already begun thinking about wage leveling, or "equal pay for equal work" across industries and from firm to firm regardless of their competitiveness and profitability. In their view, a more rational wage structure built on "job evaluation" pay-grading principles would help eliminate the intensely competitive "free-for-all" in wage bargaining that had been centralized only up to the industrial level.[2] Distributing contract wage increases in a way that reduced arbitrary differentials would, they thought, limit the inflationary dynamics of uncontrolled, competitive bargaining relations associated with strong unionism in a full-em-

---

[1]On both counts—overall expenses on labor market measures and especially the share of active supply-directed measures in the budget—Sweden easily takes first place in international comparisons. Gösta Rehn, "Swedish Active Labor Market Policy: Retrospect and Prospect," *Industrial Relations* 24 (Winter 1985), 65, 74; see also Anna Hedborg and Rudolf Meidner, *Folkhemsmodellen* (Stockholm: Rabén & Sjögren, 1984), 123, and Meidner, "Limits of Active Labour Market Policy," manuscript (Stockholm, Arbetslivscentrum, 1983). Cf. Anders Björklund, "Rehn/Meidners program och den faktiska politiken," 15–34 in *Arbetsmarknadspolitik under debatt: 10 forskares syn på arbetsmarknadsproblem* (Stockholm: Liber Förlag, 1982).

[2]Standard job evaluation schemes grade work by skill, responsibility, and difficulty.

ployment economy.[3] As an LO witticism of the 1940s held, there were only two kinds of wages in Sweden: low wages and slipping (*eftersläpande*) wages.[4] Low-wage earners demanded extra, which by necessity retarded the (relative) development of others, which in turn justified extra increases in the latter's pay.

Wage setting, guided by consensual principles for determining when wages were "low" and when "equilibration" (*nollställning*) truly was justified for retarded wages, promised to shift the "Phillips' curve" downward. Stabilization objectives, in other words, would be served by altering what the two economists called "psychological" determinants of the inflation-unemployment trade-off, so that the level of inflation structurally associated with a given level of unemployment could be reduced.

Leveling would also serve export-led growth stimulation by inducing structural change. If relatively unprofitable firms incapable of paying decent rates were forced out of business, capital and labor would be freed for the more dynamic and growing export-oriented sectors of the economy. Logically, then, Rehn and Meidner—and others in what Prime Minister Tage Erlander called the "gang of querulants" (*kverulantgänget*) opposing the more orthodox Keynesianism of the Social Democrats—called for the government to retrain and redeploy the labor force. Solidaristic wage policy would keep wages down in high-pay, expansive sectors, while the mobilization of labor toward those sectors would check the upward wage drift resulting from labor shortages, thus taking some pressure off profits and facilitating expansion.

One of Rehn and Meidner's most controversial suggestions was to squeeze profits with a combination of restrictive fiscal policy and free and unrestricted (yet centrally coordinated) wage bargaining. Pinching profits this way would help reduce the wage-push inflationary effects (transmitted by wage rivalry and drift) of sectorally high profits resulting in part from wage leveling. Tax-based forced savings—collective capital formation—would finance continued growth when the combination of high wages and high taxes kept profit-based, self-financed investment down. Keeping profits down by holding aggregate demand under strict control would in turn relieve union leaders of the responsi-

---

[3]See Rehn, "Idéutvecklingen," in Landsorganisationen, *Lönepolitik och solidaritet* (Stockholm: LO, 1980), 39–41 for a description of these phenomena during the late 1940s.
[4]Rehn, "Finansministrarna, LO-ekonomerna och arbetsmarknadspolitiken," in Jan Herin and Lars Werin, eds., *Ekonomisk debatt och ekonomisk politik* (Stockholm: Norstedt, 1977), 206.

bility for exercising wage restraint: employers under these conditions would play the restraining role, especially in severing the root of much evil—wage drift.[5]

Because Rehn and Meidner recognized that some kind of peak-level coordination by LO was necessary for wage leveling, many have wrongly concluded that the machinery of peak negotiations with SAF was finally built in the 1950s to satisfy the egalitarian ambitions of LO unions and the economic policy objectives of the LO executive. As Nils Elvander has written, "the solidaristic wage policy was for LO the decisive motive for the transition to central negotiations beginning in 1956."[6] In fact, as research by Axel Hadenius shows, the exact opposite is true: centralization was the means not for obtaining egalitarian objectives but rather for ensuring wage restraint, economic stabilization, and forestalling SAF lockouts, government intervention, and possibly electoral failure for the Social Democrats. The resulting egalitarian structure of contract increases was a compromise hammered out in order to obtain the consent of low-pay unions reluctant to give up their bargaining autonomy and power in a full-employment economy unless they received some distributional payoff.[7]

Supporting this view is the fact that the 1951 LO congress decision that officially adopted the Rehn-Meidner model was a dead letter from the start because of tacit opposition from the Metalworkers' Union and the high-pay craft unions. By no means was it a clear policy mandate, either with regard to solidaristic wage policy or with regard to economic policy. The standing "contract council" (avtalsråd) that Rehn and Meidner proposed for centralized vetting of LO unions' wage demands was indeed set up but never fulfilled its function. The LO executive, instead, took over the norm-setting role from the start because of its intensely political rather than technocratic nature. The contract council

---

[5]Rehn held that high profits make businesses lazy and wasteful, whereas moderated profits keep the pressure on them to increase productivity. A detailed description in English of the Rehn-Meidner model integrating wage, fiscal, and labor market policies is Rehn, "Swedish Active Labor Market Policy," 62–89. See also Andrew Martin, "Trade Unions in Sweden," in Peter Gourevitch et al., eds., Unions and Economic Crisis (London: Allen & Unwin, 1984), especially 202–18. For the original version of the Rehn-Meidner model, see Landsorganisationen, Fackföreningsrörelsen och den fulla sysselsättningen: Betänkande och förslag från Landsorganisationens organisationskommitté (Stockholm: LO, 1951).

[6]Nils Elvander, Intresseorganisationerna i dagens Sverige (Lund: CWK Gleerup, 1972), 114. Anders Victorin echoes Elvander, saying leveling was the "decisive motive for resumption of central negotiations in 1956." Lönenormering genom kollektivavtal (Stockholm: Allmänna Förlaget, 1973), 73.

[7]See Axel Hadenius, Facklig organisationsutveckling: En studie av Landsorganisationen i Sverige (Stockholm: Rabén & Sjögren, 1976). Elvander later incorporates Hadenius's argument in Den svenska modellen: Löneförhandlingar och inkomstpolitik, 1982–1986 (Stockholm: Allmänna Förlaget, 1988), 34.

was eventually dismantled.[8] The high-pay unions had gone on record as supporters of the reform, but their support was superficial and their resistance decisive. Attitudes about the Rehn-Meidner proposals, as about the 1941 statute reform, were stratified according to the distributional position and independent bargaining strength of the delegates' different unions.[9]

Furthermore, the form that solidaristic wage policy actually took in 1952 and 1956 onward was not what the economists had advocated in 1951. The LO-SAF agreements of the 1950s through 1969 aimed primarily at reducing average pay differentials between national-industrial bargaining units. They did not bring the disaggregated reduction of occupational and skill differentials across industries for which the economists' "equal pay for equal work" principle called. Initially, individual unions were given great freedom to distribute their average allowable increases within their bargaining units in any manner they desired or could manage in negotiations with their respective bargaining partners. Here the LO executive officers, and especially their economists, had no say whatsoever.

In sum, wage leveling and peak centralization preceded active labor market policy, and therefore put the Rehn-Meidner ideas on the agenda, rather than vice versa. The mechanism that might be said to have driven the policy process in this area was the wage policy trilemma. The trilemma describes the punitive costs that follow the determined pursuit of certain distributional objectives to the neglect of others and identifies motives of union leaders to seek political means to neutralize those punitive forces. Active labor market policy became the "policy support" that LO leaders sought in order to maintain peak control and leveling. A government policy of this nature could help maintain the distributional terms of the cross-class coalition that brought peak centralization into being.

From the Trilemma to Labor Market Policy

Peak-level authority in the hands of the LO executive was established under two conditions: full employment and leveling. Full employment had brought high wage drift for some unions and bargaining power for others, especially low-pay unions, to catch up. Eager to put an end to the result, variously known as an inflationary "free-for-all" (*huggsexan*), "wage race" (*lönekapplöpning*), and "whip-sawing" (*lönesaxning*), em-

[8]On the short history of the contract council, see Rudolf Meidner, *Samordning och solidarisk lönepolitik* (Stockholm: LO/Prisma, 1974), 17–19.
[9]See Hadenius, *Facklig organisationsutveckling*, 75–81.

ployers corraled the unions into the centralized arrangement with lock-out threats. The price they paid was an egalitarian wage policy, which was not wholly disadvantageous to dominant high-wage employers in SAF. LO's price, in turn, was some degree of wage restraint in exchange for leveling. In other words, LO policy—in essence a Front I policy—was initially thrust upon it by forces from "above" and "below"—from employers and government, and from low-pay unions.

The long-term economic consequences of this "restrained leveling" policy of the late 1950s and the 1960s, could have meant the end of centralized bargaining and therefore the chances for leveling as well.[10] What LO leaders ultimately had to avoid was a vicious circle of events set off by their wage policy. High increases in the low-pay sectors and low increases in high-pay sectors would produce structural unemployment in low-pay sectors. When egalitarian settlements left behind "excess profits" in the profitable, high-pay sectors, employers let wages drift rapidly upward because of their favorable liquidity or to attract labor for the increased production motivated by high profits. The increases in pay differentials resulting from high wage drift would intensify the demands of low-pay unions for compensation. The stronger the compensatory components of LO-SAF agreements, the more structural unemployment would be created, and the stronger the wage drift tendencies would be elsewhere. Ultimately, high sectoral unemployment would weaken the potential independent bargaining power that low-pay unions used earlier to set off inflationary wage rivalry and would therefore reduce employers' need for peak-level negotiations. Employers in SAF would then be likely to revert to more decentralized bargaining without inter-industrial leveling.

How was LO to preempt the self-destructive consequences of its favored wage policy, which gave LO the possibility of exercising centralized authority but also gradually undermined it? The answer, conveniently, was to be found in the theory and policy prescriptions already worked out by the LO economists and at least officially accepted a number of years earlier at the 1951 congress. The way to break the vicious circle was through intensive government measures for retraining and moving workers made redundant by wage leveling. The unemployment consequences of business failures or labor-saving strategies brought about by wage leveling had to be "mopped up" by government action if peak-level bargaining and the egalitarian policies supporting it were to be maintained in the long run.

[10]The situation was analogous to that of early Weimar Germany, when the inflationary effects of the distributional settlement behind centralized relations in the ZAG helped bring about its own demise.

Not until peak-level bargaining was fully under way in the late 1950s, however, did the theory behind the Rehn-Meidner policy model begin to "sink in" at the executive leadership levels of LO—even though the model had been officially adopted earlier. This is what Jörgen Ullenhag concludes from his reading of the congress proceedings and other documents. In fact, LO began forcefully to seek and actually obtain strong government labor market regulation or "policy support" for peak-level, egalitarian wage determination practices only *after* these wage policy developments had virtually been forced on LO. In vivid and entertaining recollections of the period, Gösta Rehn describes how reluctant the Social Democrats were to accept his and Meidner's ideas about labor market policy until the late 1950s and early 1960s, when Finance Minister Gunnar Sträng, former leader of the very low-pay Agricultural Laborers' Union and one who was "totally sold" on the theory, was finally able to put them into practice.[11]

The delays in full-scale implementation of government labor market policy can be attributed in part to the fact that not until well into the 1960s did solidaristic wage policy begin to take noticeable effect on the interindustry structure of wages. Leveling picked up even more steam in the 1970s. By 1969, too, LO-SAF agreements began strongly favoring egalitarian distribution of pay increases *within* and not just between bargaining units—that is, within and between firms as well. Studies by both union and industry economists show a striking pattern of uninterrupted wage leveling, and all agree that collective bargaining, certainly not market forces alone, was responsible.[12] International comparisons confirm this conclusion.[13] (See Appendix.)

Expansion and development of the instruments of labor market policy therefore *followed* developments in pay policy. Most important in compensating for the effects of solidaristic wage policy were the innovative "supply-directed" training programs, which represented only a very small portion of total expenditures by the Labor Market Board

[11]Jörgen Ullenhag, *Den solidariska lönepolitiken i Sverige* (Stockholm: Läromedelsförlagen, 1971), 85; Rehn, "Finansministrarna," 222.

[12]See Meidner, *Samordning och solidarisk lönepolitik*, 45–59; Ingvar Ohlsson, "Den solidariska lönepolitikens resultat," 185–201 in Landsorganisationen, *Lönepolitik och solidaritet* (Stockholm: LO, 1980); Karl-Olof Faxén, "Wage Policy and Attitudes of Industrial Relations Parties in Sweden," *Labour and Society* 2 (January 1977), 63–74; Svenska Arbetsgivareföreningen, *Lönespridning: Arbetare tjänstemän 1972–1980* (Stockholm: SAF, 1981); and N. Anders Klevmarken, *Lönebildning och lönestruktur: En jämförelse mellan Sverige och USA* (Stockholm: Industriens Utredningsinstitut, 1983).

[13]Klevmarken, *Lönebildning och lönestruktur*, 38–48; Hedborg and Meidner, *Folkhemsmodellen*, 142–45. In 1980, economist Villy Bergström could write that "crudely put, solidaristic wage policy has given us the world's most expensive textile workers and relatively cheap auto workers." "Lönepolitik, ekonomisk tillväxt och strukturförändring," in Landsorganisationen, *Lönepolitik och solidaritet*, 103.

135

before 1960, gradually amounting to over 40 percent of a constantly expanding budget by 1982.[14]

Would the realization of the Rehn-Meidner ideas ever have taken place had they not been propelled onto the policy agenda by pressures emanating from the LO-SAF bargaining arrangement and its ultimately disruptive market consequences? The question cannot be answered definitively. But it seems likely that the presence of both LO and SAF officials on the Labor Market Board helped make the policy reality, especially because the policy promised to clean up after the effects of the Front I distributive settlement underlying LO and SAF leaders' centralized control. Power maintenance motivations probably helped unify LO and SAF behind active labor market policy. Arne Geijer's leadership of LO probably also contributed. Geijer, former chairman of the Metalworkers' Union, had based his earlier and at times intense criticism of LO-coordinated, interindustrial leveling on the metal industries' difficulties in attracting and finding skilled workers. Now converted to centralism and egalitarian wage policy, Geijer found justification for abandoning market fatalism in a government policy that restructured market forces by generating labor skills that free enterprise alone would not provide.

It should be noted that the more theoretically arcane aspects of the Rehn-Meidner model—fiscal restraint and collective capital formation—received less enthusiastic implementation than the labor market measures.[15] Through the roaring growth of the 1960s, LO wage policies and their effects had presented no compelling reasons for such exotica—unlike the labor market policies, where the reasoning was obvious to union leaders relatively uninitiated or uninterested in the theory. Rehn cites the case of the Textile Workers' Union, whose representative at the 1961 LO congress requested stronger support from LO, so that the union could catch up with the wages of other unions, and for pressure on the labor market authorities to help textile workers thrown out of work as a result to find jobs in industries with more promising futures.[16] Similar direct experiences and resulting pressures

[14]Rehn writes of substantial "ideological lags" between the pressure applied by LO officials for "supply-directed" (training workers in skills in short supply) as well as "demand-directed" (job creation at points of labor surplus) programs and their expansion. Rehn, "Swedish Active Labor Market Policy," 81–82.

[15]Rehn, "Finansministrarna," 218, 222–23. Development of the national pension fund system in the 1960s, complying to a degree with the demands of the active labor market policy for "collective capital formation," can be explained best by factors other than the force of ideas in the Rehn-Meidner model. See Hugh Heclo, *Modern Social Politics in Britain and Sweden: From Relief to Income Maintenance* (New Haven: Yale University Press, 1974), 228–53; Gøsta Esping-Andersen, *Politics against Markets: The Social Democratic Road to Power* (Princeton: Princeton University Press, 1985), 145–78.

[16]Rehn, "Finansministrarna," 218.

did not suggest to the unions the other, more esoteric features of the model.

In conclusion, use of the trilemma to explain why an active labor market policy appeared on the Swedish political agenda should help dispel two common misunderstandings about the relationship between the Swedish labor confederation's bargaining structure, its wage policy, and its politics. The first, dealt with above, suggests that LO adopted peak centralization in order to achieve leveling, not vice versa. The second, concerning the Rehn-Meidner model, suggests that LO eventually adopted egalitarian wage policies in order to fulfill the requirements of its unorthodox policy of stabilization and growth through labor market intervention. Casten von Otter, for example, suggests that LO adopted solidaristic wage policy to resolve the dilemmas of full employment and price stability, which is what Rehn and Meidner recommended.[17] This is in fact not the case. Even Andrew Martin, a leading expert on LO and Swedish economic policy, at times leaves the impression, or at least leaves open the possible interpretation, that the adoption of the Rehn-Meidner model as LO's official policy at its 1951 congress explains later decisions actually to undertake egalitarian wage policies in 1952 and from 1956 onward.[18] LO's own "autobiographies" suggest the same chain of events by mentioning the Rehn-Meidner model but not the internal conflicts that produced today's egalitarian policies, doubtless because latent divisions in the present mirror conflicts of the past. Organizational interests lie in describing recent history as one without winners and losers.[19] Past conflicts were in fact decisive, and Gösta Rehn's and Rudolf Meidner's ideas about wages and labor markets were not sufficient and possibly not even necessary factors causing LO to adopt the solidaristic wage policy.

Although the Rehn-Meidner model was conceived *before* LO actually took over egalitarian wage policy making, therefore, it is not at all clear that macroeconomic motivations invoked by the model explain what

[17]His picture is actually somewhat ambiguous. He suggests, correctly, that the solidaristic wage policy was also adopted to resolve the dilemmas of maintaining consensus among and within unions behind voluntary restraint necessary for full employment and economic growth. See his "Swedish Welfare Capitalism: The Role of the State," in Richard Scase, ed., *The State in Western Europe* (London: Croom Helm, 1980), 155.

[18]Martin, "The Dynamics of Change in a Keynesian Political Economy: The Swedish Case and Its Implications," in Colin Crouch, ed., *State and Economy in Contemporary Capitalism* (New York: St. Martin's Press, 1979), 104–5. Elsewhere, Martin presents the historical facts in better detail but remains unclear about causality: see "Trade Unions in Sweden," 203–13. A reviewer of Martin's study concluded, for instance, that the Swedish labor movement "was the first to adopt Keynesianism and the first to recognize its inflationary consequences. Their solution was a solidaristic wage policy." *American Political Science Review* 79 (June 1985), 559–60. This is exactly the wrong conclusion to draw.

[19]See for example LO's summary of the history of solidaristic wage policy in Landsorganisationen, *Lönepolitik: Rapport till LO-kongressen 1971* (Stockholm: LO, 1971) 21–38.

ensued. Had conditions not forced LO unions into central bargaining with SAF, the creative economic policy ideas of LO economists would have gone the way of all good ideas scattered on unfertile institutional ground. Over the long run, they would have been discarded and forgotten. Certainly they would never have met with the enthusiastic support they ultimately enjoyed.

In no way, therefore, did the LO experts drive the evolution of institutional structure and policy. It may be true that the actual policy developments we have seen might have failed to transpire in the absence of experts and their ideas. But the opposite would have been more likely: if the political and organizational developments had not been in the making, it is unlikely the ideas would have emerged. In some sense, the production of the economic policy program was strongly driven by organizational and wage policy developments, and the same holds even more strongly for the transformation of policy ideas into Social Democratic government policy. The Front I policy of restrained leveling, which LO adopted in the 1950s and 1960s, not only justified but also received critical support from active labor market policy.

THE WINDING ROAD TO FUND SOCIALISM

Active labor market policy in Sweden—and no doubt the growing public sector as well—helped absorb labor made redundant by egalitarian wage policy. But it could do nothing about excess profits and wage drift associated with general wage restraint combined with leveling. LO efforts at restraint, responding to pressure from SAF and the Social Democratic government, aimed at keeping general, nominal wage-cost trends roughly within the framework of productivity increases, especially in the nonsheltered sectors, throughout the 1960s and 1970s. Although LO leaders considered themselves by no means the sole guardians of full employment through their wage restraint, they recognized the shared role they had to play. Full employment, after all, was what had propelled them into power in the first place. It was probably keeping them there.

LO was only partially successful in maintaining restraint, however. Through the 1960s and 1970s, LO wage bargaining strategy and results "oscillated" regularly between Front I and Front III, from restrained to militant leveling. Restrained leveling, it became increasingly clear, set in motion forces that undermined LO's ability to maintain restraint over the long haul. While occasionally relaxing their restraints on wages, however, LO leaders clung tenaciously to egalitarian wage policy. In the face of its disruptive consequences, LO sought political solutions to allow pursuit of a steadier Front I policy. Most important of these solutions was collective capital formation in wage-earner funds.

Fund Socialism

In agitating for various versions of wage-earner funds in the 1970s, the LO leadership departed radically from its reformist accommodation to the market allocation of privately generated capital for ownership and investment, just as with active manpower policy it had rejected the autonomous market allocation of labor and commodified job training. The consequences for Swedish politics were enormous. In reaction, about three months before passage of actual legislation in 1983, about seventy-five thousand Swedes, including large numbers of corporate executives and entrepreneurs, took to the streets of Stockholm in protest against the new socialist ambitions of the Social Democrats and LO.[20] Not since the immediate postwar period had Sweden seen such intense political conflict over the fundamental question of how to allocate income, wealth, and control in society—in order to generate more equality, democracy, economic security, and growth.[21]

LO's various plans for collective capital formation all called for a portion of productive income from private enterprise to be channeled into funds solely or partially managed by union officials or elected workers' representatives.[22] The first two versions called for the wage-earner share of profits (20 percent) to stay in the firm where it was generated, issued as shares held permanently by the funds. Later versions called for cash payment to the funds, financed by a dual tax on wages and profits. In the later versions, the funds would buy and sell shares on the open market. In all versions, voting rights connected to

[20]One year after this "march of directors," as Swedish Leftists called it, employers organized similar marches throughout Sweden, in which over 100,000 participated. In Göteborg, Communists and trade unionists organized a counterdemonstration. *Dagens Nyheter,* 5 October 1984, p. 6.

[21]On the postwar debate about nationalization and state planning, see Leif Lewin, *Planhushållningsdebatten* (Stockholm: Almqvist & Wiksell, 1967).

[22]The three official, prelegislative versions of wage-earner fund plans produced by LO were published as Landsorganisationen, *Kollektiv kapitalbildning genom löntagarfonder: Rapport till LO-kongressen 1976* (Stockholm: Prisma/LO, 1976); LO and SAP, *Löntagarfonder och kapitalbildning: Förslag från LO-SAPs arbetsgrupp* (Stockholm: Tiden, 1978); and LO and SAP, *Arbetarrörelsen och löntagarfonder: Rapport från en arbetsgrupp inom LO och socialdemokraterna* (Stockholm: Tiden/LO/SAP, 1982). The first version is in English as Rudolf Meidner, *Employee Investment Funds: An Approach to Collective Capital Formation* (London: Allen & Unwin, 1978).

fund shareholding were to be divided up between the funds themselves and the employees of the individual firms where the funds had holdings. Depending on the rate at which profits and wages were to be taxed, all of the plans—except for the final, legislated version—explicitly or implicitly assured eventual controlling ownership for wage-earner funds in major enterprises of the Swedish economy. Hence a revolution in ownership and control was to be accomplished peacefully, incrementally, and legally. It was also to take place without interruption to Swedish prosperity and growth, because capital formation and investment were not to be disrupted, and were even to be encouraged, by the fund system.

LO's new policy offensive was not the culmination of a profound ideological change in the ranks and leadership. Proposals for wage-earner funds came from above, not from below. The change in policy did not accompany or follow any major turnover in LO leadership. Gunnar Nilsson, LO chairman in the early 1970s, was a candidate groomed by the earlier leadership under Arne Geijer, who retired. Rudolf Meidner, LO's chief researcher and economist, played a central role in introducing wage-earner funds, as he did with active labor market policy. Also, there was limited spontaneous support from members, and the leadership generated little broad-based public enthusiasm for such a complicated scheme.

There was also great continuity in the objectives that wage-earner funds and active labor market policy were designed to further. Just as active labor market policy came to fruition on behalf of wage leveling, and not vice versa, so egalitarian wage policy remained the pivotal concern underlying LO's campaign for wage-earner funds. Every one of the LO fund proposals from 1975 through 1984 cited support for solidaristic wage policy as a primary motivation.

The connection between egalitarian wage policy and the fund idea shows up early in the Swedish debate. The postwar depression in the 1920s had set in motion within LO the first, rather bitter controversy on centralization and egalitarian wage policy, resulting from a "catastrophic" divergence in wage developments between industries.[23] Calling LO congress motions for centralization "a crude attempt to establish a dictatorship in the Swedish trade union movement," the Food Workers' Union attacked the Metalworkers' Union and the General and Factory Workers' Union in 1926 for blaming rising food prices on high wages in what was at the time a crafts-based food industry. The real cause of the high prices was, according to Hugo Pettersson of the

[23]Rehn, "Idéutvecklingen," 26–27.

Food Workers' Union, employers and their ravenous thirst for profits.[24] Restricting his members' wages would not solve the problem; it would only increase the accumulation of private wealth outside the working class. Foreshadowed here was the later "excess profits" debate, which caught fire only after the kind of centralized wage policy rejected by Pettersson had actually come into effect.

About a decade later, the Metalworkers' Union became the temporary standard bearer for leveling, entering a motion for "socialistic wage policy" at the 1936 LO congress. The size and growing prominence of the union ensured that the idea would be taken seriously, especially by the smaller and lower-pay unions, whose commitment to the idea outlived the Metalworkers'. Responding to the growing pressure for leveling and peak centralization five years later, a motion from the high-pay Foundry Workers' Union once again adumbrated the problems of excess profits: "When . . . workers in the more fortunate industry groups abstain from their chances at further improving their position and at the same time remain incapable of transferring the resulting sacrifice [*uppoffringsvärdet*] to the lower-paid worker groups in other industries, then one can question whether such a wage policy ought to be recommended."[25]

This question could not, understandably, be answered at the time. Another ten years later, a motion to the 1951 LO congress from the Västervik local of the growing Municipal Workers' Union suggested the bold idea of a "wage leveling fund" (*löneutjämningsfond*) for transfer and redistribution of "sacrificed" earnings from high-pay to low-pay sectors, appealing to two egalitarian principles: taking what can be gotten from profits where they are earned, and handing over a portion of those "wages" to other workers in less fortunate circumstances. The motion met with a chilly response from the LO executive council and the congress as neither feasible nor appropriate.[26]

Clearly LO was not ready to pave the way for egalitarian wage policies by dealing with anticipated problems *in advance*. Solidaristic wage policy and peak bargaining were ultimately forced upon LO by a coalition of external and internal forces and did not require transfer funds. When that happened, the classic objections of the Foundry Workers' Union to the Metalworkers' initiative began to reverberate within the Metalworkers' Union itself, the arch-rival of the Foundry Workers' Union and the union that would ultimately absorb it.

[24]See Erik Åsard, *LO och löntagarfondsfrågan: En studie i facklig politik och strategi* (Stockholm: Rabén & Sjögren, 1978), 53.
[25]Quoted in ibid., 63.
[26]Ibid., 70.

Now was the time for concrete designs for a fund system to emerge. The first proposal, published in 1957, came not from below but from above and outside—from Per Edvin Sköld, the Social Democratic finance minister. Sköld, relatively uninterested in solidaristic wage policy and excess profits, more concerned about the inflationary consequences of union power in a full-employment economy, launched the idea of negotiations between unions and employers over union-controlled trust funds. He looked on such funds as a solution to the trade-off between full employment and price stability. The funds, he proposed, should receive yearly sums amounting to the difference between productivity-based wage increases and the amount over and above those increases that unions (given their powerful bargaining position under full employment) would have negotiated as nominal wage increases. The response from LO functionaries—Rudolf Meidner among them—was indifference.[27]

It was not until the 1970s that interest picked up among LO leaders. By then, however, the Social Democratic party and its government had dropped the fund idea. By 1970, solidaristic wage policy had become a reality and had begun to make a striking impact on the blue-collar pay structure. As the 1969–71 strike wave showed, too, egalitarian pay policies produced some unpleasant side-effects on LO unity. In a joint motion submitted to the 1971 LO congress, six locals from the Metalworkers' Union argued that the main disadvantage of solidaristic wage policy was that "out of concern for employment we could not take out greater overall increases than the majority of industries could have tolerated. This has resulted in an extortionate increase of wealth of owners in the more expansive industries. Members in these industries have not always been satisfied with the effects of solidaristic wage policy when it comes to the skewed distribution of profits . . . [benefiting] their own firms."[28]

The locals then called for investigation of a fund system that would skim off profits left behind by solidaristic wage policy. Two other motions from Metalworkers' locals in Stockholm and Oxelösund also criticized solidaristic wage policy for its benefits to the most profitable firms and called for progressive corporate taxation to offset what came to be called the "backside" of wage egalitarianism—"excess profits" (*övervinster*).[29] Finally, the Metalworkers' leadership presented a mo-

[27]Per Edvin Sköld, *Sparande och medinflytande* (Malmö: Arbetets debattforum, 1957); Björn von Sydow, "Löntagarfonder 1957 och 1977—och Per Edvin Sköld," *Tiden* 9 (1977), 558.

[28]Motion 318, in Landsorganisationen, *Protokoll Del 2: 18:e ordinarie kongress 4–11 september 1971* (Stockholm: LO, 1972), 832.

[29]On these motions, see Landsorganisationen, *Kollektiv kapitalbildning*, 10–12, and Åsard, *LO och löntagarfondsfrågan*, 94–97.

tion proposing "collective capital formation," without elucidating how it ought to be financed. The proposal offered a way of satisfying industry's increasing need for capital in the 1970s without the undesirable distributional effects of self-financing from retained profits. Implicit if not altogether clear here were allusions to the contradictions of solidaristic wage policy: in generating solidarity behind LO coordination, a precondition for restraint, the policy generated excess profits and therefore internal dissent against that restraint.

The motions from Metalworkers' locals at the LO congress of 1971 show how the problems of solidaristic wage policy were viewed from "below," whereas the motion advanced by the union's executive officials integrated macroeconomic, macropolitical, and internal union considerations.[30] As is customary, the diverse motions were "addressed" (*behandlade*) and voted on in the form of an omnibus "report" (*utlåtande*) from LO's executive council. Passed without opposition, the report recommended commissioning a study on the merits of establishing "branch funds" with three basic purposes: (1) neutralizing excess profits that result from the solidaristic wage policy; (2) pooling the capital and creating the capital market institutions for social steering of investment and industrial development; and (3) increasing wage earners' influence in economic enterprises, basing that influence on union-owned and controlled equity accumulated in the system.

Wage-Policy Oscillation

What explains the transition in official LO policy from indifference to enthusiasm for wage-earner funds? The answer lies in the learning process set in motion when, as LO assumed centralized power, it was "cornered" into an egalitarian leveling policy and frustrated in its simultaneous attempts to maintain restraint.

LO wage policies in the 1960s and 1970s, defined as the shifting and, in part, unintended outcomes of centralized bargaining, *oscillated* between restrained leveling and more militant egalitarianism. This portrayal owes much to Andrew Martin, from whose research one can identify four major policy cycles, dated 1964–68, 1969–72, 1973–76, and 1977–80.[31] In each successive policy cycle, and with increasing intensity, restrained Front I policies were followed by militancy on Front III. The net medium-term effect was to contribute to a serious

[30]Meidner and his coauthors note the "strong connections" between the Metalworkers' leadership motion and those of its locals in Landsorganisationen, *Kollektiv kapitalbildning*, 12.

[31]See Martin, "Wages, Profits, and Investments in Sweden," in Leon Lindberg and Charles Meier, eds., *The Politics of Inflation and Economic Stagnation* (Washington, D.C.: Brookings, 1985), especially 436–40.

secular decline in the profit share, especially in the critical export sector. Because of wage drift and at times intense wildcat strike activity (especially in 1970–71 and 1974–75) during Front I phases, and because of LO's reaction to these phenomena with aggressive Front III policies, the result was a "ratchet effect" on wage levels and a long-term downward pressure on profits.

The learning process for LO leaders conveyed three major lessons about the impossibility of pursuing a stable Front I policy. First, there was wage drift, or the uncontrolled upward movement of some workers' wages during contract periods, for the most part counteracting the achievements of solidaristic wage policy. Second, there were wildcat strikes and vocal dissent within LO unions against restraint and its consequences. Finally, there was the feverish intersectoral wage-distributive rivalry—between LO unions and white-collar unions outside LO—exacerbated by wage drift, an independent cause of wildcat strikes. All three occurrences, magnified if not solely generated by Front I policies, forced LO periodically, if reluctantly, to abandon Front I and put a squeeze on profits—without at the same time reducing pressure for wage leveling.

Wage Drift Cycles

Wage drift is the most powerful irritant in any system of wage determination where agreements about contractually guaranteed increases are negotiated above the firm level but where individual employers retain considerable autonomy in setting actual wages.[32] Any centralized and restrained wage policy, egalitarian or not, will by intention neglect to increase wages in sectors that could bear higher wage increases without detriment to competitiveness and profitability. In expansionary sectors, labor market pressures will tend to force wage increases up. Also, higher profits in those sectors may induce workers and their local leaders to agitate for more than what was centrally negotiated, while at the same time employers—perhaps with large orders and low inventories—are more likely to concede increases.

Egalitarian restraint, or Front I policies, will only exaggerate this situation. Often, high-pay firms and sectors are also the most expan-

---

[32]*Wage drift* in Sweden is the difference between contractual increases at the beginning of a contract period and total increases at the end of the period. One way to think of wage drift is to see it as the market's "correction" of negotiated wages, although this description hardly captures the complexity of sociological factors determining enterprise-level wages.

sionary, and there wage drift will be strongest.[33] Also, egalitarian agreements such as those negotiated by LO, which aim at leveling pay structures within as well as between firms, often set off firm-level rivalries between wage-earning groups when higher-pay workers try to recapture lost ground. Employers desirous of smooth local relations may grant extra-contractual increases to high-pay groups in order to reinstate differentials. Local, enterprise-level union officials, recruited often from the ranks of such workers yet eager to gain the approval of all, attempt to gain selective increases above contractual ones without cutting back on the special contractual increases for low-pay members. Hence, firm-level increases in pay often exceed the size of increases negotiated at the peak and centralized industrial levels.[34] Upward drifting of wages from any one of these sources may, furthermore, spread as "secondary" drift. Competition over labor, as well as employee unrest over widening interfirm differentials caused by isolated wage drift, may transmit pressure over entire regions and industries.

Not surprisingly, then, shortly after the beginning of each of LO's wage-policy oscillations in the 1960s and 1970s, wage drift as a proportion of total wage increases accelerated.[35] In 1964, wage drift more than doubled contractual wage increases for industrial workers, and it remained higher in 1965 as well. These increases continued a fairly chronic pattern that had started in the early 1960s (with the exception of 1962, when contractual increases exceeded drift) and contributed to looming conflicts between LO and white-collar unions. The 1964 agreement, covering two years, followed a year of high drift relative to contract increases, but out of loyalty to the Social Democratic government's plea not to impair an incipient recovery from the 1962–63 slowdown, LO negotiated a restrained agreement. An immediate boom in wage drift resulted.

Possibly fearing the same in 1969—again during an upturn when the previous year's drift exceeded contract wage increases—LO negotiated

---

[33]On the causes and origins of wage drift, see Gösta Edgren, Karl-Olof Faxén, and Clas-Erik Odhner, *Lönebildningen och samhällsekonomi* (Stockholm: Rabén & Sjögren, 1970), especially 135–58; Per-Olof Edin, "Löneläge och lönsamhet, en studie av solidarisk lönepolitik och övervinster," Appendix 4 in Landsorgansationen, *Kollektiv kapitalbildning*, 193–200; Nils-Henrik Schager, "Den lokala lönebildningen och företagens vinster: En preliminär analys," from *Löntagarna och kapitaltillväxten 3: Tre expertrapporter från utredningen om löntagarna och kapitaltillväxten* (Stockholm: Ekonomidepartementet, 1979); Hans T:son Söderström and Eva Uddén-Jondal, "Does Egalitarian Wage Policy Cause Wage Drift?" Institute for International Economic Studies (Stockholm, 1982); and Anders Röttorp, "Löntagarfonder smygvägen," *Svenska Dagbladet,* 1 November 1982.

[34]On local negotiations for interpreting and implementing centrally negotiated contracts, and for regulating local problems, see Horst Hart and Casten von Otter, *Lönebildning på arbetsplatsen* (Stockholm: Prisma, 1973), 63–88.

[35]Martin, "Wages, Profits, and Investment," 436–40.

the highest contract increases since the inflationary Korean War years. Wage drift kept below contract increases this time. But problems arose in the second year of the two-year agreement, which provided for only a moderate increase in 1970. The unexpectedly strong acceleration of the boom in 1969 and 1970 translated the contract terms for 1970 into a Front I policy, and once again drift exceeded contract increases: 7.2 percent, as compared to 3.4 percent for LO workers in industry.

Recession and increased unemployment, with reduced profits and drift in 1972 and 1973, was followed by a repeat of the same pattern. In relative haste, LO negotiated moderate increases for 1974 (distributed as usual in an egalitarian fashion) despite strong productivity growth and a powerful recovery of profits in 1973 from the low levels of the previous two years. The profit share returned to 1960 levels. Persuaded by the relatively high unemployment in 1972 and 1973 (when Sweden's recovery lagged behind the rest of Europe's) and the Arab oil embargo, LO officials pulled in the reins so as not to jeopardize an export and investment-based recovery of employment and growth. Unexpectedly, profits and prices boomed unabated in 1974.[36]

The resulting wage drift in 1974—8.1 percent, as compared to contractual increases of 5.1 percent—brought overall nominal wage increases to a level higher than any reached since the Korean War, while real earnings increased only modestly by postwar standards. Because of the inegalitarian structure of drift and the inherently inegalitarian accumulation of profit-based wealth and decline of the wage share in 1974, LO's policy, measured by its own standards, amounted to complete failure—except that it did help unemployment decline from peak levels in 1972 and 1973. The tighter labor market in itself contributed to the high tide of wage drift.

The next time wage drift exceeded contract increases was again after a Front I agreement, covering 1978 and 1979. Accommodating a devaluation by the bourgeois coalition government as a way to redistribute income between wages and profits in favor of the latter, LO negotiated what even the center-right government called a "responsible agreement"—despite the usual elements of egalitarianism in its structure.[37] The share going to profits during these two periods increased considerably. Unlike in the mid-1970s and earlier, by contrast, investment and production picked up only very sluggishly. Em-

---

[36]This was attributable in part to the highly synchronized booms of other OECD countries while Sweden lagged behind, especially in wage growth. Exporters, especially of raw materials, benefited from increases in competitive prices on world markets. See ibid., 426.

[37]See ibid., 455.

ployment continued a steady decline from its 1975 peak—a low peak by postwar standards. Therefore, the drift tendencies in analogous situations earlier did not show up to the same extent, although in 1978 (but not 1979) drift accounted for more than half of total wage increases. Under the new economic circumstances—a sluggish international economy—a policy of greater restraint and relaxation of the squeeze on profits would have been necessary to qualify as a Front I policy; only then would investment increase fast enough to recover earlier employment levels.

A Front I policy under these conditions, however, risked not only the drift levels of the mid-1970s but also a continued decline in *real* wages, something that LO members had already experienced during a period of moderation in 1977–79 (the first time since about 1958). Furthermore, rank-and-file discontent, another correlate of restraint, had once again begun to show up in the form of wildcat strikes in 1979 and 1980, as they had earlier in 1969–71 and 1974–75.

Wildcat Strikes

Each time LO pursued Front I policies in the 1960s and 1970s, unofficial strikes followed, causing the leadership to recoil from earlier intentions to hold wages down. After the start of a Front I contract period, close to the time when a recovery in profits, investment, and employment occurred, localized rank-and-file discontent with firm-level wage developments broke out in waves of wildcat strikes.

This was the case, as we have seen, in 1969–71 and again in 1974 and 1975. Even in 1964, when official data from the Central Bureau of Statistics did not differentiate legal and illegal strikes, overall levels of strikes rose significantly, if only moderately. The proportion of the year's (recorded) 14 strikes and 34,000 lost working days attributable to wildcats cannot be ascertained.[38] Many wildcats may have gone unrecorded. In 1970, according to an independent compilation of data, there were at least 283 strikes, of which 278 were wildcats, accounting for about 37,600 of 38,800 working days lost. In 1974, too, there were at least 244 wildcat strikes out of about 259 strikes in all, and wildcats accounted for about 31,000 out of 50,000 lost working days. Even under the recessionary conditions of the late 1970s, there was another, smaller wave in 1979 of somewhat fewer than 200 wildcat strikes; of the total registered loss of working days, 27,824 out of 28,664 were due to

[38]Data collection on strikes, especially on wildcats, was very crude until the 1970s. See P. O. Johansson and Ann-Britt Hellmark, *Från LKAB till ASAB* (Stockholm: Arbetslivscentrum, 1976), 28–33.

wildcats. Private industry, in which there were no official strikes, accounted for fully 25,558 or roughly 90 percent of those days.[39]

These wildcat waves all followed Front I policies of restrained leveling and accompanied economic upturns and wage drift. A major cause of these strikes, as I argued earlier, was uneven drift. The strikes in turn helped spread secondary drift to areas that felt somewhat weaker labor market pressures on wages, particularly in 1974 and 1975. Then, highly uneven drift in the raw-materials-exporting sector may have contributed to rank-and-file militancy in engineering, where most of the wildcats occurred.[40]

Widening differentials within the industrial blue-collar sector were not the only force driving up the rate of wildcat strikes. The combination of high profits, a tightening labor market, and high drift added fuel to another problem emerging in Swedish labor politics during the 1960s and 1970s: wage differentials between blue-collar groups and salaried workers, both within particular firms and on average.

Blue against White

Earlier analysis of the LKAB miners' wildcat strike in the winter of 1969–70 demonstrated the problem quite clearly. The strike occurred in the second of the wage-policy cycles under analysis. Ten years later, during the Front I phase of the policy cycle (coinciding with a short upturn in 1979), several major wildcat strikes of similar character broke out in other high-pay but stagnant sectors. Iron and steel works in Halstahammar and Oxelösund and the shipyards in Göteborg suffered major wildcats when discontent with the stagnation of wages relative to white-collar earnings could not be contained.[41]

This localized blue-collar versus white-collar conflict during 1979 and 1980 was only one symptom of tensions building at all levels. LO's 1980 wage-policy report described an "increasing mutual surveillance," even at central levels, by LO and white-collar unions in the private sector, as well as by large public- and private-sector confederations or bargaining "cartels." These cartels had consolidated in the 1970s among both unions and employers, in both the public and the private white-collar sectors.[42] LO officials complained increasingly about their

[39]For 1970 and 1974 see ibid., 37, 56; for 1979 see Statistiska Centralbyrån, *Statistisk årsbok 1985* (Stockholm: SCB, 1986), 202.

[40]Johansson and Hellmark, *Från LKAB till ASAB*, 57.

[41]Bertil Jacobson, "Vad hände under 1980 års konflikt?" in Anders Broström, ed., *Storkonflikten 1980* (Stockholm: Arbetslivscentrum, 1981), 32.

[42]Landsorganisationen, *Lönepolitik för 80-talet: Rapport till LO-kongressen 1981* (Stockholm: LO, 1981) 56.

inability to set the pattern for white-collar salary developments by means of their leverage on SAF, which also negotiated with salaried workers' unions, and by means of their leverage on the Social Democratic government, which negotiated with public-sector workers. LO's 1976 report identified a powerful inflationary mechanism in "the direct competition between rival organizations." Each group "always thinks that the other got too much and feels compelled to demand more." Negotiations had become "incredibly complicated" and forced negotiators to "run greater risks, for short-sighted tactical reasons, of neglecting essential long-term concerns, for example those regarding stabilization policies." Negotiations became long and drawn-out as each side refused to make decisive moves without assurances that others would not leapfrog over them.[43]

The questionable fairness of maintaining the differential pay and benefits of high-pay groups outside of LO relative to LO's own members was the subject of the increasingly tense relations between LO and other unions in the 1970s. Of special interest here is the fact that overt conflict was precipitated by the question of wage drift and how to compensate for it. White-collar and public-sector workers experienced little to no drift in the 1970s, resembling in this respect many low-pay manual workers in industry. For this reason, leaders of white-collar unions, especially the Union of Salaried Employees in Industry (Svenska Industritjänstemannaförbundet, SIF) and the negotiating cartel for SIF and other private-sector white-collar workers (Privattjänstemannakartellen, PTK), tried with increasing resolve to stake early claims on the room available for overall pay increases with demands for "earnings development guarantees" amounting to up to 100 percent of the wage drift in LO bargaining units.

Such contract clauses aimed to reinstate differentials present at the beginning of previous wage rounds, thereby preemptively capturing a portion of what LO might obtain for its members in total noninflationary wage increases. In this manner, too, white-collar unions could enter wage rounds on an equal footing, prepared to accept increases in percentage terms roughly equivalent to what LO workers got, knowing that they would be "compensated" for LO workers' future drift. For this reason, LO came under pressure from its own members, and some high-pay groups in particular, to achieve even *higher* percentage increases than white-collar unions.[44]

---

[43]Landsorganisationen, *Löner, priser, skatter: Rapport till LO-kongressen 1976* (Stockholm: LO, 1976), 227.

[44]A further problem with drift compensation clauses for white-collar workers is that, to the extent that LO members' compensation clauses do not fully reinstate the past

The potential losers from white-collar militancy are generally the higher-paid skilled groups within LO. Because of the expense of compensating others for drift and because of the egalitarian structure of across-the-board increases, these groups tended to receive the smallest percentage increases distributed in the contractual agreements, which would then be exceeded by increases for white-collar workers in their own firms. However, they are also the groups who on average benefit from the highest wage drift in the coming contract periods, and so they can recoup much of their losses on their own.

Skilled and other high-pay blue-collar workers were therefore not an inevitable source of dissatisfaction. Only when their independent bargaining strength or their firms' profitability and expansionary potential flagged, checking their upward wage drift, did "hot spots" of discontent seem to appear among them. This was indeed the source of the growing anger among LKAB miners before 1969 and among steel and shipyard workers ten years later. Adding insult to injury was the fact that individual LO workers saw they continuously lost ground with respect to individual salaried workers, despite relative stability in *average* differentials. (Seniority differentials and upward mobility are limited in the blue-collar sector, where the seniority-based, automatic raises characteristic of white-collar scales are rare.)[45] This phenomenon could combine with the structure of contract increases and wage drift guarantees for blue- and white-collar groups, imposed on a workplace whose high-pay manual workers received little or no drift, to produce an explosive mixture.

RESOLVING THE HORIZONTAL TRILEMMA

The blue-white conflict manifested during Front I phases shows LO facing both vertical and horizontal variants of the trilemma simultaneously. Internal leveling and general restraint let profits as well as white-blue collar differentials drift upward. Where one fails to occur,

---

contract's egalitarian results, a portion of LO's newly negotiated increases must be used to "fill out" what was not compensated. The higher the drift, the larger this portion must be, since LO's own wage drift guarantees typically provide less than 100 percent drift compensation. To the extent, therefore, that drift guarantees for the white-collar and public sectors are better than LO's, what remains for the white-collar workers to distribute among themselves for *general* across-the-board increases will tend to exceed what LO can distribute from its equivalent percentage increases for the same.

[45]Landsorganisationen, *Lönepolitik för 80-talet*, 59–60.

the other may.[46] Competition and conflict between LO and white-collar unions thus contributed to LO's inability to sustain a Front I policy and to its oscillation toward a more militant Front III policy before a full recovery of profits, investment, growth, and employment. Thus during the 1970s, LO leaders became increasingly preoccupied with exerting control over white-collar pay setting—in effect, to extend the scope of peak bargaining—in order to keep white-collar pay down with respect to LO wages, especially those of skilled workers. This was one way to help "resolve" LO's trilemma.

Applying State Power

LO could have dealt with conflictual relations with the white-collar unions by using its influence on the Social Democratic government. Statutory intervention could restrict white-collar wage settlements that threatened to undermine LO's distributional accomplishments and capacity for restraint, thereby escalating horizontal wage conflict and its threats to macroeconomic stability. After the experiences of 1964, for example, Arne Geijer reflected aloud, even in front of a Social Democratic party convention, about the distasteful but perhaps unavoidable recourse of statutory intervention: "The only thing that could stand in the way of a development of that nature is for wage-earner groups, both high and low, to come together and agree on principles for wage policy which are defensible from both an egalitarian standpoint and from a broad macroeconomic perspective."[47]

It is probably more than mere coincidence, then, that a social Democratic government intervened against white-collar groups within a few years. The occasion was a 1971 strike by professionals and higher civil servants organized in SACO and SR, who had watched their relative pay slip with respect to LO and white collar unions in both public and private sectors—because of blue-collar wage drift and egalitarian agreements in the public sector that prevented them from obtaining

---

[46]The 1979 wildcat strikes in structurally stagnant, low-profit sectors such as steel and shipbuilding during the economic upturn confirm these points. A combination of overall wage drift exceeding contractual increases in 1978, on top of a restrained agreement for 1979 entailing real wage reductions of 2.3 percent in industry, generated local conflicts fueled by rivalry between blue- and white-collar workers and expressed by rank-and-file militancy against employers and internal dissent against LO's negotiating policies. Here are *all three* "symptoms" of a Front I policy expressed in a few local conflicts.

[47]Arne Geijer, "Inkomstutjämning och lönepolitik," 172, reprinted in Erik Zander, ed., *Fackliga klassiker: En antologi kring facklig demokrati, ideologi och lönepolitik* (Stockholm: LO/Rabén & Sjögren, 1981), 162–72.

commensurate increases from the public budget. The government negotiating agency calmly threatened a lockout against army officers. Through emergency legislation the government then imposed a mediation decision without SACO and SR signatures, making the government a temporary instrument of LO egalitarianism. This action convinced SAF to settle on LO's high terms that year.

But this overt flexing of state muscle would never recur, much less induce the various competitors in following wage rounds to coalesce on a permanent, institutionalized basis. Formation of negotiating cartels within the public sector and among private-sector, white-collar groups did occur, which increased chances for further concentration of peak bargaining, yet without more than temporary results. After 1976, too, the electoral defeat of the Social Democratic government eliminated one powerful political factor that might have advanced the trend on LO terms.

Coercive and Collaborative Approaches

One way of preempting the disturbing consequences of Front I policies was to tame the white-collar unions by recruiting SAF into a coalition against them. There was a precedent for such a strategy in the taming of construction unions within LO in the 1930s, when the Metalworkers' Union had analogous interests in extending its control of pay setting. Such a coalition would make wage drift less of an irritant or catalyst for destabilizing wage rivalry. Aggressive bargaining tactics, aimed at using SAF to impose LO's distributional policies on other unions was one way of setting up de facto peak control.[48] With temporary, strategic abandonment of restraint, LO has hoped from time to time to force SAF to accept its distributional objectives and in turn force them on the white-collar unions, even resorting to lockouts for that end.

First signs of a new militancy by LO leaders against the white-collar unions appeared in a meeting of the representative council in 1964, when chairman Arne Geijer began an increasingly vocal campaign against the tactics of white-collar unions in TCO. That year, salaried workers had managed to obtain significantly larger increases than LO had agreed to. In another meeting in late 1965, Geijer openly renounced restraint. "With fresh memories of the unrest of 1964 in

[48]SAF had in 1967 called for fully centralized determination of overall wage developments and distribution, but within an institutional framework that LO leaders found unacceptably restrictive of their freedom of action and of their control over distributional outcomes. See Martin, "Trade Unions in Sweden," 241–42.

mind," Axel Hadenius writes, the LO leadership trumpeted demands that were admittedly "so lavish that the total increase would without a doubt exceed what was macroeconomically justifiable. Clearly, the objective was to guard against falling behind salaried groups from the start." Membership pressure apparently outweighed other economic and political considerations. Experiences with the recent Front I policy had led to the conclusion, pronounced publicly by LO's representative council, that "there is no evidence indicating that stronger restraint by LO groups in today's tight labor market would induce other groups to show similar restraint."[49]

In 1969, LO had tried (and by and large managed) to hold private white-collar and public-sector unions in line by refusing to sign any agreements with SAF until others had negotiated their increases. It thereby in effect centrally coordinated the process without institutionalized control. The result was a relatively restrained overall agreement. But the boom and the wage drift that followed in LO bargaining units seemed to break the hold LO had asserted. In 1971 it once again backed away from Front I restraint in negotiations with SAF in order at the same time to match the egalitarian structure of increases just negotiated in the public sector and, in the aftermath of the LKAB strike, to close the blue/white-collar gap. The public-sector unions in LO had managed in separate negotiations with the government bargaining agency to push through a strongly egalitarian increase—accepted by the government in order to quell a brewing police strike—that LO could match in the private sector only in a way that would exceed the framework set by stabilization objectives.[50] Moreover, the wildcat strikes of this time, beginning at LKAB, pressured LO away from any kind of restraint that might have allowed wage gaps with white-collar groups to increase.

The period following the next Front I agreement in 1974 was marked by further vicissitudes for the LO and white-collar unions in their attempts to resolve their mutual problems. Ingvar Seregard, head of PTK, the newly formed negotiating cartel (the practical equivalent of a confederation) of white-collar unions in the private sector, went on

[49]Hadenius, *Facklig organisationsutveckling*, 101–2. Problems with earlier years' restraint appeared when the Transport Workers' Union bolted from the peak-level bargaining arrangement, hoping to do better alone, especially to compensate for its low drift during a high-drift period. It did not do any better apparently, thanks to SAF's efforts to hold employers in that sector in line.

[50]Information on these wage rounds is based on Hadenius, *Facklig organisationsutveckling*, 105–6; Martin, "Trade Unions in Sweden," 247, 265–66; and Svante Nycander, *Kurs på kollision: Inblick i avtalsrörelsen 1970–71* (Stockholm: Askild & Kärnekull, 1972), 166–70.

record in LO's weekly newspaper *Fackföreningsrörelsen* saying, in mid-1975, that PTK had even been "prepared to accept LO's getting more than salaried workers."[51] Hopes of "total coordination" in the private sector broke down, however, in part over the question of wage-drift guarantees, when PTK demanded 100 percent compensation. As an editorial in *Fackföreningsrörelsen* put it, "the villain in the drama" was the high wage drift for certain LO groups. At the time, Harry Fjällström, chief LO negotiator, pinned his hopes on perfecting a uniform system of wage drift guarantees for both LO and PTK, with SAF help. His uniform system did not transpire.

As in 1975, so in 1978 a breakdown of attempts at coordination accompanied high wage drift. In both years, LO abandoned restraint in order to keep up with white-collar demands centered on wage drift compensation. Again, intentions and results corresponded to Front III objectives. By the late 1970s, then, it was becoming increasingly clear that collaborationist impulses (which had managed to prevail only in the low-drift years between 1976 and 1978) could not withstand the strain of high wage drift and compensation demands, which were the seemingly inevitable product of successful Front I policies. LO's desire to bring white-collar unions to order in peak-level coordination showed little success. It was, in any case, an objective that required full and unambivalent SAF support. SAF's interests in forging a coalition with LO against PTK were, however, temporary and ambiguous.[52]

The wildcat strikes of 1979 were "fresh in the memory" of LO and PTK negotiators when, in the autumn of that year, attempts to coordinate negotiations with SAF and therefore fully expand the scope of peak-level private-sector negotiations for both blue- and white-collar workers broke down.[53] One way or another, with higher increases or

[51]*Fackföreningsrörelsen* 27 (1975), 19.

[52]In the late 1970s, SAF did lead, with LO behind it, in blocking PTK attempts to strengthen wage drift compensation for white-collar workers. Elvander, *Den svenska modellen*, 49–50, 60. But SAF's readiness to concede ground on the wage-distributional front on LO's terms, which they had been doing since the 1950s, was rapidly vanishing, as evidenced by the reformulation of official policy published in 1979 under the title "Fair Pay: Wage Policy Program." In stark terms, SAF pronounced its increasing displeasure with peak coordination as a tool for altering wage-distributional relations: "Central instruments for guiding the distribution of pay . . . are to be rejected." SAF's new attitude reduced chances for total coordination between LO and PTK. Svenska Arbetsgivareföreningen, *Rättvis lön—lönepolitiskt program* (Stockholm: SAF, 1979), 15. The views expressed in this document were of course hardly new. What had changed was SAF's perception of the costs of wage leveling. See Håkan Lundgren, *Utjämning eller utveckling: Ett inlägg i den lönepolitiska debatten* (Stockholm: SAF, 1972), which lays out many of SAF's reservations about leveling. See also Assar Lindbeck's lecture, "Reformera lönebildningen!" in *SAFtidningen*, 17 March 1983, p. 8.

[53]Jacobson, "Vad hände under 1980 års konflikt?" 32.

with differential wage-drift guarantees, LO sought to give blue-collar workers the lion's share of the "room for pay increases" at the expense of what PTK could get for white-collar workers. PTK's negotiating delegation could not accept this aim, and two years of improved relations between LO and PTK suffered a setback. The breakdown contributed to the massive strikes and lockouts of 1980, shutting down all of private industry and much of the public sector for two weeks and resulting in a government-mediated wage agreement that once again moved away from Front I. The final outcome further threatened Sweden's continued economic recovery at the very time that the second Arab oil price shock was beginning to take effect.

Collaborative efforts to generate consensual norms for inter- and intraconfederal wage distribution were another potential and less coercive means of bringing about peak-level control of white-collar contract developments in a way that would not undermine LO's Front I efforts at redistribution and restraint. All such efforts have failed, however, even the most modest plans for collaborative design of government wage and salary statistics that could provide a mutually agreeable "objective" basis for less arbitrary—and less contradictory—wage and salary comparisons. Ever since the 1950s, LO economists have called for the development of "difficulty-graded" (*svårighetsgraderad*) pay data that class blue- and white-collar workers along a common scale from unskilled, light jobs to heavy or otherwise demanding jobs requiring great skill and responsibility. Comparison of pay differentials *within each category* (but across confederations) would then provide a consensual basis for distributing pay increases and wage drift compensation— so long as the principles for designing the classificatory and ranking scheme were also consensual.[54]

In the late 1960s, LO, TCO, and the Central Bureau of Statistics began to develop the groundwork for this new scale in the form of a sophisticated "occupational nomenclature." The white-collar unions agreed to cooperate, however, only on the condition that no difficulty grading of occupational groups would be undertaken. If this grading was ever to happen, it would be negotiated later. In 1971, LO and SAF had actually begun discussing how to go about developing a scale, but collaboration quickly broke down in the context of that year's conflictual wage round. Furthermore, even the collaborative efforts on neutral nomenclature under the auspices of the Central Bureau of Statistics broke down in the beginning of 1979, when it had become clear

[54]From the beginning, Meidner, Rehn, and others recognized that wage standardization and leveling within LO could in the long term proceed only if parallel developments were taking place outside it. Difficulty-based pay statistics would be essential.

that the different sides "could not agree on how to proceed."[55] There was therefore no remaining chance for LO to resolve its horizontal trilemma by expanding the scope of peak bargaining and, through domination of that process, keep control of white-collar pay.

RESOLVING THE VERTICAL TRILEMMA

As the desire grew in the 1970s to extend peak-level bargaining as a way of coping with Front I problems on the horizontal trilemma, other economic and political factors made attempts to resolve the vertical variant more compelling as well. Above all, Sweden's declining position in a more competitive international economy had shown that LO would have to participate in the rescue attempt, even if it meant bringing down the growing wage share of recent years. LO's Front III policies had not been the sole cause of the trouble.[56] But throughout the labor movement, there was considerable consensus that the unions would collectively have to abjure all militancy in the future if Sweden's competitive position was to improve.

The growth of the state sector and the tax burden on factor income in the private sector, combined with the bankruptcy of relatively unproductive sectors (whose unemployment was increasingly soaked up by expensive public relief measures), meant that average unit labor costs would have to do more than just stay in line with international developments. Total production—not just productivity—would have to increase to sustain a large and growing public sector and maintain private-sector employment. Increased capacity and output would require higher investment levels, which suggested the need for a stable reduction in relative unit labor costs and an increase in the profit share. Increased competitive capacity would further stem the tide of spending on imports which surged with each phase of growth, upsetting external balance and pressuring governments to choke off growth with deflationary measures.[57]

[55]On 1971 see Landsorganisationen, *Löner, priser, skatter*, 223; on 1979 see Landsorganisationen, *Lönepolitik för 80-talet*, 115.
[56]See Jonas Pontusson, "Labor Reformism and the Politics of Capital Formation in Sweden" (diss., University of California, Berkeley, 1986), 222–70.
[57]See Assar Lindbeck, *Swedish Economic Policy* (London: Macmillan, 1975), 232. The chronic tendency for balance of payments deficits to grow with each boom or accelerated growth period (1965–66, 1969–70, 1974–75, and 1979–80) was symptomatic of Swedish industry's structural weakness. Capacity expansion and cost competitiveness in the export and import-competing sectors would have to accelerate during Front I phases to unusually high levels to capture larger shares of export markets and to accommodate demand from growing disposable income that would otherwise leak abroad.

Complicating the matter even further was the decline in recent years in self-financed investment, or the proportion of fixed capital formation in industry paid for out of retained earnings or new stock issues. This decline was manifested in a steadily declining equity/debt ratio from around 30 percent in 1970 and 1971 to about 26 percent in 1981 for manufacturing industry (from 29 percent to 24 percent for all businesses with more than two-hundred employees).[58] Such high levels of debt had reduced enterprise risk taking on expansionary projects. Under those conditions, if profits were to provide sufficient new risk-bearing capital, they would have to increase even more than otherwise.[59] But allowing profit ratios to rise to the levels required for these investments would only add to the drift pressures and internal discontent that undermined LO's ability to sustain its restraint.

Government policy contributed to the overheating effects of high profits. Worrying about balance of payments problems, the government pursued restrictive policies during recessions—for example, in 1967–68 and 1971–73, and again in 1976–78—and then failed to tighten the fiscal reins when LO restrained wages to help bring the economy out of recession. The restrained agreements of 1964, 1969, and 1974 were therefore all followed by inflationary and drift-inducing booms in profits and demand that the government either failed to rein in or even exacerbated with badly timed stimulation and devaluation.[60]

This "pro-cyclical" tendency in economic policy making accelerated the activation of the trilemma's punitive mechanisms for Front I policies. Increasing dispersion of profits magnified the punishment. A widening variation in profitability levels in Swedish industry, partly a consequence of the stagnation of certain industries, partly exacerbated by decline in equity-debt ratios, weakened LO's resolve to relax its grip on profits in order to generate investment.[61] From the standpoint of conservatives, this dispersion of profits would be salutory for the Swedish economy in the long term. But even the prominent economist Erik Lundberg admitted that the "unusually large dispersion of profits,"

[58]Statistiska Centralbyrån, *Företagen 1981: Ekonomisk redovisning* (Stockholm: SCB, 1981), 39–51.
[59]Krister Wickman, "Kapitalbildning och investeringsutveckling inför 1980-talet," in Kjell-Olof Feldt et al., *Ekonomisk politik inför 1980–talet* (Stockholm: Tiden, 1977), 35.
[60]Ibid., 231, and Martin, "Trade Unions in Sweden," 238, 249, 291.
[61]See Lars Wohlin, "Företagens soliditet och försörjning med riskkapital," *Ekonomisk debatt* 7 (1980), 493. Lars Bertmar et al. show evidence of increasing profits dispersion, especially in terms of return on equity, from 1966 to 1976 in "Löner, lönsamhet och soliditet i svenska industriföretag," from *Löntagarna och kapitaltillväxten 3: Tre expertrapporter från utredningen om löntagarna och kapitaltillväxten* (Stockholm: Ekonomidepartementet, 1979), 69–86.

which he welcomed, "makes it hard for LO to keep wage negotiations on course with respect to its solidaristic objectives."[62]

A widening profit spread sharpened the "excess profits" problem of egalitarian wage policy, making restrained and egalitarian wage policy increasingly hard to accept on the part of workers in high-profit firms.[63] LO leaders got their first taste of the problem in 1974, when unusually high profits in a few sectors benefiting from the international commodity price boom set off explosive wage drift and wildcat strikes.[64] Unfortunately, everyone seemed to agree, profits characteristic of that time were necessary to maintain full employment and growth in the 1980s.

More disturbing than strikes from the standpoint of LO officials, perhaps, was the effect of the profit spread on wage drift and compensation mechanisms. LO economist Per-Olof Edin made the connection most clearly:

> That the dispersion of profits has increased means that the difference between firms that can pay the best wages and those that have the lowest capacity to pay has increased. . . . Increased dispersion of profits increases the risks of wage drift, at the same time that some firms are doing badly and cannot even bear average acceptable wage costs. It then becomes more and more difficult to use wage policy to manage distributional problems and at the same time bring about restrained wage-cost increases for needed expansion and growth.

After wages drift up in the high-profit firms, "corresponding increases spread to other sectors of the labor market" automatically and with the help of drift guarantees. The solidaristic wage policy is maintained "retroactively," yet Front I policies are undone: "Excess profits can then be avoided, but the system has the great defect of pushing up the overall wage level to the heights bearable only to those firms that at the time have the ability to pay the best." In other words, "the wage-cost level is adjusted to the most profitable firms, thereby damaging employment and growth and increasing inflation."[65]

---

[62]Andrew Martin, "Distributive Conflict, Inflation and Investment: The Swedish Case" (Cambridge: Council for European Studies, Harvard University, 1980), 80; Erik Lundberg, "Är vi verkligen solidariska?—en kritisk granskning," in Landsorganisationen, Lönepolitik och solidaritet, 83.

[63]In LO economist Anna Hedborg's words, "in a society with a successful solidaristic wage policy, the tolerance for private profits distributed in a highly unequal manner must be very low." "Löntagarfonder—en konsekvent fortsättning," in Landsorganisationen, Lönepolitik och solidaritet, 168.

[64]Martin, "Wages, Profits, and Investment," 426.

[65]Per-Olof Edin, "Fonder, tillväxt och lönsamhet," in Ekonomisk debatt 5 (1981), 370–71.

Facing wildcat strikes and wage drift on Front I, and increasing unemployment on Front III, LO could have relaxed its pressure for egalitarian agreements. Beating a retreat on that front was made somewhat more attractive by the political pressure from the employers' confederation, emboldened by slowly increasing unemployment levels and by the changing electoral balance since 1976 in favor of the bourgeois parties.

In fact, LO began making incremental moves toward the employers' position in 1980, when it introduced the idea of age and experience premiums for blue-collar workers, much like those applied in the white-collar sector. These increases were to be deducted from calculations of wage drift, thus preventing other LO members and, more important, public-sector and white-collar workers from demanding "compensation." Employers in manufacturing would benefit in two ways. Skilled workers' wages could drift upward relative to all others, helping replenish a short supply in the labor market. This upward trend in relative wages would not set off costly compensation demands from other wage and salary earners, including government employees, whose increases would come out of corporate income or payroll taxes. Finally, some of the tensions between LO and other union cartels would relax, as judgment about what portion of wage drift should be compensated became more consensual.[66]

These changes, however, were small. LO leaders were unwilling to depart more radically from egalitarian wage policy, despite intense pressures from SAF. For LO leaders, maintenance of peak control had no doubt become an end in itself, and they concentrated all efforts on maintaining and developing it along with its mutually supportive strategy, solidaristic wage policy. No traces of the earlier cautious, experimental attitudes about peak-level bargaining remained from the 1950s and early 1960s.[67] The choices that remained entailed either throwing

[66]Landsorganisationen, *Lönepolitik för 80-talet*, 61. At least one could expect SAF to impose the new measurement and comparison procedures on other unions. White-collar unions typically calculate aggregate increases by "standardizing" or controlling for shifts in the age structure and changes in average length of employment. In this manner, upward salary growth—salary drift—may not register in the statistic. Ibid., 59. This is especially likely to happen when new hiring fails to keep up with attrition, or when younger employees are laid off faster than old, which are likely occurrences in the 1980s.

[67]The leadership had however refused to seek more constitutional authority to bolster the consensual foundations of LO unions' voluntary support for LO leadership in wage bargaining. In response to motions calling for strengthening LO vis-à-vis its member unions in 1971, LO's wage policy committee wrote that it is "not through statutory changes that unity increases, but rather the understanding of members that wage policy successes for all members can be achieved only with common efforts and common responsibility. The solidaristic wage policy proceeds under those conditions." Landsorganisationen, *Lönepolitik: Rapport till LO-kongressen 1971* (Stockholm: LO, 1971), 173.

caution to the wind and abandoning hopes of keeping wages in line with full employment objectives or somehow resolving the acute vertical trilemma of the 1970s and 1980s.

Resolving the trilemma could not be accomplished with the means at hand in collective bargaining. LO needed the power of the state behind it to alter the market environment in which collective bargaining functions, so as to ease the binds of the trilemma and defuse its threats to continued centralized control. Wage-earner funds became the political side of the two-prong strategy adopted by LO's leading policy makers, along with the ever hoped-for "total coordination" with the white-collar unions.[68]

At the heart of LO wage-earner fund plans that evolved after 1976 was a tax on excess profits, to break the nexus between Front I restraint and the distributional disturbances of wage drift. Financing wage-earner funds out of the proceeds of this tax represented a kind of forced savings: a portion of productive income would be rechanneled away from its three traditional destinations—disposable consumer income, private capital earnings, and public-sector revenues. Leaving the administration of the funds in the hands of union representatives and allowing them to invest in equity capital in industry, with voting rights accruing to the fund and being partially distributed to workers in the firms where the equity is held, would provide the motivation for restraint and acceptance of continued LO control of peak-level wage bargaining. This moral incentive would complement the "mechanical" effects of the profits tax, which—supposedly—would weaken the profit-drift-conflict nexus that undermines long-term restraint.

Supporting this view, Per-Olof Edin of LO laid out the organization's conception of how to neutralize the disruptive effect of Front I's high profits. With collective profit sharing, or a tax on profits over a certain level to finance wage-earner funds,

we figure on the possibility of limiting the ability of those firms that happen to be most profitable at any given time to drive up wage levels. It will be possible for wage earners and their organizations to cooperate in restraining wage developments, for now they will retroactively receive a more reasonable distribution of the profits that were created. Hence we're saying that the final result . . . of profit sharing and how it influences wage policy, wage drift, and the labor market will be that the total profit volume

[68]The latest developments on the latter campaign came in late 1983, when LO independently proposed a system of "difficulty-graded pay statistics" (*svårighetsgraderad lönestatistik*). See *Dagens Nyheter*, 28 September 1983, pp. 1, 8; 29 September, p. 8; and 1 October, p. 8.

in Swedish industry will increase. Our purpose . . . is to change profitability in an upward, not downward, direction.[69]

In other words, the net effect would be increased aggregate savings levels, most of the savings still composed of retained profits or reinvested dividends but now including a significant component of "collective capital" made available as risk-bearing equity to cash-starved industry. Furthermore, the wage-earner funds would be mandated to make relatively moderate demands for dividends—as described in the second LO-SAP plan in 1981. This moderation would make the issue of stock to them more attractive, and a potentially larger share of profits earned could stay in the enterprise than would be the case with fully private investments.

These arguments emerge as central in the final 1981 version of wage-earner funds advocated by LO and the Social Democrats in a joint publication, *The Trade Union Movement and Wage-Earner Funds.* There the party and the unions argue that "if the industrial growth problem confronting us today demands an increase in profitability in industrial enterprise, we must find some method of breaking the vicious circle beginning with high profits, leading to higher wage drift, which leads to higher inflation and which leads to lower profits and growth." Further:

> To make wage-policy restraint reasonable is one of the purposes of profit-sharing through wage-earner funds. . . . It might perhaps seem surprising at first that a wage-earner organization and a wage-earners' party proposes a measure which has among other purposes the aim of holding down wages. . . . The reasonable union ambition can be described as follows: We should always strive for the highest possible wage level which is consistent with full employment and reasonable growth. . . . [But] since it is in practice socially and from a union standpoint impossible to hold back wage demands if certain firms are doing extremely well, excess profits must [also] be reduced. Some form of profit sharing can support solidaristic wage policy.[70]

THE TRILEMMA AND THE SOCIAL DEMOCRATIC AGENDA

The founding conditions of LO power in the labor market were wage leveling and full employment. Originally, LO's egalitarian wage

---

[69]Quoted in Hugo Hegeland, *Fondsocialism och förmögenhetsfördelning* (Göteborg: Karima, 1982), 26. As Erik Lundberg put it, wage-earner funds were supposed to increase the system's—that is, wage earners'—"tolerance" for profits. "The Rise and Fall of the Swedish Model," *Journal of Economic Literature* 23 (March 1985), 30.

[70]LO and SAP, *Arbetarrörelsen och löntagarfonderna,* 58, 59–63.

policy had a pragmatic purpose: to forge a coalition of interests among low-pay unions in LO, SAF, and the Social Democratic government behind peak-coordinated wage restraint. There is little doubt, though perhaps equally little hard proof, that wage leveling as a principle legitimating LO power took on independent, self-justifying moral force during the 1960s and 1970s. It is hard otherwise to explain LO's powerful fixation on leveling and its rather extraordinary success in limiting opposition and revolt by high-pay workers and unions.

But, as the trilemma analysis suggests, unions are generally unlikely to want or be able to pursue a leveling strategy as consistently as the LO leadership actually did from the 1950s until the early 1980s. The Swedish exception confirms the rule, in that the unions were subjected to heavy government and employer coercion. While the Social Democratic government pressured LO, it also opened opportunity for LO to pursue legislative strategies that would complement and support Front I leveling by neutralizing its self-defeating consequences. The active labor market policy was one example; wage-earner funds became another.

Within the Swedish labor movement, it has become an article of faith that union unity—manifested by peak LO control, wage restraint, and absence of militant wage scrambles—and Social Democratic dominance have been mutually reinforcing. Decentralization would mean the end of solidaristic wage policy and its by-product—unity within the entire labor movement. Andrew Martin describes the connections well:

> The LO's negotiation of central agreements on the basis of claims agreed on in advance by its component unions provides a mechanism for avoiding wage rivalry among them, or at least preventing it from breaking out in open, competitive bargaining. In this way, the identification of LO members with the particular unions, occupations, sectors, or even work places to which they belong, and which bargaining confined to such sub-confederal units tends to encourage, can be inhibited. Instead identification of LO members with a single, unified labor movement, of which the SAP is the political vehicle, can be fostered. Cohesion in wage bargaining can thus be expected to reinforce political cohesion, enhancing the SAP's capacity to tap union activists' energies and increasing rank-and-file receptivity to this claim, transmitted by the activists, to be the exclusive political instrument for advancing their interests.[71]

Gunnar Nilsson, former chairman of LO, argued too that the integral unity of LO, and LO leadership over its member unions based on

[71]Martin, "Wages, Profits, and Investment," 424–25.

their consent and not statutory rules, had given it the leverage to develop cooperation even with white-collar unions, despite all the strains between them. "And there the party both participated actively and benefited from what happened at union levels."[72] Last but not least, stable, centralized power over wage policy resulting from LO centralization, despite drift and other disruptions, gave the party, when in power, an enormous advantage in designing economic policy.

Party politicians have thus had strong interests in giving LO leaders what they thought they needed to protect union unity and peak-level collective bargaining. To the extent that the trilemma structured LO's political agenda, in other words, it also put innovative economic policy on the Social Democratic agenda.

This explanation of the appearance of collective capital formation on the Swedish political agenda contrasts sharply with an alternative, which sees fund socialism as a sign of labor movement strength and the surfacing of the immanent transformative drive of social democracy. Here I join Jonas Pontusson in his independent but related critique of works by Walter Korpi, John Stephens, and Ulf Himmelstrand.[73] Pontusson characterizes their view as suggesting "that social democracy's accommodation to capitalism was a historically necessary compromise that paved the way for structural reforms of a more radical nature." The implication, therefore, is that Sweden was somehow "ahead" of other countries in the necessary stages in the transition to socialism. Pontusson holds, as I do, that "LO's wage-earner funds proposal must first and foremost be seen as a response to the immediate problems associated with its wage-bargaining strategy"—more a defensive move than an attack from a new position of strength.[74]

[72]Bengt Lindroth, "LO, framtiden och fonderna" (interview with Gunnar Nilsson), *Tiden* 3 (1981), 163. Nils Elvander, in his comparative study of the Scandinavian labor movements, attributes much of the Social Democrats' electoral strength in Sweden, compared to its neighbors, to support among white-collar workers, especially lower-level ones, making up for a gradual decline in "class voting" among LO members in all three countries. Elvander, *Skandinavisk arbetarrörelse* (Stockholm: LiberFörlag, 1980), 312, 320, 333.
[73]See especially Walter Korpi, *The Working Class in Welfare Capitalism: Work, Unions and Politics in Sweden* (London: Routledge & Kegan Paul, 1978), and *The Democratic Class Struggle: Swedish Politics in Comparative Perspective* (London: Routledge & Kegan Paul, 1983); John Stephens, *The Transition from Capitalism to Socialism* (London: Macmillan, 1979); and Ulf Himmelstrand, *Beyond Welfare Capitalism* (London: Heinemann, 1981).
[74]See Pontusson, "Behind and Beyond Social Democracy in Sweden," *New Left Review* 143 (January–February 1984), 86. He points out that the actual changes in the balance of organizational power opposed what Korpi and others assumed, as (1) the Social Democrats had lost control of government for the first time in forty-four years in 1976; (2) there was strong, broad-based public opinion against funds; and (3) the organizational power of capital was increasing with ongoing concentration. Ibid., 82–87. He might also have mentioned the growing strains within LO, quietly building up within the Metal-

I also differ considerably with Gøsta Esping-Andersen, who sees the Swedish Social Democrats' support for wage-earner funds as part of a general drive for "economic democracy." This drive, he suggests, was geared to creating a new majoritarian coalition of wage and salary dependents, replacing the defunct farmer-labor coalition that made Social Democracy dominant in Sweden and elsewhere in Scandinavia. Indeed, according to Esping-Andersen, wage-earner funds "constitute the centerpiece of social democracy's realignment plan."[75] My interpretation differs in that it identifies a different "coalition" on which the Social Democrats focused. Instead of trying to forge a new electoral coalition, the party sought market restructuring through wage-earner funds as a way to inhibit the breakdown of an *old* interest-group coalition of unions and employers behind the structures and policies of peak bargaining. As Pontusson argues, LO did not have, nor did it seem to deem necessary, a broad popular movement behind the funds. At the time legislation was passed, only 22 percent of voters polled were clearly for wage-earner funds, 61 percent against.[76]

The course of the debate within the labor movement as wage-earner funds left Rudolf Meidner's drawing board, surfaced on the political agenda, and passed through the legislative process, shows that the promises of socialism and economic democracy in wage-earner funds waned in importance as LO's project gathered political steam. What motivated the Social Democratic leaders was much simpler. They wanted to give LO leaders something in return for wage restraint and, in particular, something the unions regarded as necessary for maintaining the preconditions of restraint under full employment: that is, membership and constituent union support for continued peak-level egalitarian wage policy.

This point comes out more or less explicitly in LO's repeated justifications of wage-earner funds as "complementing LO's solidaristic wage policy." But from the beginning, public attention focused on other matters, affecting academic analysis along the way. Meidner's initial plan excited many rank-and-file union and party activists, many of them from the New Left generation, partly because of its promise that funds would take over controlling ownership in industry within a gen-

---

workers' Union and aimed particularly at LO unions in the public sector, and the generally conflictual atmosphere between LO and white-collar unions in both public and private sectors.

[75]Esping-Andersen, *Politics against Markets*, 290.

[76]At most, 55 percent of Social Democrats supported funds. Pontusson, "Radicalization and Retreat in Swedish Social Democracy," *New Left Review* 165 (1987). Pontusson maintains LO genuinely sought to challenge capital but was too institutionally and ideologically inhibited to mobilize the necessary popular support.

eration and partly because of its emphasis on empowering workers at the shop level.[77] In the 1975–76 plan, "revenue" from the 20 percent tax on profits was actually to stay within the firm, presumably to be invested as usual but now with ownership and control over its use shared between the firm's employees and the administrators of the central funds. Dividends were to be earmarked for educational and other support services, backing up effective firm-level codetermination. In that way, extra profits "left behind" by wage leveling would not simply become income or assets for existing owners. Workers would now be rewarded with more than moral satisfaction for wage solidarity (that is, wage restraint).

By 1983, however, "redistribution" and "economic democracy," which seemed to have taken center stage in Meidner's formula, had been upstaged by other concerns raised after the Social Democratic leadership joined the debate in the latter 1970s. The 1971 LO congress decision to appoint a commission to report at the next congress in 1975 had surprised and angered the Social Democratic leadership. Indeed, opposition parties took power in 1976 after a campaign aimed at demonstrating Social Democratic guilt by association for LO's radical proposal.[78] LO and the party learned their lesson and henceforth committed themselves to strategic cooperation on the matter in the future.

Cooperation brought the publication in 1978 of a new plan, *Wage-Earner Funds and Capital Formation*, produced with the collaboration of future finance minister Kjell-Olof Feldt and former Social Democratic minister of trade Carl Lidbom. Meanwhile, Rudolf Meidner quietly excused himself from the debate. Meidner was strongly disappointed by the addition of a fourth objective for wage-earner funds, "contributing to collective savings and capital formation for productive investments," to the three original ones of "supporting the solidaristic wage policy," "counteracting the wealth and power concentration which results from profit-based self-financing," and "strengthening wage-earner influence via co-ownership."[79] This fourth objective was to be met with a new tax on both wages and profits for the national pension system and with the creation of another layer of "development" funds,

[77]At the 1981 Social Democratic convention, one member recalled that 1976 brought a new "enthusiasm and agitation in the movement" and that there was "enthusiasm on the streets and squares" on the part of people who "wanted to fight for wage-earner funds and economic democracy." Sveriges Socialdemokratiska Arbetarepartiet, *Protokoll/C: 1981 års Socialdemokratiska Partikongress* (Stockholm: SAP, 1982), 15.

[78]It is doubtful that wage-earner funds decided the election against the Social Democrats—the nuclear power issue was probably more important.

[79]Meidner's name was now at the bottom of the list of co-authors of the new proposal, a sign of support but not active contribution and enthusiasm.

in addition to wage-earner funds, which would buy and sell on the regular stock market. The wage-earner funds would be financed and administered more or less as Meidner had conceived them earlier, except that they would be set up on a regional and not a branch basis. This change provided potentially smaller chances for individual unions to monopolize control of funds operating only in their respective industries.

For Meidner, wage-earner funds should not be instruments for collective capital formation, nor should attempts to bring them into being ride on incomes policy and macroeconomic concerns. In his view, the three original objectives were to be "neutral with respect to costs, wages, and prices." In other words, the funds should "not exacerbate the problems of providing the investment which the authorities consider desirable" but should not resolve them either.[80]

Whereas the 1978 proposal mostly complicated the earlier one by adding on new purposes and new structures, the 1981 proposal simplified the plan once more. As in the first plan there was to be only one set of funds, and this time they would be financed with revenues from new taxes, one an increase in existing payroll taxes for the pension fund system, the other—discussed earlier—the tax on profits over a certain level (an operationalization of the "excess profits" concept). Compulsory collective savings and the instrumental use of taxation to regulate and calm the wage determination process came to the fore. Abandoned was the older idea—associated with the 1976 and 1978 proposals—of tapping into profits at much higher rates but allowing them to stay within the firms where they were generated.

With the abandonment of Meidner's approach, the Social Democratic leadership lost support from many rank-and-file union and party activists, who saw the essence of economic democracy in the earlier idea of obligatory issue of shares to the wage-earner funds. At the 1981 party and LO congresses, which accepted the 1981 revision, numerous motions were entered criticizing the "drifting," "slipping," or "twisting away" from, or "watering down" and "emasculation" of, the idea's initial purposes. Various motions called for the removal of increased capital formation from the plan or demanded that workers be given a

[80]See Meidner, *Employee Investment Funds*, 17. In his view, LO's coordination of collective bargaining, legitimated by success with solidaristic wage policy, along with government tax policies and the already existing system of nationalized pension funds, should provide the necessary conditions and instruments for maintaining savings and investment at satisfactory levels. Wage-earner funds would help in this process only indirectly—by eliminating one basis of opposition to solidaristic wage policy, "excess profits," and thereby bolstering LO's moral authority in peak-level wage determination.

share in firms' capital growth, or that the funds should ultimately "take over the means of production."[81]

Evidence exists that leading Social Democrats had long held strong private reservations about wage-earner funds. Olof Palme, it is said, personally would have been happy to see the fund idea disappear from the agenda. In 1976, he was "furious" with LO for springing the original proposal on the party, and a "stormy" exchange took place between himself and LO's Gunnar Nilsson. Before the 1979 election, Palme expressed the sentiment that wage-earner funds ought to be put aside for some coming generation to carry out.[82] Later, however, he frequently spoke out loyally and with ostensible enthusiasm for the idea, suggesting how intense union and party pressure from below must have been. During the election campaign of 1982, Palme repeatedly asserted his policy of "an outstretched hand" to the center parties for negotiation and compromise on some form of wage-earner funds, a gesture that displeased many within LO and that was spurned contemptuously by the Right.[83]

Kjell-Olof Feldt, a coauthor of the first joint proposal in 1978 and finance minister after the Social Democrats returned to power in 1982, took up the banner for wage-earner funds during the televised election debate. A year later, however, on the first day of debate in the Riksdag preceding the first funds legislation, Feldt was surreptitiously photographed by a powerful telephoto lens as—piqued by the "rancorous and sterile debate"—he whimsically scribbled a verse that was most unflattering to funds and their advocates. Reproduced (of all places) on the front page of the Social Democrats' Stockholm daily *Stockholms-Tidningen,* the verse caused considerable mirth on the Right and astonishment on the Left.[84] Only the newspaper's increasing skepticism

---

[81]Landsorganisationen, *Protokoll Del 2: 20:e ordinarie kongress,* 803–20; Sveriges Socialdemokratiska Arbetarepartiet, *Motioner 5: 1981 års Socialdemokratiska Partikongress* (Stockholm: SAP, 1982), 3–23.

[82]"Partiet som tvekar: Ännu oklar valtaktik," *Veckans affärer,* 17 September 1981, pp. 56–57.

[83]See for example his speech at the SAP congresses in 1978 and 1981. Sveriges Socialdemokratiska Arbetarepartiet, *Motioner 1: 1978 års Socialdemokratiska Partikongress* (Stockholm: SAP, 1979), 273–78, and *Protokoll C: 1981 års Socialdemokratiska Partikongress* (Stockholm: SAP, 1982), 13, 40–43; and Palme, "SAF's nej till fondsamtal ett misstag," *Dagens Nyheter,* 15 September 1983, p. 2.

[84]Translated roughly as "Wage-earner funds are a damned load of shit / But look how far we've shoveled it," Feldt's version was "Löntagarfonder är ett jävla skit / Men nu har vi baxat dom ända hit." Feldt's angry reply was that it was an "extremely private satire" provoked by the intense debate and that it "reveals nothing about my views concerning the funds." *Dagens Nyheter,* 22 December 1983, p. 10. Cf. Feldt's statements in the press in *LO-Tidningen,* 3 March 1981, p. 6, and *Veckans affärer,* 25 November 1982, pp. 72–76.

about wage-earner funds in 1983, and perhaps hopes of improving its flagging subscribership, can explain this editorial decision.

Ambivalence notwithstanding, Social Democratic support for a certain conception of wage-earner funds extended deep into the established leadership. Supporters included Gunnar Sträng, former finance minister and early supporter of leveling along with Rehn and Meidner's ideas. Sträng ultimately came forward with reserved support for wage-earner funds as a complement to tax policies for capital formation and redistributive ends. "Wage-earner funds with the necessary modifications," Sträng wrote in 1977, "must become practical policy." Particularly attractive to him was the idea of the "structure" or development funds in the 1978 version, which would be financed with a tax on value added and which can be seen as a "further extension of the AP [pension] funds."[85]

Relatively slow to come around was Industry Minister Thage Peterson, who in 1983 finally declared that "my own doubts have been cleared away by six months of governmental responsibilities."

> If we are to come up with the enormous industrial investments that are needed in the future we cannot rely on the traditional stock market. More is needed if Sweden is to keep up. . . . It is a question of sound, common sense here. We cannot defend to wage earners the fact that corporations are taking in bigger and bigger profits while at the same time we want wage increases to stay low.[86]

Peterson, who like Palme called for compromise and consensus with opponents to the Right, claimed further that "intelligent entrepreneurs" could understand the logic in siphoning off what might have gone as wage increases into funds, which would then be made available on the capital market for investment.

Worthy of note is the relative lack of interest among Social Democratic leaders in the economic democracy aspects of wage-earner funds, their only moderate interest in the distributional purposes of the funds, and the heaviest concentration of attention on capital formation and wage restraint. From Gunnar Nilsson's standpoint in 1981, LO and the party had overestimated the strength of rank-and-file pressure for economic democracy in the early 1970s as the party pushed an extensive series of labor law reforms through the Riksdag, often with the aid of the center parties. Rank-and-file interest in implementation of the reforms and use of their new rights and resources had not been easily

[85]Sträng, "Avslutande kommentarer," in Feldt et al., *Ekonomisk politik*, 148–49.
[86]Quoted in *Dagens Nyheter*, 5 May 1983, p. 8.

mobilized. That LO in the 1980s would proceed more "moderately and soberly" in the push for more economic democracy was an "absolute" certainty, Nilsson believed. "We must use a great deal of the 1980s partly to defend the reforms, but also to anchor them in broad practical application."[87]

From this it seems clear that neither rank-and-file nor leadership pressure for economic democracy was the powerful force driving wage-earner funds along. The LO leadership maintained its commitment to economic democracy, but Olof Palme had from time to time made his view clear that labor law and substantive innovations in collective bargaining were preferable to ownership as a source of progress in economic democracy. Positive experiences of past coalition with bourgeois parties on these principles probably strengthened his view. Thus in 1983, when wage-earner fund legislation was passed against a united oppositional front, the leadership of the Social Democratic labor movement was under no compulsion, either from conviction or from rank-and-file pressure, to push for more radical workplace democracy reforms.

Short-term economic objectives and long-term electoral interests were, on the other hand, paramount. Out of power in 1979, Social Democratic and LO economists displayed, according to Martin, "widespread apprehension" that wages would surge back upward during the mild upswing as capacity utilization and profits rose.[88] The labor movement would get little joy when the bourgeois government suffered in the expected recessionary aftermath, for no doubt the government would blame the unions, as would a large and possibly growing segment of the public. Worrisome was the fact that even with relatively high unemployment, the same old destabilizing tendencies (high profits, wage drift, wildcat strikes) set in before investments, which tend to lag considerably behind profits, began to increase. Hoping to return to power soon, the Social Democrats expected to suffer from this syndrome as well.

Back in power in October 1982, after weathering an intense campaign focused almost exclusively against the joint LO-SAP wage-earner fund proposal of the previous year, the new government set about quickly to transform the idea into some form of reality. All indications are that their actions toward wage-earner funds were taken despite, not

[87]Quoted in Lindroth, "LO, framtiden och fonderna," *Tiden* 3 (1981), 169. Problems in mobilizing membership activity led to a large report commissioned in 1976 and presented to the 1981 LO congress, with recommendations for adapting union organization to the new tasks of codetermination and economic democracy. See Landsorganisationen, *LO 80-Rapporten: Rapport till LO-kongressen 1981* (Stockholm: LO, 1981).

[88]Martin, "Wages, Profits, and Investment," 456–57.

because of, the electoral outcome, which had gone in their favor despite and not because of wage-earner funds.[89]

There can be little question that a major policy step taken immediately helped propel wage-earner funds up the agenda. The government's 16 percent devaluation, undertaken with a nod of consent from the unions, gave a powerful boost to export industry's competitiveness and profits, which by June of 1983 were growing at an estimated annual rate of over 5 percent while imports stayed stable.[90] That summer, the Konjunkturinstitut estimated that the profit share in industry had reached its highest level in almost a decade, a level characteristic of the "good years" in the 1960s. According to Swedish industry representatives, this level—20 percent of value added—had to be maintained over a long period if expansion of industrial capacity was to take place.[91]

By December, however, LO economists were already predicting that the continuing profits explosion would bring about "complete revolt" on the shop floor; wage drift and inflation would soon pick up speed, they argued, and undermine the effects of the devaluation, the cornerstone of the Social Democrats' crisis program.[92] Furthermore, they pointed out, investment had not yet picked up and employment was not benefiting. Capacity utilization was still relatively low while large inventories were being cleared.

For the period following the devaluation, Palme had called for continuing stagnation in real wages, which in fact occurred.[93] Trying to make wage restraint sweeter for LO under these conditions, the government passed a provisional 20 percent tax on corporate dividends for 1983. Meanwhile, intensive study of a permanent "profit-sharing fee" was under way, led by LO's Per-Olof Edin (now in the Finance Ministry). Finance Minister Feldt, like Edin, expressed strong worries that the high profits would "turn into excessive wage drift," which despite growing unemployment had remained high at around 8 percent for the year.

[89]A Sifo survey after the election found that 73 percent of the voters answered "no" when asked if they believed that the voters had given a mandate to introduce funds. Even a majority of Social Democratic voters and LO members—65 percent and 66 percent respectively—answered no. Of those voting for the Social Democrats or the Communists, only 49 percent approved of the government's actions on the funds, which by then amounted only to a publicized plan for a profit-sharing tax; the full plan would come out that winter. *Dagens Nyheter*, 15 June 1983, p. 6.

[90]*Svenska Dagbladet*, 15 November 1982, p. 26; *Dagens Nyheter*, 23 June 1983, p. 6.
[91]*Dagens Nyheter*, 6 July 1983, pp. 1, 7.
[92]*Dagens Nyheter*, 8 December 1983, p. 10.
[93]*Veckans affärer*, 21 October 1982, p. 94. Palme's "crisis package" included, along with the devaluation and wage stagnation, an increase in the value-added tax and unemployment insurance fees as well as other measures amounting to at least a 2.5 percent reduction in real disposable income. *Dagens Industri*, 11 November 1982.

Particularly distressing was the fear that profits would not be used for the development and strengthening of Swedish industry and that "wage-earners will be intensely watching over what companies are doing with the devaluation profits they amass in 1983."[94]

Early in May, Edin formally presented the fruits of research and drafting of a "profit-sharing fee" that had been released to the press about a month earlier. Calling for a 20 percent tax on "real profits" ("nominal profits" minus adjustments for inflation) exceeding either Skr 500,000 or 6 percent of wage costs, Edin's proposal emphasized the need to support the solidaristic wage policy and emphasized as well that, technically, profit sharing did *not* have to be linked in any way with economic democracy considerations. The informal April announcement was followed within two weeks by formal Riksdag action implementing the provisional corporate tax on dividend payments mentioned earlier, which, like Edin's tax, was justified by its "contribution to a restrained wage round."[95]

Between the Social Democrats' massive devaluation and these first, relatively small steps in LO's direction, the 1983 wage negotiations had taken place. The consequences were devastating for LO and, perhaps for reasons mentioned earlier, costly for the party as well. For the first time ever, peak-level negotiations proceeded without the Metalworkers' Union. That union, enticed by engineering employers in SAF (Verkstadsföreningen), went off on its own because, in addition to other "sweeteners," the employers' offer exceeded LO's initial bid, making it impossible for Leif Blomberg, a new and untested leader of a union with strong latent divisions, to resist.[96]

In sum, not only did the real wages of LO workers continue to decline but LO leaders in the peak-level process had suffered a blow

[94]Quoted in *Veckans affärer*, 25 November 1982, p. 75.

[95]*Dagens Nyheter*, 10 April 1983, p. 6, 13 April 1983, p. 8, and 28 April, p. 7. From LO's standpoint, Edin's profit-sharing tax, which ultimately would be integrated with the fund legislation to follow in December, was too "generous" to industry, but LO gave qualified support. *Dagens Nyheter*, 8 July 1983, p. 7. Rudolf Meidner and Social Democratic economist Villy Bergström had earlier registered their own skepticism about the adequacy of the provisional tax on dividend payments to neutralize the disruptive distributional effects of the devaluation profits, especially considering the likelihood of only slow increases in investment and employment. *Svenska Dagbladet*, 5 May 1983, p. 3.

[96]The press reported that the settlement of 2.2 percent in overall increases corresponded "exactly" to what LO had demanded earlier. *Dagens Nyheter*, 6 March 1983, p. 1. However, before and throughout the negotiations LO had actually demanded 2.1 percent. Ibid., 11 November 1982, p. 10. SAF, while still negotiating for Verkstadsföreningen before it bolted, had insisted no increases were possible. Ibid., 25 January 1983, p. 7. When the LO-SAF negotiations "stranded," the Metalworkers' and Verkstadsföreningen carried on with separate negotiations immediately. Ibid., 8 February 1983, p. 10. On the events surrounding the breakdown of LO-SAF coordination, see Elvander, *Den svenska modellen*, 78–135.

they may have feared for a while. The ultimate outcome of the contractual agreements was the least egalitarian in recent memory. Metalworkers received higher-than-average contractual increases—distributed internally in a less egalitarian fashion than in the past—whereas other LO unions received significantly less on average and a weak wage-drift guarantee.[97] The fact that the Metalworkers received higher-than-average increases also promised somewhat lower drift in industry, which would reduce the level of drift compensation to be paid to white-collar and public-sector workers. From SAF's standpoint, division and restraint in LO were all it could ask for, short of the disappearance of wage-earner funds from the agenda.

Disappear they would not however, for in June 1983, LO's new chairman Stig Malm was still exhorting the government to come forth with legislation by the end of the year. The year before, Feldt had suggested a target of 1985.[98] Malm, worried about the following year's wage negotiations, expressed the wish that the profit-sharing tax were larger, so that it could have a "restraining effect on the wage round." The press called the coming wage round "the most important since World War II" and predicted that "if LO fails to hold the unions together . . . its influence will decline—not only in wage policy but also in other socioeconomic affairs." Despite the decentralized format, LO would still try to maintain control over levels and distribution. The government admitted that room was available for some real wage improvements without hurting Sweden's competitive position, but not without at the same time increasing unemployment (because of ongoing labor-saving rationalization and therefore increases in productivity).[99]

The culmination finally came on December 22, 1983. Aided by 21 abstentions, 20 of them from Communist members of the Riksdag, the Social Democratic proposal for wage-earner funds won with 164 votes for and 158 against.[100] More than ten years of debate ended—perhaps only temporarily—with a partial victory for LO officials, economists, and ideologues and even less of a victory for those who saw in wage-earner funds the first step toward socialism and economic democracy.

As proposed by the second installment of Edin's legislative drafting efforts, and publicized first in July, five regional funds were to be set

[97]Anders Olsson, Madeleine Wänseth, and Tom Burns, *Det svenska löneförhandlingssystemet, Rapport 1: Projektet Löneförhandlingar i Sverige* (Uppsala: Sociologiska Institutionen, Uppsala University, 1984), 30–38.
[98]*Dagens Nyheter*, 8 June 1983, p. 12; *Veckans affärer*, 25 November 1982, p. 72.
[99]*Dagens Nyheter*, 4 December 1983, p. 12.
[100]One supportive vote came from a Center party member who pushed the wrong button.

up at the beginning of 1984—as Malm had called for.[101] Their boards of directors would consist of nine members. At least five would be union-affiliated wage earners, to be appointed by the government. The funds would be financed, as proposed in the 1981 LO/SAP proposal, by a combination of increased pension fees and the "excess profits" tax in the form proposed earlier in the year by Edin.[102] The increased pension fees would amount to an increase in the payroll tax of about 0.2 percent, to increase to no more than 0.5% by 1990. At the time, the government expected the funds would receive about 2 billion Swedish crowns per year until 1990 (when the taxes expire unless renewed), which would be invested by the funds primarily in equity shares in manufacturing industry. Each fund would be committed to paying the equivalent of a 3 percent return on its capital to the pension fund system to help maintain its funding levels. In line with all earlier proposals, the legislation required the funds to delegate 50 percent of the voting rights in stockholders' meetings to the firm-level union organization for those stocks held by the funds in the respective firms. Finally, no wage-earner fund would be able to acquire more stock in a firm if it already held 8 percent of existing voting rights.

The last restriction, along with the seven-year "sunset" clause and the relatively small amount of money collected by the tax on profits, amounted to a substantial retreat from the original ambitions of LO and even the party regarding distribution and economic democracy. Restricting control to 8 percent for each fund limits total control of the fund system in any one firm to 40 percent. In the first two proposals of 1976 and 1978, the objective had been gradual but eventual assumption of controlling interest; in the 1981 proposal this ambition was toned down, but at least no limits were mentioned. Together, these restrictions meant that only "a first step" had been taken, and perhaps the only one we will ever see, toward the original objectives of wage-earner funds.[103]

CONCLUSION

The trilemma suggests that when leaders of a union or union confederation feel compelled to pursue a coherent, long-term objective

[101]*Svenska Dagbladet*, 1 July 1983, p. 6.

[102]About 5,000 companies, including corporations as well as other industrial, financial, and insurance firms, were expected to be affected. *Dagens Nyheter*, 22 December 1983, p. 10.

[103]Stig Malm, interviewed after the vote, suggested his willingness to resume the debate once again in five or six years. Asked if he was satisfied, he replied, "Don't think I'm so enthusiastic that I'll go home, uncork a bottle of champagne and celebrate." Ibid.

somewhere on the multidimensional battlefield of distributional conflict, they will tend to seek, and in the long term require, extraordinary support from the state in order to persevere. Solidaristic wage policy was just such an objective for LO in Sweden. As I have argued, the very idea of wage leveling generated debates and ideas that foreshadowed both active labor market policy and wage-earner funds as necessary complements even before leveling became a fixed element of LO wage policy in the 1950s. Full employment was a second priority in LO's survival strategy, entailing, as the trilemma suggests, a lowering of sights on wage share maximization. A full employment economy had generated conditions that convinced Swedish employers to prefer peak-level bargaining for all manual workers in the private sector; the loss of full employment would result in weaker unity within both the unions and the employers' associations and therefore fissiparous tendencies in the peak-level bargaining system. The 1983 breakdown of peak-level bargaining, planned and desired by employers in the decisive engineering sector and following a period of unemployment that was high by Swedish standards, confirmed this fear. LO's desire to maintain peak control therefore conditioned its efforts to achieve full employment along with wage leveling—hence LO attempts to pursue Front I strategies as a general, long-term policy.

Front I strategies entailed costs, however. In particular, these costs resulted from excess profits left behind in certain sectors of the economy, often the dynamic, export-oriented engineering sector. High wage drift and then wildcat strikes there, accompanied by rank-and-file opposition to peak-level bargaining, ensued with fairly predictable regularity as Front I wage agreements were imposed to deal with exogenous forces, both cyclical and structural, that threatened full employment. Wage-drift guarantees and reactive retreat from Front I then aimed to reinstate distributional successes and to calm localized rank-and-file discontent. The long-term result, according to Andrew Martin but translated into my terms, amounted to something more like a Front III policy of leveling plus profit squeeze rather than leveling plus full employment. To the extent that full employment was nevertheless maintained, it was due to the efforts of the government to soak up unemployment with labor market measures and expansion of the public sector. These efforts had their own costs and drawbacks for wage bargaining, however, as the tax burden increased and the effects of the tax system swamped the contract negotiation process in determining real wage-income and wage-cost developments.

Dealing with the destabilizing consequences of Front I policies—and thereby making it possible to pursue them long enough for profits, investment, and growth to bring Sweden into balance with the changing international economic environment—therefore required, in LO's view, first and foremost the neutralization of excess profits. Wage drift and ensuing interunion and interconfederation rivalries could thereby be reduced, relieving some of the economic and political pressures on the unions to abandon restraint. The aspect of wage-earner funds that promised to neutralize excess profits—"collective profit sharing"— thus promised to "resolve the trilemma" by squeezing profits without at the same time choking off the supply of capital needed for investment and growth. Creating another class of income that was neither wage nor profit—neither income for consumption nor private accumulation of wealth—would, it was hoped, allow LO to cover Front I and Front III simultaneously, thereby achieving all three egalitarian objectives.

Thus the appearance of wage-earner funds on the political agenda in Sweden had, according to this analysis, three causes, in combination sufficient for its explanation. First, as a structural cause, were the predictable workings of the trilemma associated with peak-level bargaining arrangements and revealed by the repetition over time of punishments and "recoil" from Front I policies. Second were the ideological as well as "institutional maintenance" objectives of LO leaders in maintaining peak control, which, as they saw it, required wage leveling first and full employment second. Pursuit of this Front I policy required in turn the active efforts of a sympathetic government willing and able to take measures to "clean up" after the effects of a Front I policy. Legislative action had to be taken to counteract the disruptive effects of excess profits and ensuing wage drift associated with Front I. The third condition, then, for the appearance of wage-earner funds high on the political agenda was a government that stood to benefit from the same aims LO pursued.

The Social Democrats, interested in the short-term electoral benefits of investment and growth led by high profits, and recognizing the long-term electoral benefits of LO unity based on successful peak-level wage bargaining, showed considerable reluctance but ultimately lined up behind what LO declared it needed to maintain its authority. A most pressing need was wage restraint to support the effects of a massive devaluation of the Swedish currency on profits and future investment. The expected benefits would apparently outweigh the negative but limited electoral effects of support for wage-earner funds, which only a minority of even the Social Democrats' supporters clearly understood and wanted. Short- and long-term "maintenance" considerations thus motivated the party in adopting wage-earner funds—with some significant modifications. LO's own organizational maintenance objectives were in this sense prior to the party's, and for this reason, the trilemma structured the Social Democratic agenda in the same way it did the LO agenda.

The flaw of wage-earner funds lay in the rather unsurprising fact that they deeply antagonized employers in SAF, mobilizing and unifying the economic and political Right to a degree highly unusual in Sweden.[104] Sweden's postwar political economy—a mutually supportive mixture of economic policies promoting labor mobility and export-oriented industry, on the one hand, and a cross-class interest-group coalition behind peak-level centralized bargaining, on the other—had become obsolete. Wage-earner funds represented LO's attempt to shore up centralized bargaining by checking growing internal opposition in the labor movement. Inevitably the attempt failed, by antagonizing employers and shattering the cross-class coalition underlying the passing order. To resolve the vertical trilemma is to use state power for negating forces that preserve inequality. LO's past organizational, distributional, and policy successes had been based on cross-class coalitions. No such coalition could be found to resolve the trilemma and thus bring about socialism.

[104]Social Democratic power in Sweden rests in part on unity among unions, as comparative research shows, and in part on strong divisions in the right in partisan politics. Francis G. Castles, *The Social Democratic Image of Society* (London: Routledge & Kegan Paul, 1978), 1–45 and 103–42.

CHAPTER SIX

Divided by the Trilemma:
Unions in West Germany

Wage-earner funds emerged as the strategy the Swedish unions used to bring state power to bear in defense of peak-level centralized bargaining. Under conditions of structural crisis, the trilemma translated the reformist impulse to defend egalitarian distributive accomplishments into a drive toward a more fundamental transformation—away from capitalist private enterprise and ownership.

Swedish unions in LO, the major confederation, united behind wage-earner funds. For the German unions, in contrast, the redistribution of income, wealth, and control between capital and labor through collective capital formation turned out to be one of the most divisive, if not explosive, issues debated in the postwar period. "Seldom has there been an issue in such dispute among the German unions as multifirm collective asset formation [*Vermögensbildung in Arbeitnehmerhand*] for workers," according to Germany's major business daily in 1972.[1] Though it has received far less international attention than Swedish wage-earner funds, the German controversy has also been central in Social Democratic politics, in this case dividing rather than unifying the labor movement.

By and large, factional conflict over the issue closely followed a stable Left-Right or militant-conservative divide within the DGB. And as the trilemma analysis would suggest, disagreements in the political sphere arose in part from divergent constraints and strategies in wage bargaining. In this chapter, I show how the immediate bargaining problems of individual and autonomous DGB unions explain much about long-

[1]Karlheinz Kleps, *Lohnpolitische Konzeptionen und Vermögensbildung: Ein Weg aus der stabilitäts- und verteilungspolitischen Sackgasse* (Baden-Baden: Nomos Verlagsgesellschaft, 1982), 245; "Streit im DGB über Vermögenspolitik," *Handelsblatt*, 29 February 1972.

term strategic and political conflicts within the German labor move-ment. Polarization over the idea of collective capital funds shows that political division in the German labor movement is generated by the contradictions of distributional policy. As autonomous agents in collec-tive bargaining, different unions in Germany suffer the trilemma in different ways and adopt different political strategies as a result.

COLLECTIVE CAPITAL AND UNION ACCOMMODATIONISM

In the German debate, the two most prominent advocates of collec-tive capital formation among the seventeen DGB unions were also clearly conservative or, in Andrei Markovits's characterization, "accom-modationist." As early as the 1950s, the Textile and Garment Workers' Union (Gewerkschaft Textil-Bekleidung, GTB) and the Construction and Allied Industry Workers' Union (Industriegewerkschaft Bau-Steine-Erden, IG Bau) lined up with other unions in opposition against the militant "activism" of the German Metalworkers' Union (IG Metall) both in politics and in collective bargaining. The origins of this postwar division, as Markovits suggests, lie in the fact that IG Metall, under the early dynamic leadership of Otto Brenner, "had repeatedly broken union solidarity by dictating a tempo and program which most other unions simply could not follow."[2] IG Metall's militancy and success were for many unions a hard act to repeat, constrained as they were by different organizational and economic problems. Attempts to keep up brought threatening reprisals from employers; failure to keep up stir-red opposition from membership groups.

Analysis of the recent interests and strategies of the union represent-ing relatively low-pay textile and garment workers in the context of "competitive" relations with IG Metall provides a first test of the propo-sition that the trilemma can help explain fundamental differences and conflicts over political strategy within a national labor movement. In the case of the GTB, unlike LO in Sweden, the motivational basis behind its advocacy of collective capital formation in the late 1970s and early 1980s arose from the horizontal rather than the vertical variant of the trilemma. In the course of the 1970s, GTB leaders found it in-creasingly difficult to maintain a degree of both internal and external wage-distributional equity without accelerating loss of jobs in a crisis

[2]See Andrei S. Markovits, *The Politics of the West German Trade Unions: Strategies of Class and Interest Representation in Growth and Crisis* (Cambridge: Cambridge University Press, 1986) for an in-depth look at the major postwar issues and events dividing the unions into "accommodationist" and "activist" camps. Quotation at 90.

industry and perhaps provoking employers into actions that would weaken the union further. The GTB's leadership thus turned to collective capital formation through "investment wages" as a way of coping with, if not fully resolving, the trilemma.

The GTB Initiative: An Investment-Wage Fund

The performance problem in recent years for a union like the GTB, whose relatively low-pay members work in a declining industry, is described well by the horizontal trilemma. The industries in which GTB members work all suffer disproportionately from the long-term stagnation of domestic and international demand due to lower-wage competition from abroad. The textile industry in West Germany, for example, despite productivity increases far higher than the average in manufacturing and despite pay increases well below productivity trends, lost 37 percent of its jobs between 1970 and 1979. Productivity rose so fast that even modest growth in output had to be accompanied by drastic cuts in employment.[3] The garment industry was worse off in every respect, due in part to slow productivity growth.

Moreover, these were industries with a high proportion of low-wage earners, mostly women. GTB membership in the 1970s was roughly 53 percent female, compared to only about 13 percent for IG Metall.[4] This preponderance of women helps explain the fact that, until the mid-1970s—and even sporadically thereafter—the GTB has often pressured for egalitarian pay increases. From about 1962 to 1972, both the structure of contract wages and actual wage income for GTB members leveled faster and more consistently than for IG Metall's members, even though extra increases for low-pay groups were relatively more expensive for the textile and garment industries, and even though the metal industries had more leeway in general for pay growth.

In the ten years before the 1973 oil price shock and the following recession, pay differentials in the textile and garment industries had collapsed strongly and consistently (see Figure 4). In the auto and electronics industries, the two IG Metall sectors with the highest pro-

[3] Textiles' share of net industrial production in Germany dropped from 3.8 percent to 3.4 percent as growth in other industries far outstripped growth in textile production. Andreas Achenbach et al., *Arbeitskampf an neuen Fronten: Zu den Aktionen und Streiks im Bereich der GTB, HBV, GEW und RFFU 1979* (Frankfurt/M: IMSF, 1980), 24.

[4] Reinhard Jühe, Horst-Udo Niedenhoff, and Wolfgang Pege, *Gewerkschaften in der Bundesrepublik Deutschland: Daten, Fakten, Strukturen* (Cologne: Deutscher Instituts Verlag, 1977), 78. Of those employed in textiles, about 53 percent were women; in the garment industry, about 81 percent were women. Achenbach et al., *Arbeitskampf an neuen Fronten*, 25.

Figure 4. Average earnings for unskilled women as a percentage of the average for skilled men in the textile and garment industries in West Germany

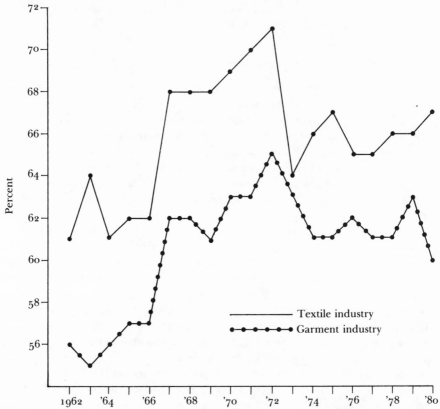

Source: Statistisches Bundesamt Wiesbaden, *Fachserie 16 Löhne und Gehälter, Reihe 2.1 Arbeiterverdienste in der Industrie,* for years 1962–80. For 1962–66 and 1972–80, the data are for average gross weekly earnings; for 1967–72, for average gross hourly earnings. Data are from the months of November for 1962–63, October for 1965–76, July for 1977, and October for 1978–80. Wages for West Berlin not included.

portion of women, the trend was erratic both before and after 1973 (see p. 80).[5] The greater consistency of effective leveling in textiles and garments reflects in part similar patterns in contracts negotiated by GTB and IG Metall.[6]

As the problems of the textile and garment industries worsened in

[5]In the auto industry, employment in the 1970s was about 11 percent female (including about 2.5 percent white-collar workers); in electronics about 30 percent were female (including about 4 percent white-collar workers).

[6]See Manfred Piecha, "Tarifliche Stundenlöhne und Lohngruppenrelationen in ausgewählten Tarifbereiche 1960–1976" (Düsseldorf, WSI-Tarifarchiv, 1977).

the mid-1970s, the GTB's leveling policy reached an impasse. Responding to the industry's need to hold down labor costs and at the same time attract and hold skilled manual workers, the union relaxed its pressure for leveling. In one regional bargaining district, Hessen, for example, the union even added two extra pay classifications at the top of the scale in 1980, after having eliminated classifications at the bottom in earlier years.[7]

Most other regional bargaining units of the GTB had by the late 1970s abandoned wage egalitarianism without actually endorsing disproportionate increases for the top pay groups. The straight percentage increases they demanded, however, often meant in practice a policy of increasing differentials. Wage drift, already discussed in the context of Swedish wage policy, explains why. Afraid to call strikes and fail miserably against employers who wanted to cut labor costs, the GTB accepted low and nonegalitarian contract increases relative to the results negotiated by other unions. Individual employers were then free to give extra-contractual increases to skilled workers (wage drift), thus maintaining rates for skilled workers relative to other industries. The outcome has been a widening of skill and sex differentials.

Increases in actual hourly earnings for skilled manual workers in textiles have, for the most part, kept up with the rates in engineering (*Investitionsgüterindustrie*)[8] in the 1970s—after general decline in the 1960s. (See Figure 5.) Unskilled women's wages suffered a far greater decline with respect to the earnings of their counterparts in engineering. After a precipitous drop in 1973, moreover, they did not recover with respect to wages for skilled men in textiles for the rest of the decade.

These observations make it clear that the GTB confronted the three contradictory objectives of the horizontal trilemma: (1) stemming the decline of, if not improving, employment in the textile and garment industries; (2) maintaining relatively egalitarian pay standards pressed on the union from below; and (3) keeping pay increases, especially for skilled workers, in line with those negotiated by other unions. Fulfillment of any two would bring about immediate and painful costs in terms of the third. Staving off unemployment while maintaining egalitarian pay would mean holding back the wages of skilled workers, risking rebellion and a loss of labor skills that the industry could not tolerate. Saving jobs and paying skilled workers well would mean shav-

[7]Interview with Fritz Kaiser, Bezirksleiter (Regional Secretary), Bezirk Frankfurt, Gewerkschaft Textil-Bekleidung, Frankfurt am Main, 9 June 1982.
[8]Investment or capital goods industry, predominantly machinery, electronics, automobile manufacturing, shipbuilding, and other metal processing.

Figure 5. Unskilled women's earnings in textiles as a percentage of unskilled women's earnings in engineering; skilled men's earnings in textiles as a percentage of skilled men's earnings in engineering.

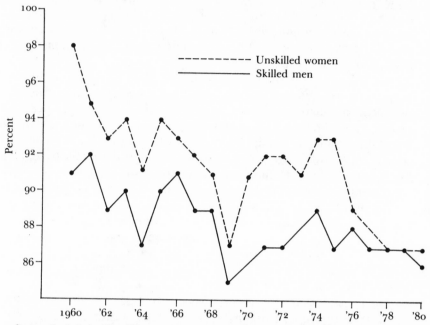

Source: Statistisches Bundesamt Wiesbaden, *Fachserie 16 Löhne und Gehälter, Reihe 2.1 Arbeiterverdienste in der Industrie,* for years 1960–80. For 1960–66 and 1972–80, the data are for average gross weekly earnings; for 1967–72, for average gross hourly earnings. Data are from the months of October for 1960–61, 1963–76, and 1978–80, November for 1962, and July for 1977. Wages for West Berlin not included.

ing relative pay for the large number of unskilled workers. Maintaining an egalitarian pay structure while also paying skilled workers up to the standards of other industries would mean, of course, tightening an already intense squeeze on profits that threatens future jobs, union membership levels, and therefore the power and credibility of union leaders.

The 1982 wage round illustrates the GTB's predicament and the logic of its response. Unwilling to strike, the GTB was forced to accept a 3.9 percent increase in pay in the textile industry, lower than IG Metall's settlement for 4.2 percent, which became the target for other unions. An alternative might have been to accept 4.2 percent for skilled workers and considerably less for the unskilled. Finding that uniform 4.2 percent increases were beyond reach and further official retreat on the wage-leveling front unpalatable, GTB leaders pressured employers—without success—to compensate workers for the difference (in this case, between 3.9 percent and 4.2 percent) with an "investment wage" fund. For employers, in the GTB view, the extra 0.3 percent would be made available as investment capital for the industry and would not have the same effect as a similar wage cost increase, for it would presumably not affect liquidity.[9]

The wage policy predicament of GTB leaders differed in critical respects from that of the Swedish labor confederation and so affected their efforts to pursue wage equity. In the case of the GTB, powerful market and employer pressures pushed it toward Front II (restraint plus differentiation) instead of LO's Front I (restraint plus leveling). As the trilemma predicts, extraordinary circumstances forcing a union into consistent pursuit of—or in this case, resignation to—one policy over time will, at the same time, move it to pursue unusual policies to compensate for objectives that thereby suffer long-term neglect.

The GTB's response to this acute trilemma, like LO's, was a plan for collective capital formation, issued in 1978. This plan called for members to abstain from disposable wage increases negotiated by other unions in exchange for an "investment wage" (*vermögenswirksamer Lohnbestandteil*), which would make up the difference. This portion of "wages" would remain as capital in the textile and garment industries to benefit employment. It would be administered by a joint union-management fund.[10]

Three peculiarities of the GTB conception of collective capital formation are worth emphasizing. First, in its 1978 proposal the union called for a *negotiated*, not legislated, collective fund system. As I shall show, hopes for the coalition of organizations and parties needed for legislation had been dashed by the mid-1970s. Second, and more interesting, is the insistence that "all details [of the fund system] must be planned so that low-income earners benefit more than high-income earners."[11] It is clear that in the aftermath of recent GTB negotiations,

[9]According to economist Karl Pitz of IG Metall, who recounted these events to me, strong consensus also prevailed among policy experts in the other DGB unions that the GTB leadership was excessively optimistic. Their response was paraphrased by Pitz as: "You'll never get 3.9 percent plus 0.3 percent, because your bargaining power [*Kampfkraft*] could only get you as far as 3.9 percent. If you had gotten a fund, then you would have gotten 3.9 percent minus 0.3 percent, or 3.6 percent cash plus 0.3 percent investment wages. The volume of your increase would again have been 3.9 percent." Interview with Pitz, Frankfurt, 15 June 1982.

[10]Gewerkschaft Textil-Bekleidung, "Programm der Gewerkschaft Textil-Bekleidung—beschlossen auf dem 13. ordentlichen Gewerkschaftstag vom 1.–2. Oktober 1978 in Mannheim," in *Informationen für Vertrauensleute der Gewerkschaft Textil-Bekleidung* 21 (November 1978), 32–33.

[11]GTB's program also maintained that "a sensible solution to the problem of wealth concentration can only be collective [*überbetrieblich*]. It should not be achieved via legislation, but rather planned and implemented by partners in collective bargaining." Ibid., 33.

skilled workers were getting raises by means of wage drift that more or less followed those for IG Metall's members. In effect, the GTB had been for some time pursuing what was from an egalitarian standpoint at best a Front I policy of external leveling and internal differentiation—but with little benefit for employment. At worst, the policy was one of internal differentiation, external slippage, and overall restraint—a retreat from any policy front on the trilemma. In any case, the greatest losers in the bargain were low-pay workers. In compensation perhaps, although the quid pro quo was never explicitly stated by the union, shares in the jointly managed investment fund would go disproportionately to low-pay groups.

The GTB's unusually acute trilemma offers a clear reason for this unique egalitarian embellishment on collective profit sharing. What the union proposed was a substitute, to compensate for its de facto—and certainly not celebrated—reversal on egalitarian pay policy.[12] By saving abstained-from wage increases and channeling the assets thereby created into the hands of those at the greatest disadvantage, the union would be able to give back with one hand what it took with the other.

The third feature that distinguishes the GTB's plan significantly from the Swedish model is the idea of investment wages—in essence, a payroll tax. Since the problem with GTB wage policies was not "excess profits" resulting from egalitarian wage policy and differentiated restraint but rather increasing wage differentials between unskilled workers in GTB industries and others, the solution was also different. LO's plan was supposed to tap excess profits; the GTB's was supposed to tap the wealth created by more generalized abstention from wage-increase trends set in healthier industries.

The difference between the Swedish and GTB concepts of a fund system is interesting. Instead of helping legitimate a retreat from egalitarian pay—implied in the GTB plan—the LO plans presupposed the opposite: continuation of egalitarian wage policy and special benefits to high-pay workers, especially many metalworkers who benefited the least from the solidaristic wage policy. Hence it was the Swedish Metalworkers' Union that led the push for collective profit sharing and sought a way to reconcile its membership to the LO-imposed wage policy. Benefits for metalworkers disadvantaged by LO policy were not to be direct material benefits but rather an increasing share in the

[12]Neglect of leveling through the late 1970s and into the 1980s did not mean that the leadership or active membership had lost interest. In 1986, a unanimous GTB congress supported a motion calling for disroportionate pay increases for low-pay groups. Gewerkschaft Textil-Bekleidung, *Protokoll: 15. ordentlicher Gewerkschaftstag 1986* (Düsseldorf: GTB, 1987), 317 and 428.

184

rights of ownership—through voting of equity shares—acquired in some distinct proportion to their restraint and the excess profits that appeared as a consequence.[13] Hence the variations in the plans closely follow differences in the leading actors and the peculiar collective bargaining problems—the trilemmas—they faced. Variations in their attempts to find an escape corresponded to the different character of their predicaments.

THE HISTORY OF THE FUND DEBATE IN GERMANY

In the early 1980s, GTB leaders remained the most prominent and tenacious advocates of collective capital formation and hence were increasingly isolated within the DGB. Although others still expressed interest in the idea, DGB debate on the subject had practically vanished by the mid-1970s. For example, in a passage on income and wealth distribution, the DGB's 1981 Basic Program (*Grundsatzprogramm*) contained only one curt, vague reference to the idea—a simple gravestone marking the passage of an idea that had appealed to many in the DGB.[14] The retirement of DGB chairman Heinz Oskar Vetter—a noted advocate of collective profit sharing—and his replacement by Ernst Breit of the Postal Workers' Union (Deutsche Postgewerkschaft) in 1982 also marked a shift.[15] Breit's union was one of the five that voted against collective profit sharing in the 1970s.[16] The Union of Mining and Energy Workers (IG Bergbau und Energie), Vetter's own, had supported it.

[13]This feature was present in the 1975 Meidner Plan, but not in later plans.
[14]"Important preconditions of a wider distribution of wealth is a higher share of national income for workers, the abolition of tax privileges for high incomes, special inducements for savings and asset formation for middle- and low-income groups and *the participation of all workers in productive assets.*" This emphasized portion contains the Basic Program's complete reference to collective profit sharing. Hans-Adam Pfromm, *Das neue DGB-Grundsatzprogramm: Einführung und Kommentar* (Munich: Günter Olzog Verlag, 1982), 77.
[15]See Christian Götz, *Heinz Oskar Vetter: Christian Götz befragt und porträtiert den Vorsitzenden des Deutschen Gewerkschaftsbundes* (Cologne: Europäische Verlagsanstalt, 1977), 90–93, and Heinz Oskar Vetter, *Gleichberechtigung oder Klassenkampf: Gewerkschaftspolitik für die achtziger Jahre* (Cologne: Bund Verlag, 1980), 63–65.
[16]At the DGB congress that elected Breit, his only reference to collective profit sharing was in his final speech in which he praised Vetter for his activity and contributions. He declared that Vetter, through his influence in the DGB and in party politics, had laid the ground for "further discussions with the parties" on the question of legislation. Whether Breit himself would lead them is left unsaid. Vetter, on the other hand, spoke at some length on collective profit sharing in his farewell speech. See the minutes in Deutscher Gewerkschaftsbund, *Protokoll: 12. ordentlicher Bundeskongress Berlin 16–22 May, 1982* (Düsseldorf: DGB, 1983), 39, 553.

The same year, several months after Breit's election, a rancorous dispute broke out at DGB headquarters about the GTB's profit-sharing conception between Berthold Keller, chairman of the GTB, and the DGB's research institute (Wirtschafts- und Sozialwissenschaftliches Institut, WSI). The conflict showed how isolated advocates in the GTB had become. In its forthcoming special issue on crisis bargaining policy, WSI's journal *WSI-Mitteilungen* was to include an article by WSI economist Claus Schäfer criticizing the GTB conception of profit sharing. In a letter to Breit, Keller called it "unheard of" and "monstrous" for the DGB to take sides in an internal union debate on bargaining policy by allowing the journal to publish such an article. Keller, considered by many arrogant and authoritarian, was especially sensitive because he was soon to face reelection in his union and was the object of much internal criticism for his profit-sharing plan to save the textile and garment industries. Although he succeeded in stopping the article, Keller's efforts backfired, because the issue and the WSI critique received more publicity than Keller would have liked.[17]

Keller's extreme sensitivity can be understood in part as a result of strong discontent within his own union over the idea of funded investment wages in exchange for restraint. By the early 1980s, it became clear that internal opposition to Keller's views could extinguish the last glimmer of hope for the idea. Collective profit sharing was being edged off the political agenda by deep divisions in the labor movement, as well as by the political impossibility of its realization at the legislative level. The vast Metalworkers Union, IG Metall, because of its strenuous opposition to the idea, can be credited with making realization impossible, as well as with strengthening the internal opponents of GTB leaders. The waning of debate, however, does not indicate new unity—only a papering over of a fundamental split.

The reasons for this split over collective capital formation are threefold. First, as the GTB case showed, low-pay unions found in collective capital formation a potential remedy for the horizontal trilemma. Second, legislated versions promised to act, through subtle but powerful mechanisms that IG Metall leaders feared, as an instrument of restraint over IG Metall's autonomous and militant wage bargaining strategies. Hence they offered an additional way of resolving the horizontal trilemma. Finally, IG Metall's leaders feared this loss of autonomy for a reason directly related to the union's own vertical trilemma—the need to maintain autonomy for the sake of flexibility in response to the trilemma.

[17]"Ungeheuerlicher Vorgang: Hauskrach bei der Textilgewerkschaft," *Der Spiegel,* 4 October 1982, pp. 76–79.

Phase I: IG Metall versus IG Bau

The split, right through the middle of the unions and the Social Democratic party, was foreshadowed in the overtly hostile relations of the 1950s and 1960s between two aggressive and politically prominent union leaders, Otto Brenner of IG Metall and Georg Leber of IG Bau. Between the two unions and throughout the entire labor movement, a strong consensus prevailed on one matter: that government policy in the early postwar years had perpetrated an unacceptable concentration of industrial wealth in private hands. The postwar surplus labor supply, in combination with (1) the 1948 currency reform (which decimated the monetary savings of working-class and middle-class families) and (2) extremely generous income tax advantages for reinvested business profits, had kept the earnings and savings of the working class abysmally low. A vastly disproportionate share of the growing wealth and power associated with the German "economic miracle" benefited a tiny number of industrial asset holders.[18] By the time the labor market tightened up in the 1960s, severe distributional damage had apparently already been done, and it could not easily be undone with bargaining and strikes. By then, too, German industry was firmly fixed on the foundations of profit-based self-financing of investments augmented with external loan financing by a highly concentrated private banking industry, and without a broad-based equity market supplied by household savings.

Within the DGB, two discordant lines of thought emerged about the use of wage policy to deal with the wealth-distribution problem.[19] One of them, associated with IG Metall, called for wage militancy. "Expansive" or "active" wage policy and legislatively secured codetermination rights were for this union two prongs of the preferred strategy for diffusing wealth and power.

In direct opposition to this militant conception was IG Bau's striving for "social partnership" with capital. Within the framework of social partnership, according to the IG Bau view, redistribution required other means. In the construction industry, wage costs that exceeded productivity development (IG Metall's prescription) would simply be countered by large price increases because of the high labor intensivity

---

[18]Bruno Gleitze, *Sozialkapital und Sozialfonds als Mittel der Vermögenspolitik,* WWI-Studie zur Wirtschaftsforschung no. 1, 2d ed. (Cologne: Bund Verlag, 1969), 16; Wilfried Höhnen, "Zwanzig Jahre vermögenspolitische Diskussion," in Karl Heinz Pitz, *Das Nein zur Vermögenspolitik: Gewerkschaftliche Argumente und Alternativen zur Vermögensbildung* (Reinbek bei Hamburg: Rowohlt, 1974), 25–26.

[19]Otto Jacobi, "Tarifpolitische Konzeptionen der Gewerkschaften," in Otto Jacobi, Walther Müller-Jentsch, and Eberhard Schmidt, eds., *Gewerkschaften und Klassenkampf: Kritisches Jahrbuch '74* (Frankfurt/M: Fischer, 1974), 149–56.

of construction and the absence of import competition. Capital would recover its profit share. Not only would distributional objectives be dashed, but severe political reaction against the construction workers could be expected as well. Since building costs affect rent levels along with a large portion of industry's investment costs, cross-class coalitions antagonistic to construction workers loomed on the horizon.

Those were only the long-term problems anticipated with wage militancy in the construction industry. The fragmented structure of small-scale ownership and employment, as well as high labor turnover due to job completions and seasonal interruptions, made union organizing difficult and solidarity hard to maintain; strikes could easily backfire.[20] Faced with these structural circumstances and the unusual centralization of employer power in the two major employers' associations, the union recognized that wage militancy was fraught with great risks.

Moreover, as it turned out, IG Bau could benefit from the aggressive bargaining tactics of other unions without itself conducting similar maneuvers. The benefits of this free riding became clear especially by the 1960s, with the tightening of the West German labor market. Large numbers of skilled workers left the industry for more secure and environmentally attractive workplaces, forcing building employers to raise their wages in step with those earned by IG Metall's members. Ironically, pay for construction workers consistently had to rise faster than their productivity. Successful militancy on their part would have contravened IG Bau's own prescriptions for the labor movement as a whole: that wages should not grow faster than overall productivity levels in the economy.

Given these mixed circumstances, both auspicious and inauspicious, any favorable signals from IG Bau's leadership to local militants could have engendered severe reprisals from employers and the conservative governments of the 1950s and 1960s. Pockets of militancy, especially in the North Rhine region, were difficult enough to contain.[21] Militant posturing by the union leadership would certainly have activated those radical groups waiting for moral and material support from above.

In the postwar period, IG Bau's leadership was thus confronted with

[20]"The seasonal character of construction makes it . . . in large degree safe from strikes, because only in the summer months can strikes be effective. In this time, however, the relatively favorable earnings possibilities (overtime!) make many workers unwilling to strike." Walther Müller-Jentsch, "IG Bau-Steine-Erden: Juniorpartner der Bauindustrie," in Otto Jacobi, Müller-Jentsch, and Eberhard Schmidt, eds., *Gewerkschaften und Klassenkampf: Kritisches Jahrbuch '73* (Frankfurt/M: Fischer, 1973), 97.

[21]In 1955, Karl Jaeckel, a Communist leader from IG Bau's North Rhine district, ran against incumbent chairman Jakob Knöss and obtained about 21 percent of the congress votes—"a very respectable showing," as Markovits points out. *Politics of the West German Trade Unions*, 343.

a clear choice: militancy or "partnership" with employers. Each choice had potential rewards and risks. The chosen strategy, it turned out, was partnership—combined with purges of Communists and other radicals—and its peculiar programmatic form was a "policy of fund formation" (*Kassenpolitik*), in order to achieve redistributive egalitarian objectives.[22] This was the germ of the collective profit-sharing idea.

Viewing IG Bau as a union with egalitarian objectives is somewhat unusual in the literature, much of it written by left leaners. But IG Bau, in its own way, within its sectoral particularism, did for much of the period under discussion pursue genuine egalitarian objectives. First of all, until the 1970s, it repeatedly negotiated extra contract pay increases for low-pay groups, with leveling as an objective, conceived in part as a way to improve its seriously deficient level of organization.[23] Even more unusual and innovative was the founding, in collaboration with employers, of a set of benefit funds in the 1950s. The first of these was the "vacation fund" (*Urlaubskasse*) set up in 1951 along the lines of the one formed in 1949 by the construction union in the British Zone; it was to be jointly administered, with representation shared between the union and the two employers' associations in the primary construction industry.[24] More important was the Wage Compensation Fund (*Lohnausgleichskasse*, the LAK) created in 1955. Based on chairman Leber's initial idea presented to the 1953 IG Bau congress, the LAK was to tide over workers laid off when winter weather interrupted their jobs. The union and employers agreed that 4 percent of total gross wages negotiated for primary construction would be channeled into the fund and then be paid out to the unemployed during winter months as a supplement to inadequate government unemployment compensation.[25]

Leber found in this strategy, as Markovits points out, an accommodationist alternative to high hourly wage rates (secured through confrontational tactics) in order to compensate for winter pay loss. Another

[22]IG Bau, instead of learning to live with militancy in its ranks, conducted during the Cold War year of 1956 one of the most ruthless purges of Communists from the local rolls and offices of a union ever witnessed in the Federal Republic. Ibid., 344.

[23]Ibid., 349. In the 1970s, IG Bau went in the opposite direction, increasing pay for skilled workers disproportionately, citing problems in keeping and attracting skilled labor in the industry.

[24]The union and the two employers' associations enjoy equal representation. Ibid., 339.

[25]Negotiations over the LAK also involved the Christian Democratic government, which promised to provide meager unemployment compensation to unemployed construction workers between 15 October and 31 March. The LAK would then provide an additional DM 2.50 per day to help fill the gap between government benefits and wages. Ibid., 342.

reason, in addition to avoiding the risks of militancy, made this strategy attractive. It promised to stem the tide of workers out of the construction industry as they sought income during the winter months from jobs they might never leave, having found them more secure, more pleasant, and perhaps even better-paying than construction.[26] This feature was attractive to employers, who could only benefit from the relaxation of competition with other industries in the market for skilled labor. Furthermore, by reducing the turnover of labor between industries, IG Bau could maintain better contact with members and thereby boost membership figures.

In 1955, Leber proposed the formation of another fund, what would come to be called the Supplemental Assistance Fund (*Zusatzversorgungskasse*). The purpose of this fund, administered like the Wage Compensation Fund, was to bring construction workers' pension benefits closer to national standards. Construction workers' state pensions were low, because of frequent unemployment and job changes, which reduced the accumulated level of their contributions to the pension system. In less than three years, Leber succeeded in negotiating just such a fund, which came into being at the beginning of 1958.[27] Yearly financing for this pension fund, together with the vacation and compensation funds, accounted for 19 percent of gross wages by the early 1970s.[28]

Leber's accommodationist "fund politics" of the 1950s departed in two fundamental ways from the strategies of IG Metall. First, creation of these funds bound the union to an accommodationist position, for "strikes and confrontation would only jeopardize such institutions and their substantial assets."[29] Second, the bargaining policies of IG Bau had an undeniable "internally redistributive" character; that is to say, income achieved through collective bargaining was to be collectivized in funds and then redistributed among construction workers according to egalitarian criteria. For IG Metall, redistribution within the working

[26]Ibid., 340; Müller-Jentsch, "IG Bau-Steine-Erden," 96.

[27]Markovits, *Politics of the West German Trade Unions*, 345. Six pfennigs were to be deposited in the fund for every man-hour worked in primary construction. Workers would then be paid an extra pension upon retirement or disability of up to DM 454 per month, depending on years worked in the industry.

[28]Müller-Jentsch, "IG Bau-Steine-Erden," 100. In 1961, IG Bau abandoned its attempts to create another fund—the Advantage Equalization Fund (*Vorteilsausgleichskasse*). As Leber saw it, contributions for this fund would be collected by employers from nonunion members and the money would be used for vocational training, scholarships, and recreational facilities available to all workers in the industry. This plan for dealing with nonunionized "free riders" met with intense opposition from IG Metall as well as the construction industry employers and was quickly abandoned. Markovits, *Politics of the West German Trade Unions*, 351–52.

[29]Ibid., 340.

class, if it took place at all, was largely a function of taxation and the welfare state and not an objective to which the exercise of labor market power was suited.[30]

The cost of IG Bau's accommodationist package, including official support for productivity-based or cost-neutral pay guidelines across the entire economy, was to sanctify existing injustices in the distribution of newly created wealth.[31] IG Bau did not, however, ignore the inegalitarian implications of productivity-based pay increases. In 1964, under Leber's leadership, the union presented what was to be called the Leber Plan for the payment of "investment wages" into a jointly administered multi-employer or "branch" fund. Through negotiated arrangements between the union and employers' associations, each employer in construction would contribute 1.5 percent of its yearly wage bill; the accumulated capital would be reinvested in the industry. Workers, in whose name the money would be held in trust, would not generally be able to withdraw their accumulated shares and interest until retirement or disablement.[32]

The underlying premise in this plan was that wage bargaining alone could never check, let alone reverse, the continuing concentration of ownership in industry. Trying to do so with wage increases that exceeded productivity advances would only backfire: businesses would raise prices to protect profits, and the extra purchasing power of workers would make that tactic possible. Furthermore, the point was to increase not workers' consumption levels but rather their assets. Hence the idea of "investment wages" offered a solution. Workers' income growth should indeed exceed productivity growth, but the difference should be *saved* rather than be spent. With investment wages, the aggregate disposable income of workers would not rise to provide slack to be taken up by defensive price increases by capitalists; the plan would thus prevent economic instability and slippage back to previous patterns of distribution. With investment wages being paid throughout the economy, industry would increasingly have to seek outside equity capital from workers and their collective funds, administered jointly by unions

---

[30]Franz Steinkühler, "Angst vor den Freunden: Zerbricht das Bündis von Gewerkschaften und Sozialdemokraten?" *Die Zeit*, 25 March 1988, 13.

[31]In its 1966/68 Annual Report, IG Bau states that the idea of "cost-neutral wage policy" (*konstenniveauneutralen Lohnpolitik*), developed by the recently formed Council of Economic Experts (Sachverständigenrat), "conforms by and large to the incomes-policy principles already practiced by IG Bau-Steine-Erden before the Council . . . was appointed." Quoted in Müller-Jentsch, "IG Bau-Steine-Erden," 104.

[32]See Georg Leber, ed., *Vermögensbildung in Arbeitnehmerhand: Ein Programm und sein Echo* (Frankfurt/M: Europäische Verlagsanstalt, 1964), and Leber, "Vermögensbildung in Arbeitnehmerhand," *Gewerkschaftliche Monatshefte* 16 (1965), 66ff.

and employers. In other words, inability to raise sufficient capital from retained profits or from existing capital owners (whose income could be reduced by the payment of investment wages) would force industry to rely on capital from the proposed funds. Thus would the trend toward concentration of asset ownership, especially in industry, be checked and reversed. All of this would be achieved, furthermore, without disturbing macroeconomic stability and growth, or so it was believed.

The Leber Plan met aggressive criticism from two sides. Construction employers agreed to investment wages the following year (1965), but without some of the ingredients critical to Leber's recipe. The employers refused, for example, to set up multi-employer branch funds, even if jointly administered. (Workers' investment wages were put into individual savings accounts.) Employers feared that the union might use the proposed capital allocation instrument, in combination with its leverage from traditional bargaining power in the labor market, to control decision making in individual firms. The three funds they had already set up on a jointly managed basis were merely allocative instruments for resources to *workers* and were therefore acceptable; an investment fund, on the other hand, allocates resources to *employers*. In union hands, employers thought, that power could be dangerous.[33]

Naturally, IG Metall's objections were different. Since the 1950s, IG Metall had rejected IG Bau's accommodationism and instead called for aggressive efforts to increase wages. At its most radical—in the early 1950s—IG Metall applauded the idea of militant wage policy, whereby wage increases should not in principle follow productivity but should exhaust union bargaining power to enlarge the wage share. By the 1960s and 1970s, IG Metall's wage policy statements wavered, but they never quite rejected the idea. Consistently, the union advocated aggressive wage bargaining as a way of increasing aggregate demand and thus generating full employment and growth. Hence the principles behind IG Metall's wage militancy ranged between positive-sum Keynesianism and militant particularism (tempered with a politics of welfare-save-the-hindmost). Unions, in this view, need not try to exercise responsibility for employment levels and macroeconomic perfor-

---

[33]In contrast with the Leber Plan, the 1965 agreement required that workers take the initiative in setting up an account. Furthermore, for every person-hour worked, workers had to contribute two pfennigs for every nine that employers contributed. Finally, the accounts were blocked for five years instead of until retirement, as the Leber Plan had recommended.

mance, for business and government retain the power behind that responsibility.[34]

IG Metall's leaders never quite managed to present a decisive argument for militant wage bargaining as the sole, necessary, and sufficient instrument for factor income redistribution. But they sought in the 1960s and 1970s to bolster the union against the outspokenly accommodationist position of IG Bau and other unions—by attacking their cases for wage restraint. One indirect yet important approach entailed attacking the idea of investment wages and funds. This strategy made sense, for the Leber Plan (and later blueprints for collective profit sharing) try to *justify* restraint by offering a way of dealing with its undesired side-effects on distribution. By the mid-1970s, IG Metall had mobilized considerable intellectual resources for this task and had developed an extensive catalog of objections to "fund politics." The effort became all the more urgent from 1968 onward, as the DGB and the Social Democratic–Liberal coalition government took over IG Bau's leading role in the debate.

Phase II: IG Metall versus the DGB

In the wake of the SPD's Bad Godesberg program (1959), IG Metall gradually lost its ability to dominate policy thinking, as in the 1960s Georg Leber of IG Bau mobilized other unions oriented toward social partnership against Brenner's quasi-Marxism.[35] Indicative was the replacement of Viktor Agartz, head of the WWI—the DGB's "think tank"—and author of IG Metall's "expansive wage policy", by Bruno Gleitze, whose ideas were soon to cause IG Metall considerable grief. In particular, Gleitze was the author of the first plan for a redistributive fund system to gather widespread support within the labor movement, something the Leber Plan never managed to do.

As early as 1957, before an audience of regional DGB officials (Landesbezirk Hessen), Gleitze introduced the problem of low worker savings resulting from low pay, the related dependence of industry on profits and self-financing for economic growth, and consequently the systemic tendency toward concentration of wealth and power in the economy. Newly created wealth was accumulating disproportionately

[34]On IG Metall's "expansive" and "active" wage policy, see Viktor Agartz, "Expansive Lohnpolitik," in *Mitteilungen des Wirtschaftswissenschaftlichen Institutes der Gewerkschaften* (December 1953), 245–47; Markovits, *Politics of the West German Trade Unions*, 84–86; Kleps, *Lohnpolitische Konzeptionen*, 55–66; and Jacobi, "Tarifpolitische Konzeptionen," 149–56.
[35]Markovits, *Politics of the West German Trade Unions*, 83–106.

in the hands of those who already had it. As a solution, Gleitze suggested the formation of collective or "multi-employer social funds" (*überbetrieblichen Sozialfonds*) owned by all wage earners and supplied with equity out of corporate profits.[36] The process of accumulation in the fund would counteract the concentration of wealth, while the exercise of power through ownership would break the concentration of private economic power over economic and political affairs.

Two important features of the gradually evolving Gleitze Plan distinguished it from the Leber Plan. First, a tax on profits instead of wages would fill the funds over time. Investment wages, many had concluded in the course of the debate, would have the undesirable consequences of enhancing oligopoly tendencies. Low-profit, labor-intensive firms in competitive industries would suffer, and many would go out of business; high-profit, capital-intensive, and oligopolistic firms would pay relatively little and easily pass on the extra wage costs to consumers. The effect on industry structure would be unwanted, and the net redistributional effect of the system would be weaker.[37] Collective profit sharing (*überbetriebliche Ertragsbeteiligung*) would not have the same distorting effects.

Second, to create an economy-wide system of funds, Gleitze called for legislative action rather than collective bargaining, the method preferred by IG Bau. Since Gleitze would allow all wage earners (including those in the public sector and nonprofit institutions) to share in the future accumulation of wealth, collective bargaining would be an awkward instrument. Changes in corporate taxation and corporate and securities law were also required to accommodate a complex system of investment funds. Most important, employer opposition to anything but individualistic, firm-level investment wages or profit sharing blocked the bargaining route from the very beginning.

The germination period for Gleitze's ideas lasted about ten years, during which time he repeated and developed them for diverse audiences.[38] In the meantime, the 1960 SPD congress adopted the Deist Plan—with a sketchy blueprint of a fund (a "German National Foundation") remotely resembling what Gleitze recommended.[39] Four years

[36]Portions of Gleitze's lecture are reprinted in his *Sozialkapital und Sozialfonds,* 18–20.

[37]Advocates of investment wages argued only that *on average* prices would not be affected. For a discussion of the advantages of collective profit sharing over investment wages, see Wilfried Höhnen, "Überbetriebliche Ertragsbeteiligung als vermögenspolitische Konzeption," *WWI-Mitteilungen* 1/2 (1969).

[38]See the collection of lectures and essays in Gleitze, *Sozialkapital und Sozialfonds,* 16–40.

[39]Wilfried Höhnen describes the plan authored by Heinrich Deist, a leading Social Democratic economist, as a concretization of the recent Bad Godesberg Program of the

later, Leber had advanced his own fund plan, which was to receive neither the labor movement's nor the employers' blessings.[40] Not until the publication of the 1968 Krelle Report to the Ministry of Labor, however, did the debate pick up speed. Wilhelm Krelle and his collaborators reported their disturbing finding that only 1.7 percent of West German households owned 70 percent of all productive assets. As the situation was getting worse rather than better, Krelle's team of researchers advocated a collective profit-sharing scheme much like what Gleitze had been proposing.[41]

The following year, the SPD finally realized its long-awaited chance to govern postwar West Germany. The "reform euphoria" of its early years in power would set in motion a number of drafting efforts within the DGB, the SPD, and even the FDP, the liberal partner of the new SPD-led coalition government of 1969. That year, for example, the Munich congress of Young Socialists (Jungsozialisten or Jusos, the youth branch of the SPD) called for the socialization of profits in a central fund; in 1970, the radical SPD district of Hessen-Süd entered a motion for the creation of a People's Assets Fund (Stiftung Volksvermögen), with revenues from a profits tax and assets allocated as individual shares.[42]

By 1970, even the highest reaches of the German civil service had joined the public debate. That year saw the publication of a leaked "discussion paper" written by four permanent undersecretaries (in the Economic Affairs, Labor, Finance, and Interior ministries), which called for something much like the Deist Plan: firms earning taxable profits over DM 100,000 would be required to contribute between 2

Social Democrats, as well as a response to the CDU's own idea of "people's capitalism" through "peoples' shares" (*Volksaktien*) or widely dispersed shareholding in industry encouraged by tax advantages. One significant difference between Deist and Gleitze was the requirement that individuals buy into the fund albeit at a subsidization rate of 90 percent. Gleitze called for automatic and egalitarian distribution to all wage earners. Höhnen, "Zwanzig Jahre vermögenspolitische Diskussion," in Pitz, *Das Nein zur Vermögenspolitik*, 34–35.

[40]Legislative action in 1965 by the Christian Democratic government extended tax breaks aimed at encouraging private savings to include the recently negotiated investment wages for construction workers. By 1970 even IG Metall was taking advantage of these tax breaks for members' savings, while maintaining that they hardly helped solve any of the fundamental problems facing the working class. Other unions had responded quickly to the incentives, leaving IG Metall's members behind. See Eugen Loderer, "Qualität des Lebens statt Vermögenspolitik," in Pitz, *Das Nein zur Vermögenspolitik*, 10.

[41]Wilhelm Krelle, Johann Schunck, and Jürgen Siebke, *Überbetriebliche Ertragsbeteiligung der Arbeitnehmer: Forschungsauftrag des Bundesministeriums für Arbeit und Sozialordnung* (Tübingen: BFAS, 1968). The 70 percent figure was for 1960; by the end of the 1960s, that figure had increased to 74 percent of equity in industry. Jürgen Siebke, "Vermögenskonzentration," in Pitz, *Das Nein zur Vermögenspolitik*, 65.

[42]Höhnen, "Zwanzig Jahre," 36.

percent and 10 percent of those profits into a system of competing funds—either in cash, or as shares in the company, or as promissory notes. Individuals with a yearly income below a certain level could buy shares in the funds at a highly subsidized rate. The funds would be integrated into the existing private credit and banking system; share owners would exercise only very limited control, by way of elections to the funds' supervisory boards (*Aufsichtsräte*). The job of these boards was restricted primarily to choosing the private banking or other capital market institutions that would manage and invest the money. Shares could be cashed in only after seven years.[43] The legislative strategy was to combine the introduction of the system with tax reform in 1974.

Hopes for legislative introduction of some form of collective or centralized profit sharing were also raised by the leftward swing of the FDP. At its 1971 congress, in a dramatic reformulation of party principles known as the Freiburg Theses, the FDP committed itself to the centralized fund solution as the only suitable way to reverse the inegalitarian process of pay and wealth distribution. Combining individualism with egalitarianism, the new FDP program called for a tax similar to the one in the government's discussion paper, along with a system of competing funds. But the acquisition of shares was to be even more egalitarian: very low-income groups would receive them free, whereas the price would increase progressively for other individuals up the income scale. A time restriction on the sale or cashing in of shares was not included, although by liquidating, an individual forfeited the right to obtain subsidized shares for the following three years. Individual "certificate" holders would receive dividends, and the power of their elected representatives on fund boards would be limited in the same way as in the leaked discussion paper.[44]

The hopes of those in the Social-Liberal coalition and in the permanent civil service for legislation of this nature were temporarily dashed, however, when it became clear that Karl Schiller, as minister of economic affairs, opposed the idea altogether. Against the efforts of his own parliamentary undersecretary, Schiller obstructed further action until his resignation in 1972.[45]

[43]Åke Wredén, *Kapital till de anställda? En studie av vinstdelning och löntagarfonder* (Stockholm: Studieförbundet Näringsliv och Samhälle, 1976), 145–51. Wredén's book is an excellent source of the details of this and other plans from Germany, Sweden, and the Netherlands.

[44]Ibid., 145–51; Höhnen, "Zwanzig Jahre," 38–39.

[45]A dominant figure in the party, Schiller had effectively laid the Hannover "Deist Plan" (1960) to rest when the 1964 Karlsruhe congress passed a very tame five-point program on the subject. The 1968 Nürnberg Congress passed an even weaker resolu-

With Schiller out of the picture, the way seemed clear once again for collective profit sharing. At the 1973 party congress in Hannover, a plan almost identical to one recently developed by the DGB executive board (described below) was passed. Passage, however, did not take place without opposition from vocal elements within the party led by IG Metall. By 17 May of the next year, less than four months after the SPD and the FDP had submitted a compromise blueprint for collective profit sharing, the new chancellor Helmut Schmidt—who apparently had never been particularly interested in the idea—called off all legislative efforts. Regrettably, Schmidt said, there were a number of insoluble legal and technical obstacles.[46] He also anticipated difficulty in getting legislation past the Bundesrat, or upper chamber, and maintained that profit sharing would preempt the opportunity for increased taxes on corporate profits and for a long-awaited tax reform.[47]

In addition, the fact that IG Metall was at the time openly and vigorously opposing collective profit sharing probably reinforced Schmidt's inclinations. IG Metall and sympathizers in the Social Democratic party had openly opposed but failed to kill the collective profit-sharing idea at the party's 1973 congress. Although IG Metall had accepted a tactical compromise at the 1972 DGB congress in Berlin, it apparently did so not for lack of numbers but for the sake of avoiding open conflict at the congress. To his chagrin, chairman Loderer realized later that IG Metall had thereby lost its chance to prevent the DGB from presenting a similar model as an official, pre-election legislative demand in 1973.[48] Nevertheless, there was no question in anyone's mind that the labor movement was deeply split over the issue. Uniting

---

tion. Little came of the matter at the Saarbrücken congress in 1970, and the "tax reform congress" of 1971 managed only to set up a committee to work out a proposal. Höhnen, "Zwanzig Jahre," 35–37.

[46]See "Schmidt gibt die Vermögenspolitik auf," *Frankfurter Allgemeine Zeitung,* 15 May 1974. In its 1976 annual economic report, the Schmidt government continued to rely on these objections: "Concerning efforts toward legislation of broad popular sharing in the growth of productive assets, no satisfactory solution could be achieved. The work of the interministerial group appointed for this task has shown that a reasonable and rational grand solution faces insoluble difficulties at this time, due to legal and technical reasons. In particular, equal treatment of firms of different corporate legal forms could not be realized. On top of that, suitable measures for the assessment of the values of company shares not traded in the stock market do not exist. Furthermore, the necessary administrative costs in relationship to yield would be unreasonably high." *Jahreswirtschaftsbericht 1976 der Bundesregierung,* appendix to Sachverständigenrat, *Vollbeschäftigung für Morgen: Jahresgutachten 1974–1975* (Stuttgart: Kohlhammer, 1975), 13.

[47]See "Schmidt gibt die Vermögenspolitik auf," *Frankfurter Allgemeine Zeitung,* 15 May 1974.

[48]The congress resolution called for further study of the issue, which would, Loderer hoped, give him time to prevail or at least prevent the DGB from taking a clear stand.

the Government and Transport Workers Union (ÖTV), the second-largest DGB union, and three other small unions against collective profit sharing, IG Metall's coalition led the majority of delegates—allocated according to strict proportional representation by membership levels—to DGB congresses. (On the other hand, in the Bundesauschuss, the intercongress decision-making body responsible for the 1973 demand, the same unions could muster only 52 votes against the 55 for collective profit sharing in 1973.)[49]

Because of the deep division in the DGB, Schmidt's actions had limited repercussions for relations with the unions. From the standpoint of economic policy, the costlier choice would have been to go along with DGB chairman Heinz Oskar Vetter (who had once led IG Bergbau und Energie, the accommodationist union representing miners) against the policy wishes of the DGB's two largest unions, which wielded the greatest clout in national wage negotiations.

The plan submitted by the DGB executive council to the DGB congress in 1972, which IG Metall so assiduously fought, resembled in many ways Rudolf Meidner's 1975 plan as presented to the Swedish labor confederation.[50] By act of legislation, all firms with taxable profits over DM 200,000 would contribute progressively, depending on profit levels, 4 percent, 8 percent, or 15 percent of those profits into a central "clearing" fund. Payment would as a rule consist not of cash but rather of "obligatory directed issues" of shares in public corporations, limited liability companies, and limited partnerships. In other words, the actual cash would remain in the firm as working capital. Changes in corporate law would be necessary to make it possible for the fund to share equity holdings in companies with different forms of ownership.[51]

The central fund in this scheme would allocate portions of the acquired assets to a number of regional, noncompeting funds, independent of banks and other private capital institutions. Two-thirds of the

[49]Höhnen writes that the vote was 55 to 52, and that joining IG Metall and the ÖTV were the Union of Postal Workers (Deutsche Postgewerkschaft), the Union of Railway Workers (Gewerkschaft der Eisenbahner Deutschlands) and the Union of Teachers and Scientists (Gewerkschaft Erziehung und Wissenschaft). "Zwanzig Jahre," 45.

[50]This is not surprising, for as Meidner repeatedly points out, many details of his plan come from the DGB/SPD plans. See Rudolf Meidner, "Deutsche Einflüsse auf die schwedische Debatte über überbetriebliche Vermögensbeteiligung," in Hans Jochen Vogel, Helmut Simon, and Adalbert Podlech, eds., *Die Freiheit des Anderen: Festschrift für Martin Hirsch* (Baden–Baden: Nomos Verlagsgesellschaft, 1982), 377–88.

[51]The possibility would remain for some nonpublic firms to pay cash or promissory notes instead of issuing shares, though payment would be at a higher rate. Expected yearly yield would be DM 4–6 billion.

members of supervisory boards of these funds would be chosen in a secret vote by the shareholders of the funds (one person, one vote); one-third would be appointed by government. The fund managers would vote the shares their boards held in individual firms, and in general they would use their capital to further industrial policy as well as other social objectives.

All wage and salary earners with yearly income less than DM 24,000 would be issued equal shares or "certificates" from the fund in their region. As shareholders, they would receive yearly dividends but could liquidate their shares only in the case of personal financial emergency. (Shares could be inherited, however.) Because it anticipated difficulty in obtaining consensus on this point, the DGB executive council suggested a possible, but to them clearly inferior, compromise: after ten years, individual shareholders might sell their shares on the stock market.

Two reasons had recommended "permanent blocking periods" (*ewige Sperrfristen*) to their advocates. First, if shareholders in the funds could freely buy and sell, they would pressure fund managers to compete on the same terms with private institutions to maximize dividends or accumulated earnings. If managers did so, that would inhibit the investment of the capital in ways that would promote union objectives regarding distribution and social policy. More important, perhaps, was the point that collective profit sharing should amass "productive capital" as a component of the "workers' share" of national income. As productive capital, it could not be converted to cash for individual consumption, especially because the operative presumption was that the macroeconomically acceptable leeway for disposable wage increases would already be exhausted through collective bargaining. The profit-sharing component, then, should be that portion of the increase in workers' total income (disposable plus nondisposable) that exceeds productivity growth. But because of the high propensity of wage earners to consume, most analysts anticipated high rates of liquidation.

This fear had some basis in empirical evidence. The widespread purchase of cars, houses, boats, and so on after blocking periods had passed would naturally be inflationary; hence unions in future years would be called on to hold back wages to counteract demand-pull inflation or otherwise to pay the costs of deflationary government policy. Equally vexatious, a rapid surge in liquidations would result in a decline in the value of shares. As other workers would be unlikely to want to or have the capacity to buy up the shares others would sell, the likely buyers of these undervalued shares would be those who already possess substantial wealth. After the blocking period passed, in other words, deconcentration would be thrown into reverse. Only extremely long and restrictive blocking rules could stop this process.[52]

IG METALL'S CASE AGAINST THE FUND IDEA

IG Metall rejected without exception all forms of collective capital formation, including the Swedish versions of the middle and late 1970s, which have received far more international attention than earlier and strikingly similar German plans. LO's Rudolf Meidner had visited both the DGB and IG Metall in 1974, drawing many of his ideas from the DGB version already receiving intense criticism from IG Metall. For this reason, we need to correct Markovits's assertion that IG Metall "would have much preferred to see the implementation of some kind of asset formation . . . as formulated in the Meidner Plan." Economist Karl Pitz, of IG Metall, who was responsible for preparing much of IG Metall's argumentation against collective profit sharing, confirms this point: "Meidner followed the DGB line, and did not adopt ours."[53]

Criticism of the permanent blocking period, mentioned above and incorporated in the Swedish models, figured prominently in IG Metall's armory of objections to the DGB plan. In what was perhaps the union's most decisive policy statement on the question, issued to the press in October 1972 and hereafter referred to as the "Seven Principles,"[54] IG Metall declared:

> Economic considerations indicate that workers' shares in a collective profit sharing system must be withheld from them for a long period or even

---

[52]Construction workers had cashed in about 40 percent of their past "investment wages." Loderer, "Qualität des Lebens," 14–19.

[53]Markovits, *Politics of the West German Trade Unions*, 121; interview with Pitz, Frankfurt, 15 June 1982.

[54]Industriegewerkschaft Metall, "Leitsätze der Industriegewerkschaft Metall zur Vermögenspolitik," in Pitz, *Das Nein zur Vermögenspolitik*, 52–54. They originally appeared in *Metall-Pressedienst*, 17 October 1972, and IG Metall, *Presse- und Funknachrichten*, 18 October 1972. IG Metall leaders issued the statement after having felt "rolled over" by the DGB executive in a sitting of the council (Bundesausschuss). *Frankfurter Neue Presse*, 12 October 1972. Karl Heinz Pitz expands on the arguments from the "Seven Principles" in "Über die potentiellen Gefahren der 'grossen Lösung' des Vermögensproblems für die gewerkschaftliche Lohnpolitik," *Gewerkschaftliche Monatshefte* 21 (October 1970); "Verbindungen zwischen Vermögenspolitik, Lohnpolitik und Sozialpolitik," in Klaus Schenke and Winfried Schmähl, eds., *Alterssicherung als Aufgabe für Wissenschaft und Politik* (Stuttgart: Kohlhammer, 1980); and "Zusammenhänge zwischen Vermögens-, Steuer- und Reformpolitik," *Sozialer Fortschritt* 4 (1972).

totally in principle, if the [desired] effect of profit sharing is to be secured. Long or even permanent blocking periods must however be rejected, because they would bring only fictive benefits [to individuals], which would then necessarily lead to corresponding counterreactions.

What those counterreactions might be, and what exactly would bring them on, is not made clear.[55]

Greater force and clarity were brought to bear in the argument that the social policy and distributional objectives of collective profit sharing would be achieved more efficiently with a mixture of different approaches. The so-called grand solution that many saw in collective profit sharing would not solve anything. Worse, it would obstruct IG Metall's three preferred reform instruments for achieving some of the same objectives: (1) codetermination (for breaking the monopoly of private economic power); (2) higher corporate taxation for social legislation (which would squeeze profits and provide an alternative to more widespread ownership as the basis for greater material security); and (3) collective bargaining (for redistribution of income).

Opportunity Costs

For IG Metall, political mobilization for collective capital formation would mean foregone opportunities. Particularly painful would be the obstruction of an ongoing legislative campaign to extend to other industries the version of codetermination in place so far only in the coal mining and steel industries. *Montanmitbestimmung* in those two sectors gave unions "parity" or equal representation on company supervisory boards (*Aufsichtsräte*), as well as the power to nominate executive labor directors on executive bodies (*Vorstände*) responsible for day-to-day management. Very few legislative objectives matched this one in importance for IG Metall, whose militancy precluded institutionalized partnership arrangements, at least those negotiated at a centralized level, to provide union security. Codetermination provided the statuto-

---

[55]Industriegewerkschaft Metall, "Leitsätze," in Pitz, *Das Nein zur Vermögenspolitik*, 53. Loderer repeated the same point elsewhere, again without clarification: members "must be able to identify clearly the concrete advantages to each individual worker. If that is not possible . . . then this program stands on feet of clay." Loderer, "Qualität des Lebens," 16. On another occasion Loderer claimed that members would regard their shares as good for no more than "papering their walls." Loderer, "Auszug aus einem hektographierten Manuskript der IG Metall ohne Orts- und Jahresangabe" (speech delivered 9 November 1972), in Gerhard Leminsky and Bernd Otto, eds., *Politik und Programmatik des Deutschen Gewerkschaftsbundes* (Cologne: Bund Verlag, 1974), 175.

ry equivalent and hence was probably more compelling for IG Metall than for accommodationist unions like GTB and IG Bau.[56]

Furthermore, IG Metall has always held that a wider dispersion of privately owned equity shares in industry cannot counteract and would probably strengthen oligarchical control in industry.[57] In its Seven Principles concerning collective capital formation, IG Metall maintained that

> even collective sharing of ownership in productive capital in the hands of workers by means of funds cannot be a solution, for these . . . do not bring codetermination, and instead unavoidably work against union demands for . . . codetermination. IG Metall therefore asserts the necessity of maintaining a clear distinction between wealth-distribution policies [*Vermögenspolitik*] on the one hand and the control of economic power on the other, and rejects one-sided emphasis on productive assets in the wealth-distribution debate.[58]

Why did IG Metall argue that collective funds would obstruct rather than foster codetermination through board representation? Clearly, secret election of shareholder representatives on fund boards by wage earners receiving less than DM 24,000 per year (or practically all DGB members), and the rights of these boards to vote the stock they held, represented a form of codetermination. It is not fully clear from the writings from Frankfurt why this form was not good enough. A reasonable conclusion is that union leaders feared that union lists would not prevail in fund elections. Competing groups—parties, for example—might prevent the 80 percent success rate that the DGB unions gener-

[56]By contrast IG Bau's Georg Leber looked to friendly relations with employers to improve membership levels. His support for codetermination was lukewarm, and he expected far less from it than IG Metall did. Christian Zentner, *Das Verhalten von Georg Leber* (Mainz: v. Hase & Koehler Verlag, 1966), 142–44, 159–66, 202–5. On the organizational and membership maintenance benefits of parity codetermination, see Wolfgang Spieker, "Mitbestimmung im Unternehmen: Idee und Wirklichkeit," *WSI-Mitteilungen* 29:8 (1976), especially 442–43. Wolfgang Streeck looks at how militancy and social partnership have shaped these membership-maintenance strategies in *Gewerkschaftliche Organisationsprobleme in der sozialstaatlichen Demokratie* (Königstein: Athenäum, 1981), 195–269.

[57]As shares become more diffusely distributed among individuals, the size of voting blocks necessary for controlling shareholder meetings declines. The argument is commonly advanced by trade unionists in and outside Germany against "people's capitalism." Edward Herman partially contests this view, maintaining that ownership diffusion strengthens the strategic position of management, not the power of shareholder blocks. The critique of people's capitalism is not thereby weakened. *Corporate Control, Corporate Power* (Cambridge: Cambridge University Press, 1981), 24–25.

[58]Industriegewerkschaft Metall, "Leitsätze," in Pitz, *Das Nein zur Vermögenspolitik*, 53.

ally have with their lists in works council elections.[59] Second, unlike the Meidner Plan and all the LO-SAP proposals, no German plan ever contained a provision for the devolution of some of the voting rights held by the funds to workers in the firms in which the funds held shares.

Another consideration alluded to in the Seven Principles is that profit sharing would stiffen conservative resistance against legislative extension of parity codetermination. As Germany's major business daily put it,

> The intention behind the [profit-sharing fund] model is to strengthen codetermination. Once parity codetermination is achieved, then hyperparity [*Überparität*, or majority union control] results, since board representatives of the funds will then sit as stockholders as well. And since the funds will of course become an annex of the unions, which appoint the executive personnel, they will become the central offices for union control over business decision making.

IG Metall chairman Loderer feared these sentiments would spread and strengthen, galvanizing the Right against codetermination: "There is already an extraordinarily intense debate about 'hyperparity.' And now of all times, at the moment we are on the verge of pushing through our insistent, decades-old demands for parity codetermination, the opposition against it gets extra fuel for its fire. No one is doing us any favor with this."[60]

Another of IG Metall's major objections to collective profit sharing along DGB lines was that it would preempt opportunities made available by Social Democratic control of government for major corporate tax reforms (elimination of huge tax credits and deductions, and hence

[59]Streeck, *Gewerkschaftliche Organisationsprobleme*, 209. Even if a DGB list received 80 percent in the fund elections, one-third of fund board members would be government appointees. Thus, with a conservative government in power, the unions would be able to control at best 54 percent of the seats. This power would be further diluted by the limited holdings of the funds in a particular enterprise, at least in the near future. Codetermination promised, on the other hand, instant control.

[60]*Handelsblatt,* 19 April 1973, quoted in Loderer, "Qualität des Lebens," 20, 21. As it turned out, even without collective profit sharing, IG Metall got far less than it wanted out of the legislative extension of codetermination in 1976, due in large part to the constraints of coalition politics ("*Koalitionszwang*") with the FDP. The 1976 codetermination did not give unions parity; middle management received separate representation; no labor directors were to be appointed; and eligibility of workers' representatives was limited so that unions could not bring in people from outside the enterprise's own work force. IG Metall's perception that success was easily threatened was thus in large part justified.

increases in profits taxation). Such reform would eliminate some of the distributional injustices of government fiscal policy since the end of World War II. It would also help finance public infrastructure and the expansion of social legislation earnestly desired by all of the DGB unions, without cutting into the disposable income of workers.

Probably uppermost in the minds of IG Metall leaders was the belief that collective profit sharing would hurt the union's ability to achieve its ends through wage bargaining. One of the Seven Principles asserted that "wealth-redistributive measures that directly or indirectly constrain active wage policy or prevent a fairer distribution of the tax burden must . . . be rejected as inappropriate." As Loderer put it, "the demands for a system of collective profit sharing . . . would hang like a millstone around our necks [wie ein Klotz am Bein hängen]."[61]

On this point, the DGB and IG Metall parted company as decisively as they had on the rights of individuals to sell their shares. Because its model would require corporations to transfer equity shares (not cash) to the funds in fulfillment of their obligations to profit sharing, the DGB argued that "no cost burdens arise." In fact, according to the DGB, "profit sharing is accomplished exclusively at the expense of previous owners. Consequently, neither active wage policy nor a tax reform is endangered."[62] From the SPD came similar counterattacks against IG Metall's "specious argumentation," because corporate liquidity would supposedly not be touched at all. From the standpoint of IG Metall, however, that argument assumed "an artificial and arbitrary separation of corporation and shareholders—of capital and the owners of capital."

> It is as if one could split the two, as if they were not inextricably bound together. The idea that one could enlist today's capital owners for [redistributional] objectives without complications seems naive. You cannot take away assets from capital owners without then provoking the stiffest resistance against even further tax increases. How can one believe that you can skin a capitalist without having to pluck him too? Never in its history has the labor movement gotten as much as a pfennig free.[63]

In other words, collective profit sharing would amount to a brake on other union efforts: employers would hold it up against other de-

[61]Industriegewerkschaft Metall, "Leitsätze," in Pitz, Das Nein zur Vermögenspolitik, 52–53; Loderer, "Auszug aus einem hektographierten Manuskript," 175.

[62]Deutscher Gewerkschaftsbund, "Stellungnahme des DGB-Bundesausschusses zur Beteiligung der Arbeitnehmer am Produktivvermögen vom 4. April 1973," in Pitz, Das Nein zur Vermögenspolitik, 55.

[63]Loderer, "Qualität des Lebens," 22.

mands, deduct it from what they say they have at their disposal for taxes and wages, and add it to justifications for price increases to recover profit shares.[64]

Regarding wage bargaining, IG Metall critics of profit sharing expressed special worries. Reaffirming its old "active wage policy" principle of raising wage earners' share of national income as disposable wages, the leadership concluded that the entire twenty-year debate presupposed that profit-sharing levels would be related to wage increases. Collective profit sharing, in other words, "seeks to sneak productivity-based wage policy in again through the back door." As Loderer expressed it to a forum of top officials, "We have no intention of taking it easy on the wage front by letting academic technocrats precalculate our wage increase rates on the basis of productivity increases, while extra portions are automatically credited to our accounts. Our instrument for income distribution is active wage policy, not passive *Vermögenspolitik*." Countering a claim familiar from the Swedish debate, Loderer also insisted that collective profit sharing would not have a "relaxing effect" (*entspannende Wirkung*) on labor market conflict. Quite the contrary: employers would count their profit-sharing contributions as part of the wage bill, and workers would insist on usual increases in their paychecks, so that the range of easily negotiable pay increases would narrow.[65] At the core of IG Metall's objections, then, was the leadership's fears of more rather than fewer vexatious problems with the wage policy trilemma.

PAY DISTRIBUTION AND POLITICAL DIVISION

From the previous analysis follows the central argument of this chapter: IG Metall's leaders opposed collective capital formation as a defense against direct or indirect control by outsiders, including other unions. Fear of a loss of bargaining autonomy and flexibility derived in

[64]IG Metall's viewpoint is probably correct in considering the effects of international capital flight: "If the dependency of investment on profits can be reduced, while workers' savings take their place . . . whether as equity or loan capital, then worker capital formation can occur without additional forfeit of disposable income . . . and without attempts by industry to pass off the costs as prices or without reduction in investments. A certain leeway for this may exist. But under given constraints, we find it to be small. The strategic position of investors and shareholders, who want to achieve their expected returns in a market system with free international capital mobility, is too strong." Sachverständigenrat, *Konjunktur im Umbruch—Risiken und Chancen: Jahresgutachten 1970/71* (Stuttgart: Kohlhammer, 1970), 72.

[65]Loderer, "Qualität des Lebens," 23, "Auszug aus einem hektographiertem Manuskrupt," 175, and "Qualität des Lebens," 23.

part from the union's vastness and heterogeneity, which made it diffi-cult to generate unity behind wage policy. The precariousness of unity was in large part a result of real internal conflicts over distribution, described by IG Metall's vertical trilemma. Finally, the leaders' anxiety about loss of autonomy and flexibility to deal with internal conflicts was not groundless paranoia; it was fully validated by memories of past political challenges from within and outside the labor movement against the union's autonomy and militancy.

The union leaders who tended to favor collective profit sharing were by and large, like the leadership of the GTB, those whose unions suf-fered from the horizontal variant of the trilemma, especially when structural trends militated against closing—or even maintaining—ex-ternal wage differentials. The logic of their situation made potentially attractive anything that might restrain more militant high-wage unions such as IG Metall. Several unions, among them the most prominent advocates of collective capital funds, openly campaigned to discredit the activist or "expansive" wage policies of IG Metall and, somewhat less openly, agitated for peak-level coordination by the DGB. For ex-ample, by proselytizing for wage policy roughly linked to the average productivity trends for the whole economy, accommodationist unions aligned themselves with employers and conservatives of all parties in their hostility to IG Metall's militancy.

The goal of sectoral wage growth linked to economy-wide productiv-ity trends resurfaced as a central premise of collective capital formation in versions eagerly supported by accommodationist unions. It is fully understandable, then, that IG Metall's leaders have interpreted the idea as an attempt to impose external, if only informal, control by undercutting the leaders' ideological grounds for wage militancy when militancy suited them. Their ideology presents high wages as the only important tool for redistribution between capital and labor. Opponents within the DGB and the SPD had challenged that premise with collec-tive profit sharing.

Autonomy and Flexibility

A desire to use collective bargaining instrumentally to govern the moral economy of pay and thereby maintain unity motivates IG Met-all's leadership to protect its freedom of action against outside control. The importance of this defensive struggle manifested itself as pressure that built in the early 1970s within IG Metall for withdrawal from *konzertierte Aktion,* the semi-institutionalized, tripartite deliberations be-tween unions, employers, and the Social Democratic government introduced in 1967 by Karl Schiller, the minister of economic affairs.[66] *Konzertierte Aktion* had the effect of sanctifying "orientation data" such as macroeconomically admissible (productivity-based) rates of pay increases as "objective" and "distributionally neutral." It thereby fueled hostile press and public opinion against unions that tried to exceed such rates. IG Metall was one of several unions frequently expressing fears that orientation data and their normative influence on public opinion encroached on their bargaining autonomy.

The reasons for this desire to maintain autonomy are clear. The trilemma suggests that union leaders ordinarily cannot pursue coherent distributional strategies in a persistent fashion over time. Short-term goals will oscillate in reaction to the consequences and oversights of past policies. IG Metall, the largest and most important union in the DGB, is the most important case in point.

IG Metall's immensity, heterogeneity, and internal democracy make its dealings with the trilemma all the more difficult. The union has members with high pay in high-profit industries and members with high pay in low-profit industries. It has badly paid members in low-profit and troubled industries, and highly paid ones as well. Relatively well-paid male steel workers in the depressed Ruhr district of North Rhein–Westfalia share membership with low-pay women in electronics manufacture concentrated in Baden-Württemberg and Bavaria, where unemployment is relatively low. Even within the relatively well-off area of Baden-Württemberg, the regional leadership must appeal to the interests of low-pay assembly workers in electronics and high-pay, white-collar technicians—both groups are weakly organized—and balance those interests against the interests of militant and well-organized auto workers at Daimler-Benz in and around Stuttgart.[67] Complicating the problem is the fact that cyclical and structural trends in these different industries are often out of step. The structural trend in the 1970s, in fact, was toward increasing divergence. It is not surprising, then, that wage-distributional conflict within the union became increasingly intractable and complicated.

IG Metall's resulting inconsistency in wage bargaining policy is exact-

[66]On the history of *konzertierte Aktion*, see Markovits, *Politics of the West German Trade Unions*, 109–11.
[67]On the heterogeneity of IG Metall's regions, sectors, and membership, see Markovits, *Politics of the West German Trade Unions*, 159–63, 169–74. For differing views on IG Metall's internal democracy, see Gerhard Bosch, *Wie demokratisch sind Gewerkschaften? Eine empirische Untersuchung der Willensbildung auf den Gewerkschaftstagen 1968 und 1971 der Industriegewerkschaft Metall* (Berlin: Verlag der Arbeitswelt, 1974), and Richard J. Willey, *Democracy in the West German Trade Unions: A Reappraisal of the "Iron Law"* (Beverly Hills, Calif.: Sage, 1971).

ly what the distributional trilemma predicts. Despite the union's repeated insistence on "active wage policy," or increasing the wage share through aggressive collective bargaining, neither actions nor results bespeak unwavering commitment. Often the union negotiated real increases that exceeded productivity developments. On occasion, however, it settled for less. Wage share trends in IG Metall's industries fluctuated no differently from those in other sectors of the economy, even where less militant unions operate.[68]

IG Metall's efforts at leveling were also erratic. Bringing up the relative earnings of low-wage groups, especially women ("equal pay for comparable work"), has long been an official commitment of IG Metall. Some evidence suggests, however, that from one year to the next, the leadership orchestrated and then discouraged the formulation of local-level demands for leveling.[69] While discussion of the problem is perennial, if IG Metall congress debates are any indication, the leadership's commitment to solving the problem understandably wavered. Some of the ongoing approaches to the problem are in themselves contradictory, such as attempts to develop "unitary pay agreements" (*einheitliche Entgeltstarifverträge*) for both blue- and white-collar workers. These attempts entail raising the pay levels of skilled workers to match those of technical, salaried employees with similar skills, years of training, and supervisory responsibilities.[70] They also promise to leave unskilled and semiskilled workers further behind.

IG Metall's wage policy with respect to unemployment also showed signs of ambivalence and irregularity. Until the late 1970s, in consonance with its active wage policy line, the union consistently evaded the acknowledgement of responsibility for employment creation or maintenance, the third of the distributional objectives incorporated in the trilemma analysis. On the other hand, IG Metall's actions reveal a pragmatic recognition of the union share, albeit unwanted, in responsibility.

[68]See Projektgruppe Gewerkschaftsforschung, *Rahmenbedingungen der Tarifpolitik, Band 2: Strukturdaten der Metallverarbeitenden, der Chemischen und der Druckindustrie* (Frankfurt/M: Campus, 1979), 158–59, 386, and Markovits, *Politics of the West German Trade Unions*, 232.

[69]For example, it appears that in 1977, practically all the important locals in the IG Metall bargaining district of Nordbaden/Nordwürttemberg conveyed demands for disproportionate raises for low-pay groups. The next year, when the special regional agenda was protection against pay loss due to deskilling, practically all the same locals demanded straight percentage increases. Compare Projektgruppe Gewerkschaftsforschung, *Tarifpolitik 1977* (Frankfurt/M: Campus, 1978), 80, with *Tarifpolitik 1978* (Frankfurt/M: Campus, 1980), 43.

[70]This has been a special concern in the North Rhine–Westfalia region, among others, of IG Metall. See IG Metall, Bezirksleitung Münster, *Die Tarifkommission berichtet* (6 November 1980), a report on the progress of negotiations with engineering employers of that region.

By the late 1970s, a combination of deflationary austerity policies under the Schmidt government, high unemployment figures, and pressure from below prompted an open and programmatic revision of collective bargaining policy toward unemployment. In 1978, IG Metall adopted a militant posture behind a reduction of the workweek, in order to force employers to hire from the growing pool of unemployed. From then on, in other words, it officially recognized that collective bargaining could and should be an active instrument for creating jobs.

For IG Metall's leaders, then, collective profit sharing threatened the bargaining autonomy of the union and therefore its freedom of action to pursue these flexible policies over time.[71] Indirectly, but unavoidably, it would force the union into the straightjacket of productivity-based wage increases. Eugen Loderer expressed this fear explicitly on many occasions. Less explicit, and therefore harder to verify, was IG Metall's fear that other unions in the DGB, and the DGB itself, were trying to use collective profit sharing to undermine IG Metall's "bargaining sovereignty" (*Tarifhoheit*).

Other unions, often frustrated in the past with IG Metall's vanguard role in pattern bargaining (*Lohnrundenführerschaft*, leadership in the serial negotiating process between different DGB unions and their employer counterparts),[72] may have seen collective profit sharing as a way of holding IG Metall back, especially during one of its militant phases. If IG Metall were to force through high pay increases with collective profit sharing in operation, and other unions were compelled by membership pressures to push for the same, the profit-sharing yield might be reduced. To put it another way, profit sharing would give the less militant unions a stronger moral justification for holding IG Metall back. They would be able to assert that restraint produces widely enjoyed *positive*—not negative—distributional consequences.

One can only speculate about IG Metall's unspoken fears. Speculations are, however, strongly supported, if only circumstantially, by the following fact: two of the most prominent advocates of collective profit sharing in the DGB were unions that in the past had sought more or less openly to rein in IG Metall's wage militancy. The first was IG Bau, whose innovative role I discussed earlier. IG Bau's highly visible leader

---

[71]Even the union literature on company profit sharing claims that it encroaches on bargaining autonomy.

[72]Also called *Lohnführerschaft* and *Tariffführerschaft*. An unusually skeptical view about the existence of "wage rounds" and leadership within them is Rolf Seitenzahl, *Gewerkschaften zwischen Kooperation und Konflikt* (Frankfurt: Europäische Verlagsanstalt, 1976), 105–14.

Georg Leber openly competed in the 1960s with IG Metall's Otto Brenner for ideological leadership within the DGB, appealing to the government, press, and public opinion for leverage, trying to win over other unions to accommodationist principles of *soziale Partnerschaft* and productivity-oriented wage policy. The second was the GTB, which in recent years, as discussed above, was perhaps the most outspoken proponent of collective profit sharing. At the 1975 DGB congress, the GTB entered an unsuccessful motion calling on the DGB executive council for more "coordination" of bargaining policy and strategies.[73] This motion evoked memories of an earlier, more aggressive attack, in the late 1950s, on IG Metall's autonomy by IG Bergbau und Energie, whose leader had openly sought DGB support for "coordination" of bargaining policies across union boundaries. Coal miners in that union had been rapidly slipping relative to metalworkers in terms of wages and working hours.[74]

As one former official of the GTB recalls, a reason for the latest, rather cautious revival of the accommodationists' idea of coordination was that, like other small unions, GTB "wants to bring down the demands of the bigger unions":

> The GTB has long held the principle that the demand must bear a sensible relationship to what is achievable. It has to do with credibility. . . . IG Metall raises foolish demands—one year it even managed only 50 percent of what it demanded. That was, among other things, one of the unspoken reasons behind [the GTB's motion]. When one union demands 10 percent, the others can't simply ask for 6 percent. Employers would conclude directly that they don't want as much, and the members would say, "The others demand 10 percent, why are we only demanding 6 percent?"

That produces "unnecessary friction" and conflict within the union. But when a union demands the same as the stronger unions, it often achieves less. The result: "Trouble, resignations, hassles with the membership."[75]

Karl Pitz, IG Metall's leading expert on collective capital formation, asserts that other unions did not share IG Metall's reservations about the costs of collective profit sharing and restraint, being in a sense "free

[73]Deutscher Gewerkschaftsbund, *Protokoll: 10. ordentlicher Bundeskongress Hamburg, 25–30 May, 1975* (Düsseldorf: DGB, 1976), 199, 324–25.
[74]See "Lohnpolitik: Bremse für Brenner," *Der Spiegel*, 15 January 1958, pp. 15–16.
[75]Interview with Heinz Fuchs, Referatsleiter, Abteilung Tarifpolitik, DGB-Vorstand, 28 May 1982. The irony is that the 1975 motion was partly a response to the strike by the ÖTV in 1974, for wage demands high enough to annoy even IG Metall's leaders. IG Metall, however, did not support the GTB motion.

riders." "IG Metall has a particularly sharp awareness of problems in achieving objectives [*Durchsetzungsfragen*], since we always start . . . the wage rounds, push through a certain percentage figure, and all the others just practically copy it down. They fall in line, swim in our wake."[76]

But in recent years it had not been as easy as Pitz maintained for such unions as the GTB and IG Bau to follow IG Metall. In construction, workers' wages sank from 114 percent of the average for manufacturing in 1965 to 104 percent in 1975, and they continued down to 101 percent in 1977. In textiles, wages stagnated at about 85 percent of the manufacturing average between 1965 and 1970, dropping to 81 percent by 1975. In the garment industry the picture was far worse. There workers' wages dropped from 80 percent in 1965 to 77 percent in 1970 and to 75 percent in 1975. But in the structurally declining steel industry, IG Metall managed to keep relative wages from falling as fast as construction wages (from 115 percent of the average in 1965 to 108 percent in 1975). Even in its ailing shipbuilding sector, relative wages held steady at about 110 percent. In autos, strategically IG Metall's most important industry, relative wages actually rose from 118 percent in 1965 to 123 percent of the industry average in 1975.[77]

IG Metall's most important supporters in internal DGB discussions and votes on collective capital formation were four unions in the *public* sector. The largest and most important was the Public Service and Transport Workers' Union (ÖTV), which by the mid-1970s had brought low postwar public-sector pay fully up to par with pay levels in private industry.[78] Between 1970 and 1976, public-sector pay rose by about 87 percent. The average increase for all industry was 77 percent. Since the three other unions bargain in concert with the ÖTV, their wages and salaries would have done the same.[79] It is no surprise, then, that leaders of the ÖTV and Gewerkschaft Post, having in the late 1950s supported IG Bergbau and IG Bau in their challenges to IG Metall's autonomy—when their wages were low and conservatives were in power—had changed sides and joined in a defense of IG Metall's

---

[76]Interview, 15 June 1982, Frankfurt.

[77]See the data in Ingvar Ohlsson, "Den solidariska lönepolitikens resultat," in Landsorganisationen, *Lönepolitik och solidaritet* (Stockholm: LO, 1980), 241.

[78]Gerhard Weiss, *Die ÖTV: Politik und gesellschaftspolitische Konzeptionen der Gewerkschaft ÖTV von 1966 bis 1976* (Marburg: Verlag Arbeiterbewegung und Gesellschaftswissenschaft, 1978), 201.

[79]Projektgruppe Gewerkschaftsforschung, *Rahmenbedingungen der Tarifpolitik: Band 1: Gesamtwirtschaftliche Entwicklung und Organisationen der Tarifparteien* (Frankfurt: Campus, 1979), 244. These other unions were the Postal Workers' Union, the Railroad Workers' Union, and the Education and Science Union.

position.[80] With time and the Social Democrats' control of government pay setting, IG Metall's successes had become easy to repeat and surpass.[81]

The policy response of two relatively high-pay unions in the private sector presents some difficulty, and some support, for the general argument. Despite its wage militancy and relatively high pay, the Printing and Paper Workers' Union (IG Druck und Papier) had also, if only temporarily, shown an apparently accommodationist side in seeking negotiated or legislated collective profit sharing as an indispensable redistributive instrument to complement wage militancy. At the 1972 DGB congress, the union submitted its own motion calling for legislative action to prepare the way for a collective fund system.[82] But it was exactly at this time that the union's members were suffering a rapid relative decline in wages, down from 118 percent of the industry average in the late 1960s to 110 percent by the mid-1970s. Because of the union's increasing militancy in the late 1970s and early 1980s—at times outstripping that of IG Metall—it is by no means clear, however, that the union leadership should have felt strongly motivated by a desire to restrain IG Metall. In any event, IG Druck und Papier was never prominent among the advocates of collective capital formation, especially after the mid-1970s.

The Chemical, Paper, and Ceramic Workers' Union (IG Chemie-Papier-Keramik) has been, like IG Bau and GTB, a more prominent and influential participant in the accommodationist drive for collective capital formation, especially since the mid-1970s. The 1970s' leadership of this relatively high-pay and previously militant union steered in an increasingly conservative direction. In 1978, IG Chemie, along with the GTB, launched the idea of negotiated, jointly managed branch funds, well after the chances for a legislated fund system as proposed by the DGB leadership had disappeared.[83] After a period of mixed success with a decentralized and confrontational bargaining

[80]"Brenner: Otto der Gusseiserne," *Der Spiegel,* 4 November 1959, pp. 36–37. Also, the unions probably shared IG Metall's concern that collective capital formation would slow down public-sector growth by competing for its financial base in increased taxes on profits.

[81]It is therefore ironic that the tables were turned in 1974, when IG Metall's leadership, behind the scenes, expressed its unhappiness with a strike in the public sector. The strike had brought more for the ÖTV than what IG Metall could get that year and proved highly embarrassing to Social Democratic chancellor Willy Brandt. Brandt was meanwhile facing other troubles that ultimately led to his resignation, bringing Helmut Schmidt, a chancellor less congenial to either IG Metall or the ÖTV, to the helm.

[82]Deutscher Gewerkschaftsbund, *Protokoll: 9. ordentlicher Bundeskongress Berlin 25–30 June 1972* (Düsseldorf: DGB, 1973), Motion 29, pp. 35–36.

[83]Manfred Krüper, "Muster für einen Branchenfonds," *Gewerkschaftliche Umschau* 6 (November–December 1978), 6–7.

strategy in the early 1970s, arousing acrimonious relations within the union and between the union and employers, the leadership adopted a more passive role in collective bargaining. In part, this turnabout was probably a response to a looming employment crisis in the chemical industries. Rapid productivity growth combined with overcapacity, stagnant demand, and capital mobility in international markets must have made the union especially fearful of employment losses.

For these reasons, the union's leadership may well have feared falling behind IG Metall as far as relative wages were concerned or, alternatively, may have feared the consequences of neglecting internal leveling and maintaining employment as the price paid for maintaining external parity. Table 1 shows the trends IG Chemie faced at the time of its 1978 initiative. Productivity in the chemical industries had been rising steeply during the five years between 1975 and 1979, much more so than in the automobile industry, IG Metall's most important sector. Demand and output, however, could not keep pace, and as a consequence, employment fell considerably. By contrast, demand and output in automobiles increased, outstripping productivity growth. Employment in the auto industry therefore did not suffer at all and in fact grew considerably.

Despite the threat of unemployment and despite its increasingly passive, accommodationist posture, however, IG Chemie negotiated to maintain both external parity and internal leveling. For example, in May 1976, after a precipitous fall in relative pay in 1975, IG Chemie negotiated a 5.85 percent pay increase for the chemical industry, and for low-pay workers at least DM 85 if 5.85 percent did not bring as much. In March 1976, IG Metall had settled for only 5.4 percent and one additional vacation day for 1977. For 1977, IG Metall settled for 6.9 percent, and IG Chemie negotiated 7 percent. In 1978, IG Metall negotiated 5 percent, and this time IG Chemie negotiated only 4.3 percent but with two extra vacation days. In 1979, both unions negotiated pay increases of 4.3 percent and a gradual increase to thirty vacation days for all, by 1983 for metalworkers and by 1984 for chemical workers. Chemical workers in addition were to get an increase of DM 30 vacation pay per vacation day.[84]

IG Chemie had become the most internally conflictual union in West Germany in the 1970s, no doubt contributing to an unwillingness to relax wage pressure for the sake of improving the employment situation.[85] In the late 1970s, intramural opposition was coming to a head between militant shop stewards and the increasingly nonmilitant cen-

---

[84]Industriegewerkschaft Chemie-Papier-Keramik, *Geschäftsbericht 1976–1979* (Hanover: IG Chemie, 1980), 32–33.
[85]Markovits, *Politics of the West German Trade Unions*, 313–26.

Table 1. Economics of automobile and chemical
manufacturing in West Germany, 1975–1979
(1976 = 100)

		1975	1979
Productivity*	Chemicals	86.6	118.8
	Automobiles	95.0	104.2
Net output	Chemicals	86.5	110.0
	Automobiles	87.7	112.3
Employment	Chemicals	102.8	97.2
	Automobiles	95.2	113.1

*Measured as output per man-hour, manual workers
only.
Source: Statistisches Bundesamt Wiesbaden, Statistisches
Jahrbuch für die Bundesrepublik Deutschland, various years.

tral leadership, whose most important base of power was the conservative works council leadership of the "Big Three" firms of BASF,
Bayer, and Hoechst. Works council leaders, in turn, based their own
power on an officially accepted system of company shop stewards
(elected by union members and nonmembers alike), a situation unique
in the German labor movement.[86] In these firms, wages were likely to
keep up with metalworkers' wages regardless of what was negotiated
centrally. Restrained contract wages would no doubt increase the interfirm pay gaps between the Big Three and others, thus exacerbating the
tendencies toward internal union conflict.

It would be reasonable to think that IG Chemie's leadership began to
find collective capital formation attractive as a way of weakening the
support base of the internal opposition, thereby allowing it freedom of
action in the future to relax pressure for official pay increases in line
with IG Metall's. Evidence that it might have wanted to do so is the fact
that IG Chemie shunned all moves that might have encouraged militancy and expectations of high wage increases among its members in
the late 1970s.[87] Individually held assets in branch funds could help
make up for a gap between IG Metall's and IG Chemie's future wage
settlements. Funding of a share of profits or investment wages, re-
cycled as investments in the industry but held by workers in the indus-

[86]See Otto Jacobi, "Innerverbandliche Stellung der Vertrauensleute in der IG Chemie-Papier-Keramik," in Jacobi, Müller-Jentsch, and Schmidt, Gewerkschaften und
Klassenkampf '73, and Markovits, Politics of the West German Trade Unions, 320–21.

[87]Edwin Schudlich, "Tarifpolitik ohne Kampfgeschrei: Die Tarifbeziehungen in der
chemischen Industrie 1970–1979," in Ulrich Billerbeck et al., Neuorientierung der Tarifpolitik? (Frankfurt: Campus, 1982). See also Otto Jacobi and Hans Günter Lang, "Anpassung und Zentralisierung: Zur Entwicklung in der IG Chemie," in Jacobi, Walther
Müller-Jentsch, and Eberhard Schmidt, Arbeitskampf um Arbeitszeit: Kritisches Jahrbuch
1980 (Berlin: Rotbuch, 1980).

try and amounting to compensation for the difference between wage developments—or compensation for wage increases foregone for the benefit of profits—might conceivably reduce the potential for conflict. Second, if only indirectly, a fund system negotiated by so prominent a union as IG Chemie could become a powerful symbolic and political victory for "social partnership" and nonmilitant unionism, undermining IG Metall's theoretical grounds and the precarious public sympathy for militancy. Finally, the explicitly egalitarian features of collective capital formation, which called for equal distribution of fund shares to individual workers regardless of their pay levels or the profitability of their employers, could serve as compensation for increasing internal inequalities in pay.

Figure 6 shows some evidence that IG Chemie's leadership might well have perceived and therefore been motivated to use collective capital formation to break out of the structure of constraints described by the horizontal trilemma. Whether due to the union's desires regarding employment maintenance, employer pressure, or noninstitutional market forces—or a combination—there was a distinct if not perfect trade-off between internal leveling within the chemical industries and external leveling between chemicals and automobiles, IG Metall's stra-

Figure 6. Internal (chemicals) and external (chemicals-automobiles) wage leveling in West Germany, 1965–1980

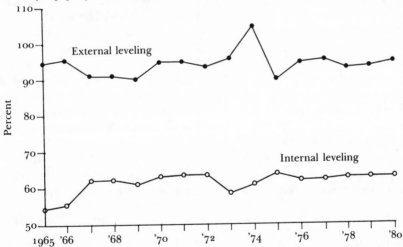

External leveling: manual workers' average wages in chemicals as a percentage of average wages in automobile manufacturing.

Internal leveling: Average wages of unskilled women as a percentage of average wages for skilled men in chemicals.

Source: Statistisches Bundesamt Wiesbaden, *Statistisches Jahrbuch fur die Bundesrepublik Deutschland,* various years.

tegically most important sector. In 1974, the exception, IG Chemie accomplished both internal and external leveling through unusually tough negotiations with employers, which brought better contract results than those for IG Metall. Fearing unemployment in the following years, IG Chemie resumed an apparent policy of trading external for internal leveling or vice versa.[88]

It must be emphasized that allowing or coping with greater external pay gaps and internal inequalities for the sake of improving the employment picture in no way figured in IG Chemie's own explicit reasoning for a negotiated branch fund system. Never did the union's leadership suggest that somehow, indirectly, IG Metall's militancy might be checked. To argue that these might *plausibly* have been underlying reasons can be justified only if the union leaders had manifest reason to conceal their underlying motives. Here, fear of fueling internal opposition by explicit resignation to—or advocacy of—increasing inequalities comes into play. Fear of upsetting the semblance of unity within the DGB by inflaming IG Metall—along with its militant sympathizers inside IG Chemie—would be an added argument against revealing motives.

THE 35–HOUR WEEK AND IG METALL'S TRILEMMA

The early 1980s brought marginalization and isolation for supporters of collective capital formation, who since the mid-1970s had limited their ambitions—largely unfulfilled—to separate deals with employers rather than legislation.[89] The new DGB leadership of Ernst Breit, who came from a public-sector union that had opposed collective profit sharing, signaled the change. IG Metall took back the initiative and at least a claim to innovative leadership in the DGB for the first time since the early 1960s, when its militancy and expansive wage policy had sent the accommodationist unions searching for an egalitarian alternative—collective capital formation.

In 1984, IG Metall called one of the most disruptive and internationally noticed strikes in postwar German history, demanding a reduction of normal weekly working hours from forty to thirty-five. Over

[88]Industriegewerkschaft Chemie-Papier-Keramik, *Geschäftsbericht 1972–1975* (Hanover: IG Chemie, 1976), 57–58.
[89]In 1975, following IG Bau's characteristic fund strategies—*Kassenpolitik*—IG Chemie established an Unemployment Benefits Fund to be administered jointly by the union and employers and financed by a one-time payment by employers (up to 5 percent of 1974's wage and salary bill). This supplementary unemployment benefits fund only remotely resembled fund models for negotiated collective capital formation. Industriegewerkschaft Chemie-Papier-Keramik, *Geschäftsbericht 1972–1975*, 374–77.

400,000 workers were directly or indirectly involved, striking, locked out, or laid off.[90] "Thirty-five hours with full compensation" (35 *Stunden mit vollem Lohnausgleich*) was IG Metall's medium-run objective. Surprised by the willingness of metalworkers to strike, engineering employers in Gesamtmetall mobilized the conservative government leaders, as well as the rest of the German employers in the BDA, in an expensive and aggressive campaign to discredit IG Metall's arguments for a reduced workweek. In the end, a compromise was worked out with the help of George Leber, former leader of IG Bau and as an accommodationist acceptable to employers as mediator. Metalworkers, according to the new contracts, were now to work, on average, 38.5 hours per week. IG Metall saw this as only the first in a series of steps toward the thirty-five-hour week. The 1986 round of negotiations, in fact, brought the weekly figure to thirty-seven.

In addition to traditional, nondistributional "humanization" objectives such as increased leisure and recuperation time for stressful and psychically unrewarding industrial work, the new and primary aim with workweek reduction was to redistribute available working hours to the growing army of unemployed.[91] Until the recession of the early 1980s, engineering had been spared the high unemployment that steelworkers and the rest of manufacturing had experienced. In 1984 unemployment had reached the point where nearly 10 percent of the entire labor force was out of work, and there were fourteen metalworkers registered unemployed for every unfilled job requiring their skills. In 1975, the ratio had been seven to one.[92] Later economic recovery brought little improvement. Contributing to IG Metall's new bargaining offensive was the vanishing of the labor movement's politi-

[90]On the strike, see Witich Rossmann, "Ohnmacht oder Gegenmacht? Gewerkschaftliche und politische Aspekte der Metaller- und Druckerstreiks," *Blätter für deutsche und internationale Politik* 29 (August 1984); Hajo Weber, "Konflikt in Interorganisationssystemen: Zur Konfliktlogik organisierter Arbeitsmarktparteien im Tarifkonflikt '84," *Soziale Welt* 37:2/3 (1986); and Markovits, *Politics of the West German Trade Unions*, 432–46.

[91]On the history of working-time struggles in Germany, see Michael Schneider, *Streit um Arbeitszeit: Geschichte des Kampfes um Arbeitszeitverkürzung in Deutschland* (Cologne: Bund Verlag, 1984).

[92]Combined figures calculated for metal producers and processers; assembly workers and related tradesmen; and machinists and related tradesmen, from Statistisches Bundesamt Wiesbaden, *Statistisches Jahrbuch*, years 1976 and 1985. For chemical workers, by contrast, the ratio was seventeen to one in 1975 and thirty-seven to one in 1984. Overall there were 2.3 million registered unemployed and at least another one million nonregistered in 1984. Hans Janssen and Klaus Lang, "Überwintern oder Überleben: Gewerkschaftspolitische Schlussfolgerungen aus dem Arbeitskampf um Arbeitszeitverkürzung," in Erwin Ferlemann and Hans Janssen, eds., *Existenz sichern, Arbeit ändern, Leben gestalten: Gewerkschaften im Kampf um Arbeitszeitverkürzung* (Hamburg: VSA-Verlag, 1985), 11.

cal influence. The change of government in October 1982, solidified by the conservative electoral shift in March 1983, had put public policy solutions out of reach for both accommodationists and activists. The government's open hostility to unionism combined with its reduced commitment to maintaining full employment to spell danger, especially for a union such as IG Metall, whose membership, infused with a spirited militancy, would not tolerate defeatism and inaction.

IG Metall's options were few. Wage restraint, especially when the economy picked up after 1983, was out of the question, for the high profit levels and real wage stagnation of the past years had massively reduced the wage share. Furthermore, as IG Metall argued, wage restraint would choke off demand, a necessary source of employment recovery. Finally, high profits were being invested, if at all, in labor-replacing technology not expansion of capacity. Wage restraint, therefore, would speed up the destruction of jobs.

Domestic demand was not the only problem. The growth potential of international demand in the early 1980s remained far below what was required for output to expand and absorb unemployed labor. A steady growth rate of 6 percent per year for a handful of years—an impossible dream—would be necessary, according to reasonable estimates, to bring unemployment down to acceptable levels within a few years.[93] German employers united as usual behind the call for profit- and investment-led growth and continued technological improvements as the road out of unemployment.[94] Astonishingly, IG Metall moved toward the view that Germany should consider bidding "farewell to the growth-society [*Abschied von der Wachstumsgesellschaft*]."[95]

IG Metall was not prepared to abandon its wage militancy and accept a long-term reduction in the wage share, nor was it willing to accept increased wage inequalities. Employers had been decrying union pressure and the long-term trend in the direction of regional, sectoral, and occupational leveling since the late 1960s. Conservatives of varying colors called for individualized profit sharing and therefore earnings differentiation for better productivity and profitability.[96] Against the

[93]Dieter Mertens, "Quantitative und qualitative Beschäftigungswirkungen von Arbeitszeitverkürzung," in Hans Mayr and Hans Janssen, eds., *Perspektiven der Arbeitszeitverkürzung: Wissenschaftler und Gewerkschafter zur 35-Stunden-Woche* (Cologne: Bund Verlag, 1984), 92.
[94]See, for example, Bundesvereinigung der Deutschen Arbeitgeberverbände, *Zwanzig-Punkte-Programm: Für mehr Beschäftigung* (Cologne: BDA, 1985), 9–21.
[95]So wrote Hans Janssen of IG Metall's executive council in "Die Arbeitszeitpolitik der IG Metall—Notwendigkeiten und Perspektiven," in Mayr and Janssen, *Perspektiven der Arbeitszeitverkürzung*, 24.
[96]Bundesvereinigung der Deutschen Arbeitgeberverbände, *Zwanzig-Punkte-Programm*, 33–34. Kleps surveys the variety of conservative approaches to individualized asset formation in Germany in *Lohnpolitische Konzeptionen*, 297–358.

conservative tide, IG Metall reaffirmed its desire for modest improvements in its internal wage structure, and it was backed up by the DGB in an informational campaign against all forms of firm-level profit-sharing arrangements.[97] One decisive objection to the company-level schemes advocated by employers and Christian Democrats was that the device would increase interfirm disparities in worker income and would therefore be *gewerkschaftsschädlich* (injurious to unions) because of its *entsolidarisierende* ("desolidarizing," or divisive) effects. This, according to one conservative, was the "primal fear," the *Urangst*, underlying all other "sham arguments" unions press against company profit sharing—the fear that the umbilical attachment of members to their unions would be severed.[98]

IG Metall's refusal to accept either increased profits or wage inequality as the solution to the unemployment problem brought it face to face with the trilemma: how to increase employment when demand is stagnating and productivity is increasing apace without letting profits and investment and/or increased pay disparities do the work. Was there an alternative to wage-induced productivity and unit labor cost advantages in international competition for export-led job creation?

For IG Metall, shorter working hours emerged in the late 1970s as the only remaining option. The progressive reduction of working hours from forty-eight per week in the 1950s to around forty by the mid-1970s had after all required and been made possible by "guest workers" from Turkey, Yugoslavia, and elsewhere in Europe.[99] At that time, the availability of international labor reserves, not just high growth and capacity utilization rates, softened employer resistance to union pressure for reductions in working time.

Influential experts within and outside the labor movement gave support to union arguments for working-time reduction as a way of reducing unemployment. It was unlikely, these experts readily conceded, that employers would add one additional worker to payrolls for every seven whose weekly hours were reduced to thirty-five—to maintain constant production levels—even if wage increases stayed within the bounds of productivity increases. By paying overtime and squeezing

[97]Claus Schäfer, "Ist Vermögensbildung nur Vermögenseinbildung? Zur Brauchbarkeit von Vermögenspolitik als gewerkschaftliches Instrument," in *WSI-Mitteilungen* 36 (July 1983), 443–53; Deutscher Gewerkschaftsbund, "Dokumentation: Stellungnahmen des DGB zur Vermögenspolitik," in *WSI-Mitteilungen* 36 (July 1983), 453–57.

[98]Jürgen Schröder, "Betriebliche Vermögensbildung—Bleibt der DGB unbelehrbar?" *Der Arbeitgeber* 30 (1978), 183.

[99]Edwin Schudlich, "Weniger Arbeit für mehr Beschäftigte: Historische Hinweise über den Zusammenhang von Arbeitszeit und Beschäftigung," in *WSI-Mitteilungen* 4 (1983), 209–17, and Schneider, *Streit um Arbeitzeit*, 170–73.

out further productivity increases, employers would partially offset the employment effects of the workweek reduction.[100]

But a realistic estimate suggested that an economy-wide reduction over five years to a thirty-five hour workweek, assuming wage costs adjusted to productivity increases, would result in a net increase of employment by 900,000 and a reduction in registered unemployment by about 630,000.[101] In 1987, even the conservative German Institute for Economic Research (Deutsches Institut für Wirtschaftsforschung, the DIW), which in the past had often testified for the employers' viewpoint that work-time reductions would not help employment, announced that the 1984 engineering contract alone—which reduced the work-week to 38.5 hours—was directly responsible for creating about 50,000 blue-collar jobs in the first year. Noting that the DIW had not counted the effects on white-collar employment (half of the labor force in engineering), IG Metall cited survey studies showing that its contract saved about 5,000 jobs and created another 97,000.[102]

In principle, workweek reductions could be distributionally neutral from the standpoint of pay differentials within the present work force, although some redistribution was implied within the entire labor force—between the employed and the newly hired. IG Metall's expectation that reductions in the workweek could be neutral in the first sense suggests that the new strategy was an adaptive response to an increasingly acute vertical trilemma. Organizational pressure from below for leveling had not subsided in the early 1980s, and it showed up as official demands for upward pay leveling and abolition of low-pay categories that employers consistently rejected out of hand.[103]

IG Metall's leaders openly hoped for distributional neutrality yet feared that employers would exploit opportunities in the new contract to widen the pay structure and divide the membership.[104] For example, it was expected that skilled workers in short supply would be highly favored with overtime pay, thus increasing inequality in both average hourly wages (because of overtime premiums) and average weekly,

[100]Edward Liebau, "Betriebswirtschaftliche Aspekte der Arbeitszeitverkürzung," 73–74, and Gerhard Bosch, "Quantitative und qualitative Aspekte des technischen Wandels," 126–33, in Mayr and Janssen, *Perspektiven der Arbeitszeitverkürzung.*

[101]Mertens, "Quantitative und qualitative Beschäftigungswirkungen von Arbeitszeitverkürzung," in Mayr and Janssen, *Perspektiven der Arbeitszeitverkürzung,* 98–99.

[102]"DIW: Beschäftigungseffekte durch Arbeitszeitverkürzung—Kalte Dusche für Gesamtmetall," *Der Gewerkschafter* 35 (July 1987), 40–41.

[103]Industriegewerkschaft Metall, *Geschäftsbericht 1983 bis 1985* (Frankfurt: IG Metall, 1986), 278, 304–5, 326–30.

[104]Janssen and Lang, "Überwintern oder Überleben?" 28–29, and Ingrid Kurz-Scherf, "Chancen, Risiken und Tendenzen der neuen Arbeitszeitbestimmungen," in Ferlemann and Janssen, *Existenz sichern,* 130.

monthly, or yearly income. IG Metall's 1984 compromise guaranteed this possibility. First, it did not insist that each and every worker work no more than 38.5 hours per week. The only restriction on employers was that workers together could not exceed an *average* of 38.5 hours in any one place of employment within a two-month period. After the agreement, however, IG Metall vigorously exhorted its enterprise-level officials in works councils to negotiate equivalent reductions for all in the implementation of the agreement. Here the union achieved some success where it had failed in central negotiations, much to the chagrin of the employers' association, which had energetically recommended "flexibility."[105]

On the other hand, the problem of increasing differentials associated with overtime was not fully resolved. This problem, to the extent it is significant, is not a necessary by-product of work-time reductions but rather an artifact of relative shortages of skilled workers. It should come as no surprise, then, that in policy on collaborative vocational training, aimed at increasing the supply of skilled workers, relations between IG Metall and Gesamtmetall did not suffer in the confrontational atmosphere of the early 1980s—indeed, quite the contrary.[106] IG Metall's approach to the trilemma, militant and confrontational in the sphere of pay determination, enhanced incentives for both sides to seek collaborative, positive-sum policy in other spheres.

The radicalism of IG Metall's new offensive for reducing weekly work-hours, as a solution to the trilemma, lay in its challenge to employers, who sought at the time to defend and even increase managerial flexibility and control. Reduction in working hours in the past was not the radical challenge it had become in the 1980s, for employers before had often granted it without a struggle. Their intense resistance now is in part attributable to the need to keep capital plant in full and continuous operation at hours when workers prefer to be their own masters. Increasingly capital-intensive industry, and the extraordinarily high labor productivity it brings, at one and the same time make the trilemma more acute and make working hour reduction as the response more radical. As with collective capital formation, so with the 35-hour work week, the intensified search for solutions to the trilemma turned centralized union officialdom away from traditional wage policy objectives—distributionism—and toward more radical challenges to capitalist ownership and control.

What are the implications of the drive for a thirty-five-hour work-

---

[105]Rossmann, "Ohnmacht oder Gegenmacht?" 951–52; Janssen and Lang, "Überwintern oder Überleben," 24–27.
[106]Markovits, *Politics of the West German Trade Unions*, 447.

week on solidarity within the DGB? Traditionally accommodationist unions have tended to follow employers' demands for "flexibility," especially in recommending work-time reductions that threaten little or no disruption of an existing organization of production which is geared to the forty-hour week. Accommodationist unions, led in particular by the low-pay and organizationally weak Union of Food Processing Workers (Gewerkschaft Nahrung-Genuss-Gaststätten), campaigned for state-subsidized early retirement (*Vorruhestand*), an approach favored by other accommodationists. This approach represented no challenge to managerial prerogatives in production management, unlike the seven-hour day, thirty-five-hour work week favored by IG Metall. It also promised a weaker effect on unemployment, according to IG Metall's supporters.[107]

Again, despite shows of solidarity from the DGB and even the accommodationist unions during the 1984 strike, old divisions and animosities were confirmed in the aftermath.[108] Just as in the 1950s and early 1960s, the accomodationist unions feared internal discontent against falling further behind—and punitive reactions from employers and government should they, under less favorable circumstances, try to follow IG Metall's militant leadership on the work-week issue. Here, the horizontal trilemma continues to operate subtly behind the scenes.

CONCLUSION

Keenly protective of their wage-bargaining autonomy, IG Metall's leaders did not turn to collective capital formation as a solution to the acute vertical trilemma they faced in the early 1980s. Past conflicts over fund plans with other DGB unions and the DGB leadership itself had left a legacy of distrust, for the idea had been in part a tool in the hands of others with designs against IG Metall's autonomy, its militancy, and, by implication, its relatively high wages.

The leadership instead turned to a radical program for working-time reduction as a solution to unemployment. This program did not require in principle either higher profits or more wage inequality. The acute wage policy trilemma could therefore be alleviated by a radical offensive to reduce managerial autonomy regarding hours of employment and production. IG Metall chose aggressive action in collec-

---

[107]On the early retirement option see Kurz-Scherf, "Chancen, Risiken und Tendenzen," 115–20; Janssen and Lang, "Überwintern oder Überleben?" 23; and Mertens, "Quantitative und qualitative Beschäftigungswirkungen," 94–95.
[108]Markovits, *Politics of the West German Trade Unions*, 443–44.

tive bargaining toward this end, for government anti-union sentiment ensured that action in the political sphere would produce no other solutions.

The implications of IG Metall's step-wise successes in working-time reduction for labor movement unity depend on the ability of other unions to match them. Failure to do so will tend to divide portions of other unions against their leaders and perpetuate leadership frustrations with IG Metall's militancy. In that case, "horizontal" distributive conflict will continue to divide German labor as it has in the past.

CONCLUSION

The Terms of Solidarity

Material conflict divides labor movements. Union leaders exercise power over the normative orientations of their members toward pay distribution and so can help unify them. Their exercise of political power over market forces, through the state, can aid them in fulfilling those norms in collective bargaining. Success in the wage struggle against employers—more pay for all—is only part of the story in motivating and achieving solidarity in centralized labor movements. Generating and fulfilling norms about fair pay matter just as much, perhaps more.

The line of argument in this book leads to an analysis of the political behavior of union leaders from theoretical reasoning about the interactive constraints they face in maintaining support through collective bargaining. In the societal sphere of union action, union leaders try to shape norms about wage-income distribution in ways that can be best fulfilled with centralized control, thereby justifying centralization. Also, they try to fulfill norm-based expectations with wage-policy successes. Limits on the achievement of union pay-structure goals, or on the defense of their successes, are described by the wage policy trilemma, which identifies systematic trade-offs between (1) internal leveling of pay for a union's members, (2) employment growth, and (3) external leveling as (a) growth in the wage share at the cost of profits, and/or (b) compression of pay differentials between as opposed to within unions. Much of union action in the political sphere can, I argue, be understood as attempts to loosen the constraints described by the trilemma if not resolve the trilemma altogether. The history of Swedish and German labor movement politics supports these ideas. The desires of union leaders to regulate the structure as well as the level of wages

224

explain much of their innovative policy ideas. These motivations also help explain the kinds of political alliances with groups beyond labor they can and want to form in order to make those policies a reality.

THE MORAL ECONOMY AND PROGRESSIVE UNIONISM

Echoing William Jennings Bryan's crusade against the gold standard, economist Martin Weitzman recently leveled a provocative attack against our "outmoded system of paying labor." Pay standards of any kind, Weitzman argues in *The Share Economy,* are the cross we now bear and to which "we have nailed untold generations of economic prosperity—many tens, even hundreds, of trillions of present dollars' worth of lost goods and services."[1] According to this economist, who is indifferent if not hostile to trade unionism, the solution to both unemployment and inflation—treating one without worsening the other—lies in the complete relaxation of wage standards and their replacement with profit- or revenue-sensitive variable pay systems. Such a proposal strikes at the heart of centralized and politically efficacious trade unionism.

Roughly thirty years earlier, Gösta Rehn and Rudolf Meidner, economists employed by the Swedish labor movement, were struggling with the same problem, but fell upon the opposite solution. In their view, wage standards fixed according to a normative consensus could reduce the inflationary wage rivalry within and between unions, a rivalry that flares up especially under full employment. The Phillips' curve would thus be shifted downward, so for any given level of employment, a lower level of inflation could be maintained. That was one element in their larger argument about the beneficial effects of union leveling objectives for economic stability, employment, and growth. These economic ideas helped secure support from leading unionists and Social Democrats for active labor market policies in Sweden, even if more powerful impulses came from union leaders' direct experience of the trilemma.

Thus the objectives of centralized unions in the moral economy—securing their own organizational safety by setting wage norms and applying collective bargaining power to fulfill them—give rise to some of social democracy's most innovative and progressive, and occasionally even radical, political programs. Richard Hyman and Ian Brough are

[1] Martin L. Weitzman, *The Share Economy: Conquering Stagflation* (Cambridge: Harvard University Press, 1984), 145–46.

only partly right in arguing that unions strengthen capitalism when they use pay norms to confine conflict to the details of its operation and not its foundations. "Trade unionism permits debate aroung the terms of workers' obedience while not challenging the fact of their subordination," they write.[2] If collective capital formation, in all its German and Swedish versions, emerged from attempts by centralized unions to proceed with pay leveling, to defend existing successes, or to compensate for retreat, then qualification of this Leftist critique is called for. Collective capital formation according to German and Swedish plans called for new, state-sponsored forms of ownership, investment control, and even workplace-level economic democracy. Reformist, trade unionist, and social democratic labor movements may have suppressed revolutionism in favor of "distributionism." But also, for the very purpose of defending their reformist goals, they have reintroduced ideas of democratic socialism, on their own terms, into political debate.

Highly centralized and egalitarian trade unionism not only gives rise to innovative ideas. It is also a source of political power—in the hands of Social Democratic or other labor parties—that can help turn those ideas into government policy. One desires to know then: Whence centralization? Clearly, as the Swedish case shows, employer strategy and government pressure play decisive roles. Clearly, too, some unions support centralization even if centralization means delegating power upward to confederation leaders, whereas others resist the concomitant loss of autonomy. The trilemma helps us discern within labor movements the basis for divisions that employers and government can exploit should they desire centralization and seek alliances with sectors of labor toward that end. In a number of cases, as we have seen, relatively low-pay unions or confederations, motivated by the trilemma, sought higher-order centralization for external leveling by controlling the pay and militancy of others. The Swedish Metalworkers' Union in the 1920s and 1930s (but not the 1940s and 1950s), low-pay unions without the LO in the 1950s, the German Construction Workers' Union in the 1950s and 1960s, and finally the German Textile and Garment Workers' Union in the 1970s all sought one way or another to establish peak-level control over other unions. Even LO, the blue-collar confederation in Sweden, since the 1960s has sought some form of "total coordination" limiting the bargaining militancy and successes of white-collar unions.

In West Germany, leaders of IG Metall have fiercely resisted all attempts to rein in the union with peak-level coordination, dividing the

[2]Richard Hyman and Ian Brough, *Social Values and Industrial Relations: A Study of Fairness and Equality* (Oxford: Basil Blackwell, 1975), 71.

labor movement on the question of collective capital formation, which other unions saw as a remedy to their trilemmas and an indirect way of controlling IG Metall. IG Metall eventually developed its own distinctive response to the trilemma—the thirty-five-hour workweek—which other militant and high-pay unions, such as the Printing and Papers Workers' Union, have followed. IG Metall's militant offensive for work-time reduction derived from its desire to counteract growing unemployment without letting profits run loose and without allowing greater internal inequalities in wage distribution to develop. In this case again, union leaders' desires to protect wage equity were directly if not obviously behind an unorthodox approach to the unemployment problem.

In Sweden, the Metalworkers' recent defection from peak-level bargaining and cross-industrial wage leveling will probably contribute to the weakening of progressive forces in the Swedish labor movement—if only by dividing unions there the same way German unions are divided. This is not to say that the union has rejected all ideas of leveling. Indeed one of the reasons for defection was the desire for external leveling between blue-collar workers in the Metalworkers' Union and white-collar workers in the same industries. This leveling, as the union sees it, has been inhibited by the bargaining structure and policies of LO and SAF at the peak level, as well as by the ability of white-collar unions to maintain their bargaining autonomy. Holding back the wages of skilled workers for the sake of others in and outside the metal industries, without at the same time limiting white-collar pay increases accordingly, only increased some pay inequities while ameliorating others. The Metalworkers' Union thus had a clear, egalitarian purpose behind reasserting its bargaining autonomy and flexibility. Now the Swedish labor movement is likely to be far less unified in its political approaches than it has been for most of the postwar period. It will be "divided by the trilemma" just as the West German labor movement has been.

Now that LO is no longer able or compelled to achieve highly egalitarian policy in peak bargaining with employers, moreover, the impulse to "resolve the trilemma" is weakened in addition to being diffused. The Social Democratic party will continue to resist attempts to produce more radical legislation or even to extend the profit-sharing tax beyond 1990, when it is slated to expire. With the weakening of solidaristic wage policy, and the loss of a large measure of peak-level control, LO leaders have lost much of the motivation to bring the debate over fund socialism back to life. Now the labor movement's leadership must face the problems of decentralization and division,

227

and the loss of an internationally unparalleled political hegemony its unusual peak-level bargaining and egalitarian pay policy once supported. What that change bodes is unclear. Swedish politics may well lose some of their distinctive egalitarian character.

THE TRILEMMA AND CROSS-CLASS POLITICAL REALIGNMENTS

In the historical process of union centralization in Germany and Sweden, centralized bargaining relations have been undergirded by cross-class alliances around distinct wage distributional formulas. If material interests were not tempered by distributional norms, interest conflicts would internally divide the broad classes of capital and labor and make stable relations between them impossible. The emergence or restructuring of centralized bargaining patterns were not the result of refashioned "compromises" between undifferentiated entities of capital and labor, after one had gained in organizational resources and power at the expense of the other. Instead, the restructuring of industrial relations is best understood as implicit coalitions between factions of labor and capital, which might even be joined by partisan political forces as well.

In Germany and Sweden, centralized unions and bargaining developed in part as a response to the mutual interests of unions and some employers in wage standards. For some employers, standards could for example help stave off price wars by setting wage floors; unions could provide such floors only if they were empowered by employer recognition and collective bargaining. Peak centralization beyond the industrial level in Sweden involved the formation of a coalition between dominant, export-oriented employers in SAF and other labor and political groups. In the first phase, assertion of peak-level control by LO fused an alliance of metalworkers, farmers, and other low-income workers with employers against high-pay construction workers. In the second phase, metalworkers fell out of the coalition but were pressured into acquiescence with a combination of lockout threats by employers and threats of government intervention by Social Democrats. Peak-level bargaining brought egalitarian pay agreements that antagonized many employers but if anything favored the high-pay, export employers dominant in SAF. It also made Rehn's and Meidner's "active labor market policy" a compelling remedy for the costs of egalitarian wage policy. Mobilizing labor away from low-pay, stagnant sectors and toward high-pay, expansive sectors was again in the interests of export industry and no doubt helped stabilize the coalition.

228

In time, the effects or costs of egalitarian wage policy also made socialization of industrial ownership through wage-earner funds compelling to LO, but in this case employers objected to the promised redistribution of ownership and control. Under those circumstances, the movement for legislation brought political polarization, shattered the cross-class coalition, and forced the unions and Social Democrats—reluctantly—to rely on Communists' abstentions in the Riksdag vote for passage. The wage-earner funds that were legislated into existence, not surprisingly, were a far cry from what LO's radical plans had called for.

Initially, collective capital formation in West Germany seemed to enjoy formidable support from a centrist coalition of economic and political groups, including the ascendant left-wing faction in the liberal FDP, large portions of the SPD, and the "accommodationist" wing of the DGB, the peak labor confederation. Divided by the trilemma, however, the DGB could not control IG Metall, which joined employers in exercising a powerful veto against collective profit sharing. This veto signaled one of the major defeats of the Social Democratic "reform euphoria" of the early 1970s.

In the late 1980s, in contrast to the 1970s, IG Metall has returned to a position of leadership within the DGB as enthusiasm about collective capital formation has subsided. Responding to its own trilemma, the union has forged ahead on the road to a thirty-five-hour workweek as a way of redistributing jobs and wage income to the benefit of the unemployed and to the benefit of a labor movement weakened by unemployment. Interestingly, IG Metall's trilemma and its workweek strategy open up the theoretical possibility of alliances with outside groups and organizations. The militant strategy received substantial moral support from the DGB leadership, though it was not strongly backed up, if at all, by the same unions whose horizontal trilemma had induced them to seek collective capital formation and control over IG Metall's militancy. On the other hand, IG Metall's rejection of export-led growth strategies against unemployment brings with it the unusual possibility—but by no means the certainty—of cooperation with the Green movement in future partisan and electoral politics. IG Metall's departure from industrial growth as cureall makes a warming of traditionally cold red-green relations a distinct possibility. The call for "humanization" of working life and enrichment of home and community life made possible by the reduction of the workweek opens the possibility of an alliance between the union and young people with feminist and "postindustrial" values who are disenchanted with traditional social democracy and attracted to the Greens. Furthermore, the thirty-five-hour workweek does not call for jobs in Germany at the expense of workers in other countries in Europe and elsewhere—as the export-led growth strategy does. What these various alliance possibilities will bring in actual political results could be significant for the shape of German and even European politics.

Recent Swedish events also show how changing and divergent responses to the trilemma pattern distributional conflict within labor movements and thereby pattern alliance possibilities. Swedish employers in SAF, especially in engineering, had by the late 1970s grown tired of peak-level bargaining, for its consequences were clear: wage leveling, LO unity, Social Democratic electoral strength, and then wage-earner funds as the means to protect them. The full story of the breakdown of peak-level bargaining cannot be told here. There is good reason to conclude that employers in engineering broke away from SAF coordination in order to entice the Swedish Metalworkers' Union into a separate deal that violated the principles of egalitarian wage policy as it had evolved in the 1970s.[3] Departure from egalitarian wage policy in the most important part of the private sector promised to weaken the moral claim for leveling between public- and private-sector unions, an increasingly annoying tax burden on private-sector profits and pay. In subsequent negotiations with SAF but without the metalworkers, LO could accomplish little along egalitarian lines for the rest of the unions.

Hence in the late 1980s, Sweden seems to be experiencing a fundamental political realignment in response to these developments in collective bargaining. The Social Democratic leadership has discouraged all optimism about extension of wage-earner funds beyond 1990, ensuring the funds will be relatively impotent as industrial policy instruments in the hands of the labor movement. The leadership has also pursued austere budget policies aimed at balancing budgets by halting government growth and freezing the relative pay levels of government workers. These policies are at cross purposes with those of the two large public-sector unions in LO, whose own militant interpretation of wage egalitarianism calls for complete parity in pay drift compensation (with metalworkers, for example), in addition to continued wage leveling between public and private sectors.

Social Democratic austerity policies conform quite well, however, with the purposes of the Metalworkers' Union, which now openly defends some increased disparities between organizational jurisdictions

---

[3]Nils Elvander tells the story in detail in *Den svenska modellen: Löneförhandlingar och inkomstpolitik 1982–1986* (Stockholm: Allmänna Förlaget, 1988), 78–98.

represented in LO. Unfriendly exchanges between leaders of the Metalworkers' Union and LO's public-sector unions have already surfaced on this point, in the press and at the 1986 LO congress.[4] Open and at times bitter distributional conflict within the labor movement of this kind, which culminated in recent years in relatively unpopular public-sector strikes against Social Democratic pay policy for the public sector, can only hurt the labor movement electorally and in parliamentary politics. On the other hand, the separate peace between the Metalworkers' Union and engineering employers—and therefore with SAF—will help compensate for the damage done, as SAF scales down its dramatic political attacks of the late 1970s and early 1980s against Social Democrats and LO. As the Metalworkers' Union and the two LO public-sector unions go it alone in autonomous attempts to deal with their own distrbutional dilemmas, Swedish Social Democrats must fashion new alliances and distributional formulas if in the future they are to match their extraordinary past political successes.

[4]See the debate in Landsorganisationen, *Protokoll, Del 2: 21 ordinarie kongress, 20–27 september 1986*, 1098–146.

 APPENDIX

Relative Pay in Swedish and West German Industry, 1960–1977

Table i. Women's hourly earnings as a percentage of men's by industry: Sweden, manual workers only, 1960–1977

Industry	1960	1965	1970	1975	1977
Manufacturing	69.3	75.5	81.3	85.1	87.3
Food	76.4	78.1	81.5	84.6	86.0
Beverages	80.1	89.4	89.8	90.5	90.8
Textiles	81.3	81.9	84.4	86.6	89.7
Garments	75.7	79.2	86.0	90.3	93.2
Leather processing	74.9	77.7	82.9	83.9	84.9
Shoes	72.4	76.6	81.5	87.4	90.1
Wood products	75.9	81.0	87.9	90.5	92.9
Paper, pulp, and allied products	70.3	76.6	80.3	83.5	84.2
Printing	70.7	69.8	74.0	80.0	82.3[1]
Chemicals and plastics	71.6	74.5	81.8	85.6	86.5
Rubber	70.3	73.4	83.9	90.7	91.7
Iron and steel	70.3	82.9	88.4	93.6	94.3
Engineering	71.9	81.3	85.0	87.8	90.0
Shipbuilding	—	—	81.9	85.7	87.2
Automobiles	73.8	97.0	94.7	96.6	97.0
Mining	—	64.9	84.7	88.5	88.9
Construction	—	55.4	55.5	65.7	69.1

[1]Excluding newspaper industry, years 1960, 1965, and 1970.
Source: Landsorganisationen, *Lönepolitik och solidaritet* (Stockholm: LO, 1980), 226.

233

Table ii. Women's hourly earnings as a percentage of men's by industry: West Germany, manual workers only, 1960–1977

Industry	1960	1965	1970	1975	1977
Manufacturing	65.9	68.8	69.6	72.3	72.3
Food	65.0	68.7	69.9	70.0	69.9[1]
Beverages	74.1	68.0	68.8	71.7	72.3
Textiles	78.7	80.0	79.8	81.4	81.2
Garments	71.3	73.6	77.0	78.6	77.9[2]
Leather processing	65.8	69.5	70.0	73.6	73.4
Shoes	75.1	77.1	79.2	79.5	79.7
Wood products	72.1	73.3	75.6	77.4	78.3
Paper, pulp, and allied products	63.6	67.8	68.5	70.6	69.8
Printing	55.1	59.2	62.1	66.0	65.9
Chemicals and plastics	65.5	67.4	69.1	73.8	73.8[3]
Rubber	70.4	70.2	72.4	78.6	79.6
Iron and steel	64.1	68.0	69.0	73.4	73.1
Engineering	69.0	70.5	71.2	76.6	74.0
Shipbuilding	—	—	71.4	77.7	77.0
Automobiles	83.2	84.0	84.1	85.6	86.0[4]
Mining	—	62.7	67.3	68.7	68.5
Construction	—	—	73.1	72.8	74.4

[1] Excluding sugar industry, years 1975 and 1977.
[2] Including shoe industry, years 1960, 1965, and 1970.
[3] Excluding petrochemicals and coal derivatives years 1960 and 1965.
[4] Including bicycle and motorcycle industries, years 1960 and 1965.
Source: Landsorganisationen, *Lönepolitik och solidaritet* (Stockholm: LO, 1980), 227.

Table iii. Relative hourly earnings in various industries: Sweden, manual workers only, 1960–1977 (Average for manufacturing = 100)

Industry	1960	1965	1970	1975	1977
Manufacturing	100	100	100	100	100
Food	89	92	95	96	97
Beverages	89	94	94	99	97
Textiles	79	82	85	87	88
Garments	74	77	79	80	84
Leather processing	91	93	90	90	92
Shoes	86	85	87	88	90
Wood products	95	96	96	94	94
Paper, pulp, and allied products	104	100	101	108	108
Printing	108	110	112	114	117[1]
Chemicals and plastics	97	95	96	97	99
Rubber	95	100	97	93	94
Iron and steel	109	106	105	109	107
Engineering	107	105	103	101	100
Shipbuilding	120	118	117	116	112
Automobiles	116	111	110	103	101
Mining	134	122	120	123	123
Construction	146	141	131	116	121

[1] Excluding newspaper industry, years 1960, 1965, and 1970.
Source: Landsorganisationen, *Lönepolitik och solidaritet* (Stockholm: LO, 1980), 239.

Table iv. Relative hourly earnings in various industries: West Germany, manual workers only, 1960–1977 (Average for manufacturing = 100)

Industry	1960	1965	1970	1975	1977
Manufacturing	100	100	100	100	100
Food	83	86	85	87	87[1]
Beverages	108	99	99	100	102
Textiles	84	84	85	81	83
Garments	74	80	77	75	74[2]
Leather processing	84	89	85	77	76
Shoes	87	87	80	77	75
Wood products	90	95	94	96	96
Paper, pulp, and allied products	92	93	94	93	94
Printing	111	118	118	112	112
Chemicals and plastics	103	106	108	110	110[3]
Rubber	103	99	99	102	100
Iron and steel	125	115	116	108	107
Engineering	102	104	103	104	103
Shipbuilding	110	110	111	110	109
Automobiles	119	118	121	123	123[4]
Mining	—	115	107	108	107
Construction	—	114	111	104	101

[1]Excluding sugar industry, years 1975 and 1977.
[2]Including shoe industry, years 1960, 1965, and 1970.
[3]Excluding petrochemicals and coal derivatives, years 1960 and 1965.
[4]Including bicycle and motorcycle industries, years 1960 and 1965.
Source: Landsorganisationen, *Lönepolitik och solidaritet* (Stockholm: LO, 1980), 241.

Bibliography

Åsard, Erik. *LO och löntagarfondsfrågan: En studie i facklig politik och strategi.* Stockholm: Rabén & Sjögren, 1978.

Achenbach, Andreas, Gert Hautsch, Johaness Heinrich v. Heiseler, Gerhard Hess, Klaus Pickshaus, Klaus Priester, and Bernd Semmler. *Arbeitskampf an neuen Fronten: Zu den Aktionen und Streiks im Bereich der GTB, HBV, GEW und RFFU 1979.* Frankfurt: IMSF, 1980.

Agartz, Viktor, "Expansive Lohnpolitik." *Mitteilungen des Wirtschaftswissenschaftlichen Institutes der Gewerkschaften* 6 (December 1953).

Annable, James E. *The Price of Industrial Labor.* Lexington, Mass.: Lexington Books, 1984.

Apitzsch, Hartmut. "Byggnadsbranschen: Produktionsförhållanden och organisationsstruktur." *Arkiv för studier i arbetarrörelsens historia* 2 (1972).

Atherton, Wallace N. *Theory of Union Bargaining Goals.* Princeton: Princeton University Press, 1973.

Bagge, Gösta, Erik Lundberg, and Ingvar Svennilson. *Wages in Sweden: 1860–1930.* London: P. S. King, 1933.

Bain, George Sayers, and Farouk Elsheikh. *Union Growth and the Business Cycle.* Oxford: Basil Blackwell, 1976.

Beckerman, Wilfred, ed. *Wage Rigidity and Unemployment.* London: Duckworth, 1986.

Bergmann, Joachim, Otto Jacobi, and Walther Müller-Jentsch. *Gewerkschaften in der Bundesrepublik, Band I: Gewerkschaftliche Lohnpolitik zwischen Mitgliederinteressen und ökonomischen Systemzwängen.* Frankfurt: Campus, 1979.

Bergström, Villy, "Lönepolitik, ekonomisk tillväxt och strukturförändring." In Landsorganisationen, *Lönepolitik och solidaritet.* Stockholm: LO, 1980.

Bertmar, Lars. "Löner, lönsamhet och soliditet i svenska industriföretag." In *Löntagarna och kapitaltillväxten 3: Tre expertrapporter från utredningen om löntagarna och kapitaltillväxten* (SOU 1979:10).

Bielefelder Kollegen. "Streik bei Rheinstahl, Brackwede." In Otto Jacobi, Walter Müller-Jentsch, and Eberhard Schmidt, eds., *Gewerkschaften und Klassenkampf: Kritisches Jahrbuch '74.* Frankfurt: Fischer, 1974.

236

Björklund, Anders. "Rehn/Meidners program och den faktiska politiken." In *Arbetsmarknadspolitik under debatt: 10 forskares syn på arbetsmarknadsproblem.* Stockholm: Liber Förlag, 1982.

Blechschmidt, Aike. "Abrisse der wirtschaftlichen Lage 1973/74." In Otto Jacobi, Walther Müller-Jentsch, and Eberhard Schmidt, eds., *Gewerkschaften und Klassenkampf: Kritisches Jahrbuch '74.* Frankfurt: Fischer, 1974.

Bloom, Gordon F., and Herbert R. Northrup. *Economics of Labor Relations.* Homewood, Ill.: Richard D. Irwin, 1969.

Bosch, Gerhard. "Quantitative und qualitative Aspekte des technischen Wandels." In Hans Mayr and Hans Janssen, eds., *Perspektiven der Arbeitszeitverkürzung.* Cologne: Bund Verlag, 1984.

——. *Wie demokratisch sind Gewerkschaften? Eine empirische Untersuchung der Willensbildung auf den Gewerkschaftstagen 1968 und 1971 der Industriegewerkschaft Metall.* Berlin: Verlag der Arbeitswelt, 1974.

Bowman, John. "When Workers Organize Capitalists: The Case of the Bituminous Coal Industry." *Politics and Society* 14:3 (1985).

Braunthal, Gerard. *The West German Social Democrats, 1969–1982: Profile of a Party in Power.* Boulder, Colo.: Westview, 1983.

Broström, Anders, ed. *Storkonflikten 1980.* Stockholm: Arbetslivscentrum, 1981.

Brown, Henry Phelps. *The Origins of Trade Union Power.* Oxford: Clarendon Press, 1983.

Brown, R. K. "The Contours of Solidarity: Social Stratification and Industrial Relations in Shipbuilding." *British Journal of Industrial Relations* 10 (1972).

Brown, William, and Keith Sisson. "The Use of Comparisons in Workplace Wage Determination." *British Journal of Industrial Relations* 13:1 (March 1975).

Bry, Gerhard. *Wages in Germany: 1871–1945.* Princeton: Princeton University Press, 1960.

Bundesvereinigung der Deutschen Arbeitgeberverbände. *Zwanzig-Punkte-Programm: Für mehr Beschäftigung.* Cologne: BDA, 1985.

Cameron, David. "Social Democracy, Corporatism, Labour Quiescence, and the Representation of Economic Interests in Advanced Capitalist Society." In John H. Goldthorpe, ed., *Order and Conflict in Contemporary Capitalism.* New York: Oxford University Press, 1984.

Cartter, Allan M. *Theory of Wages and Employment.* Homewood, Ill..: Richard D. Irwin, 1959.

Castles, Francis G. *The Social Democratic Image of Society.* London: Routledge & Kegan Paul, 1978.

Clegg, Hugh. *Trade Unionism under Collective Bargaining: A Theory Based on Comparisons of Six Countries.* London: Social Science Research Council, 1976.

——. *The Changing System of Industrial Relations in Great Britain.* Oxford: Basil Blackwell, 1979.

Crouch, Colin. "The Drive for Equality: Experience of Incomes Policy in Britain." In Leon Lindberg et al. eds., *Stress and Contradiction in Modern Capitalism.* Lexington, Mass.: D. C. Heath, 1975.

——. "Varieties of Trade Union Weakness: Organised Labour and Capital Formation in Britain, Federal Germany and Sweden." In Jack Hayward, ed., *Trade Unions and Politics in Western Europe.* London: Frank Cass, 1980.

Crouch, Colin, and Alessandro Pizzorno, eds. *The Resurgence of Class Conflict in Western Europe since 1968.* New York: Holmes & Meier, 1978.

Dahlström, Edmund, Kjell Eriksson, Bertil Gardell, and Olle Hammarström. *LKAB och demokratin: Rapport om en strejk och ett forskningsprojekt.* Stockholm: Wahlström & Widstrand, 1971.

Dahlström, Kjell-Åke. *Horndalseffekt och löneglidning: Några studier av produktivitets- och löneutveckling i verkstads- och processforetag.* Stockholm: SAF, 1971.

Das Gupta, A. K. *A Theory of Wage Policy.* Delhi: Oxford University Press, 1976.

Desai, Ashok V. *Real Wages in Germany: 1871–1913.* Oxford: Clarendon Press, 1968.

Deutscher Gewerkschaftsbund. *Anträge: 11. ordentlicher Bundeskongress Hamburg 21–26 May, 1978.* Düsseldorf: DGB, 1979.

——. *Anträge: 12. ordentlicher Bundeskongress Berlin 16–22 May, 1982.* Düsseldorf: DGB, 1983.

——. *Protokoll: 9. ordentlicher Bundeskongress Berlin 25–30 June 1972.* Düsseldorf: DGB, 1973.

——. *Protokoll: 10. ordentlicher Bundeskongress Hamburg 25–30 May, 1975.* Düsseldorf: DGB, 1976.

——. *Protokoll: 12. ordentlicher Bundeskongress Berlin 16–22 May, 1982.* Düsseldorf: DGB, 1983.

——. "Stellungnahme des DGB zur Vermögenspolitik." In *WSI-Mitteilungen* 36 (July 1983).

——. "Stellungnahme des DGB-Bundesausschusses zur Beteiligung der Arbeitnehmer am Produktivvermögen vom 4. April 1973." In Karl Heinz Pitz, ed., *Das Nein zur Vermögenspolitik.* Reinbek bei Hamburg: Rowohlt, 1974.

Dunlop, John. *Wage Determination under Trade Unions.* New York: Kelly, 1950.

Edgren, Gösta, Karl-Olof Faxén, and Clas-Erik Odhner. *Lönebildning och samhällsekonomi.* Stockholm: Rabén & Sjögren, 1970.

Edin, Per-Olof. "Fonder, tillväxt och lönsamhet." *Ekonomisk debatt* 5 (1981).

——. "Löneläge och lönsamheti: En studie av solidarisk lönepolitik och övervinster." In Landsorganisationen, *Kollektiv kapitalbildning genom löntagarfonder,* Appendix 4. Stockholm: LO/Prisma, 1976.

Elvander, Nils. *Intresseorganisationerna i dagens Sverige.* Lund: CWK Gleerup, 1972.

——. *Skandinavisk arbetarrörelse.* Stockholm: Liberförlag, 1980.

——. *Den svenska modellen: Löneförhandlingar och inkomstpolitik, 1982–1986.* Stockholm: Allmänna Förlaget, 1988.

Engels, Friedrich. "The Abdication of the Bourgeoisie." In Karl Marx and Engels, *Articles on Britain.* Moscow: Progress Publishers, 1975.

——. *The Condition of the Working Class in England.* Stanford: Stanford University Press, 1958.

Erd, Rainer. "Gewerkschaftsausschlüsse in den 70er Jahren." In Otto Jacobi, Walter Müller-Jentsch, and Eberhard Schmidt eds., *Gewerkschaftspolitik in der Krise: Kritisches Gewerkschaftsjahrbuch 1977/78.* Berlin: Rotbuch, 1978.

Erdmann, Gerhard. *Die deutschen Arbeitgeberverbände im sozialgeschichtlichen Wandel der Zeit.* Neuwied/Berlin: Luchterhand, 1966.

Ericson, Hans. *Facket mot folket.* Nacka: Förlag AB Lansering, 1981.

Eskilsson, Sture. *Löneutveckling under kontroll.* Stockholm: SAF, 1966.

Esping-Andersen, Gøsta. *Politics against Markets: The Social Democratic Road to Power.* Princeton: Princeton University Press, 1985.

Etzioni, Amitai. "The Case For a Multiple-Utility Conception." *Economics and Philosophy* 2 (October 1986).

Faxén, Karl-Olof. "Wage Policy and Attitudes of Industrial Relations Parties in Sweden." *Labour and Society* 2 (January 1977).

——. "Wages and the Community." In Organisation for Economic Co-operation and Development, *Wage Determination: Papers Presented at an International Conference.* Paris: OECD, 1974.

Feldman, Gerald. *Army, Industry, and Labor in Germany: 1914–1918.* Princeton: Princeton University Press, 1966.

Feldman, Gerald, and Irmgard Steinisch. *Industrie und Gewerkschaften 1918–1924: Die überforderte Zentralarbeitsgemeinschaft.* Stuttgart: Deutsche Verlags-Anstalt, 1985.

Feldt, Kjell-Olof, et al. *Ekonomisk politik inför 1980-talet.* Stockholm: Tiden, 1977.

Ferlemann, Erwin, and Hans Janssen eds. *Existenz sichern, Arbeit ändern, Leben gestalten: Gewerkschaften im Kampf um Arbeitszeitverkürzung.* Hamburg: VSA-Verlag, 1985.

Flanagan, Robert J., David W. Soskice, and Lloyd Ulman. *Unionism, Economic Stabilization, and Incomes Policies: European Experience.* Washington, D. C.: Brookings, 1983.

Flanders, Allan. *Management and Unions.* London: Faber & Faber, 1970.

Freeman, Richard B., and James L. Medoff. *What Do Unions Do?* New York: Basic Books, 1984.

Fülberth, Georg. "Die Entwicklung der deutschen Gewerkschaftsbewegung von den Anfängen bis 1873." In Frank Deppe, Fülberth, and Jürgen Harrer, eds., *Geschichte der deutschen Gewerkschaftsbewegung.* Cologne: Pahl-Rugenstein, 1977.

Garrett, Geoffrey, and Peter Lange. "Performance in a Hostile World: Economic Growth in Capitalist Democracies, 1974–1982." *World Politics* 38 (July 1986).

Geijer, Arne. "Inkomstutjämning och lönepolitik." In Erik Zander, ed., *Fackliga klassiker.* Stockholm: LO/Rabén & Sjögren, 1981.

——. "Lönepolitik och förhandlingsformer." In Erik Zander, ed., *Fackliga klassiker.* Stockholm: LO/Rabén & Sjögren, 1981.

——. "Större centralisering ger ej bättre förutsättningar." In Landsorganisationen, *Lönepolitiken under debatt: Aktuella frågor* 15 (1949).

Gerfin, Harald. "Ausmass und wirkung der Lohndrift." In Helmut Arndt ed., *Lohnpolitik und Einkommensverteilung.* Berlin: Duncker & Humblot, 1969.

Gergils, Håkan, Anders Thomasson, and Leif Widén. *Sex års fondopinioner 1975–1980: En översikt över opinionsläget i löntagarfondsfrågan.* Stockholm: Sveriges Aktiesparares Riksförbund, 1981.

Gewerkschaft Textil-Bekleidung. "Programm der Gewerkschaft Textil-Bekleidung." *Informationen für Vertrauensleute der Gewerkschaft Textil-Bekleidung* 21 (November 1978).

——. *Protokoll: 15. Ordentlicher Gewerkschaftstag 1986.* Düsseldorf: GTB, 1987.

Gleitze, Bruno, ed. *Sozialkapital und Sozialfonds als Mittel der Vermögenspolitik: Beiträge zur Frage der überbetrieblichen Ertragsbeteiligung der Arbeitnehmer.* WWI-Studie zur Wirtschaftsforschung No. 1, 2d ed. Cologne: WWI, 1969.

Götz, Christian. *Heinz Oskar Vetter.* Cologne: Europäische Verlagsanstalt, 1977.

Goldthorpe, John H., ed. *Order and Conflict in Contemporary Capitalism.* New York: Oxford University Press, 1984.

Gourevitch, Peter. *Politics in Hard Times: Comparative Responses to International Economic Crises.* Ithaca: Cornell University Press, 1986.

Gourevitch, Peter, Andrew Martin, George Ross, Stephen Bornstein, Andrei Markovits, and Christopher Allen. *Unions and Economic Crisis: Britain, West Germany, and Sweden.* London: Allen & Unwin, 1984.

Hadenius, Axel. *Facklig organisationsutveckling: En studie av Landsorganisationen i Sverige.* Stockholm: Rabén & Sjögren, 1976.

Hadenius, Stig, Björn Molin, and Hans Wieslander. *Sverige efter 1900.* Stockholm: Aldus/Bonniers, 1974.

Hart, Horst, and Casten von Otter. *Lönebildningen på arbetsplatsen: En sociologisk studie.* Stockholm: Prisma, 1973.

Heclo, Hugh. *Modern Social Politics in Britain and Sweden: From Relief to Income Maintenance.* New Haven: Yale University Press, 1974.

Hedborg, Anna. "Löntagarfonder—en konsekvent fortsättning." In Landsorganisationen, *Lönepolitik och solidaritet.* Stockholm: LO, 1980.

Hedborg, Anna, and Rudolf Meidner. *Folkhemsmodellen.* Stockholm: Rabén & Sjögren, 1984.

Hedström, Peter, and Richard Swedberg. "The Power of Working-Class Organizations and the Inter-Industrial Wage Structure." *International Journal of Comparative Sociology* 26 (March–June 1985).

Hegeland, Hugo. *Fondsocialism och förmögenhetsfördelning.* Göteborg: Karima, 1982.

Herman, Edward S. *Corporate Control, Corporate Power.* Cambridge: Cambridge University Press, 1981.

Hicks, J. R. *The Theory of Wages.* London: MacMillan, 1932.

Himmelstrand, Ulf. *Beyond Welfare Capitalism.* London: Heinemann, 1981.

Hirsch, Barry T., and John T. Addison. *The Economic Analysis of Unions: New Approaches and Evidence.* Boston: Allen & Unwin, 1986.

Hirschman, Albert O. "Against Parsimony: Three Easy Ways of Complicating Some Categories of Economic Discourse." *Economics and Philosophy* 1 (April 1985).

Höglund, Sten. "Centralisering och reduktion av medlemsinflytandet i en stor facklig organisation." *Research Reports from the Department of Sociology, University of Umeå* 52 (1979).

——. "Storföretagen, Svenska Arbetsgivareföreningen och beslutsordningen i arbetarnas fackliga organisationer: Arbetsgivaresynpunkter på LO:s och fackförbundens sätt att fatta beslut om förlikningsbud perioden 1925–1941." *Research Reports from the Department of Sociology, University of Umeå* 45 (1978).

Höhnen, Wilfried. "Überbetriebliche Ertragsbeteiligung als vermögenspolitische Konzeption." *WWI-Mitteilungen* 1/2 (1969).

——. "Zwanzig Jahre vermögenspolitische Diskussion." In Karl Heinz Pitz, ed., *Das Nein zur Vermögenspolitik.* Reinbek bei Hamburg: Rowohlt, 1974.

Hyman, Richard, and Ian Brough. *Social Values and Industrial Relations: A Study of Fairness and Equality.* Oxford: Basil Blackwell, 1975.

Industriegewerkschaft Chemie-Papier-Keramik. *Geschäftsbericht 1972–1975.* Hanover: IG Chemie, 1976.

——. *Geschäftsbericht 1976–1979.* Hanover: IG Chemie, 1980.

Industriegewerkschaft Metall. *Daten, Fakten, Informationen* 13 (1982).
——. *Fünfundsiebzig Jahre Industriegewerkschaft: 1891 bis 1966*. Frankfurt: Europäische Verlagsanstalt, 1966.
——. *Geschäftsbericht 1983 bis 1985*. Frankfurt: IG Metall, 1986.
——. "Leitsätze der Industriegewerkschaft Metall zur Vermögenspolitik." In Karl Heinz Pitz, ed., *Das Nein zur Vermögenspolitik: Gewerkschaftliche Argumente und Alkternativen zur Vermögensbildung*. Reinbek bei Hamburg: Rowohlt, 1974.
——. *Protokoll: 12. ordentlicher Gewerkschaftstag 18–24 September 1977*. Frankfurt: IG Metall, 1978.
——. *Protokoll: 13. ordentlicher Gewerkschaftstag 2–27 September 1980*. Frankfurt: IG Metall, 1981.
Industriegewerkschaft Metall, Bezirksleitung Münster. "Die Tarifkommisson berichtet: Bericht an die Verwaltungsstellen im Bezirk Münster und an die Mitglieder der Tarifkommission der metallverarbeitenden Industrie NRW." Münster: IG Metall, 6 November 1980.
Ingham, Geoffrey. *Strikes and Industrial Conflict: Britain and Scandinavia*. London: Macmillan, 1974.
Institut für angewandte Sozialwissenschaft. *Spontane Arbeitsniederlegungen im September 1969*. Bad Godesberg: IAS, 1970.
Jackson, Peter, and Keith Sisson. "Employers' Confederations in Sweden and the U.K. and the Significance of Industrial Infrastructure." *British Journal of Industrial Relations* 14 (November 1976).
Jacobi, Otto. "Die innerverbandliche Stellung der Vertrauensleute in der IG Chemie-Papier-Keramik." In Jacobi, Walther Müller-Jentsch, and Eberhard Schmidt, eds., *Gewerkschaften und Klassenkampf: Kritisches Jahrbuch '73*. Frankfurt: Fischer, 1973.
——. "Tarifpolitische Konzeptionen der westdeutschen Gewerkschaften." In Jacobi, Walther Müller-Jentsch, and Eberhard Schmidt, eds., *Gewerkschaften und Klassenkampf: Kritisches Jahrbuch '74*. Frankfurt: Fischer, 1974.
Jacobi, Otto, and Hans Günter Lang. "Anpassung und Zentralisierung: Zur Entwicklung in der IG Chemie." In Jacobi, Walther Müller-Jentsch, and Eberhard Schmidt, eds., *Arbeitskampf um Arbeitszeit: Kritisches Jahrbuch 1980*. Berlin: Rotbuch, 1980.
Jacobi, Otto, Walther Müller-Jentsch, and Eberhard Schmidt, eds., *Arbeiterinteressen gegen Sozialpartnerschaft: Kritisches Gewerkschaftsjahrbuch 1978/79*. Berlin: Rotbuch, 1979.
——. *Arbeitskampf um Arbeitszeit: Kritisches Jahrbuch 1980*. Berlin: Rotbuch 1980.
——. *Gewerkschaften und Klassenkampf: Kritisches Jahrbuch '73*. Frankfurt: Fischer, 1973.
——. *Gewerkschaften und Klassenkampf: Kritisches Jahrbuch '74*. Frankfurt: Fischer, 1974.
——. *Gewerkschaftspolitik in der Krise: Kritisches Gewerkschaftsjahrbuch 1977/78*. Berlin: Rotbuch, 1978.
Jocobson, Bertil. "Vad hände under 1980 års konflikt?" In Anders Broström, ed., *Storkonflikten 1980*. Stockholm: Arbetslivscentrum, 1981.
Jahreswirtschaftsbericht 1976 der Bundesregierung. Appendix to Sachverständigenrat. *Vollbeschäftigung für Morgen: Jahresgutachten 1974–1975*. Stuttgart: Kohlhammer, 1974.

Janérus, Inge. "Den juridiska traditionens seger." In Anders Broström, ed., *Arbetsrättens utveckling*. Stockholm: Arbetslivscentrum, 1983.

Janssen, Hans. "Die Arbeitszeitpolitik der IG Metall: Notwendigkeiten und Perspektiven." In Hans Mayr and Janssen, eds., *Perspektiven der Arbeitszeitverküzung*. Cologne: Bund Verlag, 1984.

Janssen, Hans, and Klaus Lang. "Überwintern oder Überleben: Gewerkschaftspolitische Schlussfolgerungen aus dem Arbeitskampf um Arbeitszeitverkürzung." In Erwin Ferlemann and Janssen, eds., *Existenz sichern, Arbeit ändern, Leben gestalten*. Hamburg: VSA-Verlag, 1985.

Jaques, Elliot. "An Objective Approach to Pay Differentials." *New Scientist* 14 (1958).

——. *Equitable Payment*. London: Heinemann, 1961.

——. *Free Enterprise, Fair Employment*. New York: Crane Russak, 1982.

Johansson, P. O., and Ann-Britt Hellmark. *Från LKAB till ASAB: Strejker och lockouter på den svenska arbetsmarknaden 1970–1974*. Stockholm: Arbetslivscentrum, 1981.

Johnston, T. L. *Collective Bargaining in Sweden: A Study of the Labour Market and Its Institutions*. Cambridge: Harvard University Press, 1962.

Jühe, Reinhard, Horst-Udo Niedenhoff, and Wolfgang Pege. *Gewerkschaften in der Bundesrepublik Deutschland: Daten, Fakten, Strukturen*. Cologne: Deutscher Instituts-Verlag, 1977.

Jung, Heinz, Josef Schleifstein, and Kurt Steinhaus, eds. *Die Septemberstreiks 1969: Darstellung, Analyse, Dokumente*. Cologne: Pahl-Rugenstein Verlag, 1969.

Kaelble, Hartmut. *Industrielle Interessenpolitik in der Wilhelminischen Gesellschaft: Centralverband Deutscher Industrieller, 1895–1914*. Berlin: Walter de Gruyter, 1967.

Kalbitz, Rainer. "Gewerkschaftsausschlüsse in den 50er Jahren." In Otto Jacobi, Walther Müller-Jentsch, and Eberhard Schmidt, eds., *Gewerkschaftspolitik in der Krise: Kritisches Gewerkschaftsjahrbuch 1977/78*. Berlin: Rotbuch, 1978.

Katzenstein, Peter. *Small States in World Markets: Industrial Policy in Europe*. Ithaca: Cornell University Press, 1985.

Kalecki, Michael. "Class Struggle and Distribution of National Income." In *Selected Essays on the Dynamics of the Capitalist Economy*. Cambridge: Cambridge University Press, 1971.

Kern, Horst. "Die Bedeutung der Arbeitsbedingungen in den Streiks 1973." In Otto Jacobi, Walther Müller-Jentsch, and Eberhard Schmidt, eds., *Gewerkschaften und Klassenkampf: Kritisches Jahrbuch '74*. Frankfurt: Fischer, 1974.

Kessler, Gerhard. *Die deutschen Arbeitgeberverbände*. Leipzig: Duncker & Humblot, 1907.

Kleps, Karlheinz. *Lohnpolitische Konzeptionen und Vermögensbildung: Ein Weg aus der stabilitäts- und verteilungspolitische Sackgasse*. Baden-Baden: Nomos Verlagsgesellschaft, 1982.

Klevmarken, N. Anders. *Lönebildning och lönestruktur: En jämförelse mellan Sverige och USA*. Stockholm: Industriens Utredningsinstitut, 1983.

Kollegen der Gruppe oppositioneller Gewerkschafter in der IG Metall. "Listenvielfalt bei Opel, Bochum." In Otto Jacobi, Walther Müller-Jentsch, and Eberhard Schmidt, eds., *Arbeiterinteressen gegen Sozialpartnerschaft: Kritisches Gewerkschaftsjahrbuch 1978/79*. Berlin: Rotbuch, 1979.

Kollegen von Mannesmann-Huckingen. "Streiks bei Mannesmann, Duisburg."

In Otto Jacobi, Walther Müller-Jentsch, and Eberhard Schmidt, eds., *Gewerkschaften und Klassenkampf: Kritisches Jahrbuch '74*. Frankfurt: Fischer, 1974.

Kolleginnen und Kollegen von Pierburg Autogerätebau Neuss. "Streik bei Pierburg, Neuss." In Otto Jacobi, Walther Müller-Jentsch, and Eberhard Schmidt, eds., *Gewerkschaften und Klassenkampf: Kritisches Jahrbuch '74*. Frankfurt: Fischer, 1974.

Korpi, Walter. *The Working Class in Welfare Capitalism: Work, Unions and Politics in Sweden*. London: Routledge & Kegan Paul, 1978.

Korpi, Walter, and Michael Shalev. "Strikes, Industrial Relations and Class Conflict in Capitalist Societies." *British Journal of Sociology* 30 (1979).

Kosack, Godula, and Stephen Castles. "Gewerkschaften und ausländische Arbeiter." In Otto Jacobi, Walther Müller-Jentsch, and Eberhard Schmidt, eds., *Gewerkschaften und Klassenkampf: Kritisches Jahrbuch '74*. Frankfurt: Fischer, 1974.

Kotthoff, Hermann. "Zum Verhältnis von Betriebsrat und Gewerkschaft: Ergebnisse einer empirischen Untersuchung." In Joachim Bergmann, ed., *Beiträge zur Soziologie der Gewerkschaften*. Frankfurt: Suhrkamp, 1979.

Krelle, Wilhelm, Johann Schunck, and Jürgen Siebke. *Überbetriebliche Ertragsbeteiligung der Arbeitnehmer: Forschungsauftrag des Bundesministeriums für Arbeit und Sozialordnung*. Tübingen, 1968.

Krüper, Manfred. "Muster für einen Branchenfonds." *Gewerkschaftliche Umschau* 6 (November–December 1978).

Kuczynski, Jürgen. *Darstellung der Lage der Arbeiter in Deutschland von 1933 bis 1945*. Berlin: Akademie-Verlag, 1964.

———. *Darstellung der Lage der Arbeiter in Westdeutschland seit 1945*. Berlin: Akademie-Verlag, 1963.

———. *A Short History of Labour Conditions under Industrial Capitalism, Volume III, Part I: Germany 1800 to the Present Day*. London: Frederick Muller, 1945.

Kungliga Statistiska Centralbyrån. *Statistisk årsbok för Sverige: Tolvte årgången 1925*. Stockholm: KSCB, 1925.

Kupferberg, Feiwel. "Byggnadsstrejken 1933–34." *Arkiv för studier i arbetarrörelsens historia* 2 (1972).

Landsorganisationen. *De centrala överenskommelserna mellan LO och SAF: 1952– 1982*. Stockholm: LO, 1981.

———. *Fackföreningsrörelsen och den fulla sysselsättningen: Betänkande och förslag från Landsorganisationens organisationskommitté*. Stockholm: LO, 1951.

———. *Fackföreningsrörelsen och den tekniska utvecklingen: Rapport avgiven till 1966-års LO-kongress*. Stockholm: LO, 1966.

———. *Kollektiv kapitalbildning genom löntagarfonder: Rapport till LO-kongressen 1976*. Stockholm: Prisma/LO, 1976.

———. *Landssekretariatets berättelse för år 1970*. Stockholm: LO, 1971.

———. *LO-80 Rapporten: Rapport till LO-kongressen 1981*. Stockholm: LO, 1981.

———. *Lönepolitik för 80-talet: Rapport till LO-kongressen 1981*. Stockholm: LO/Tiden, 1981.

———. *Lönepolitik och solidaritet: Debattinlägg vid Meidner seminariet den 21–22 februari 1980*. Stockholm: LO, 1980.

———. *Lönepolitik: Rapport till LO-kongressen 1971*. Stockholm: LO, 1971.

———. *Löner, priser, skatter: Rapport till LO-kongressen 1976*. Stockholm: LO/Prisma, 1976.

———. *Protokoll: 18:e ordinarie kongress, 4–11 september 1971*. Stockholm: LO, 1972.

———. *Protokoll: 20:e ordinarie kongress, 19–27 september 1981*. Stockholm: LO, 1982.

———. *Protokoll: 21 ordinarie kongress, 20–27 september 1986*. Stockholm: LO, 1987.

———. *Vem behöver ackorden?* Stockholm: LO, ca. 1980.

Landsorganisationen and Sveriges Socialdemokratiska Arbetareparti. *Arbetarrörelsen och löntagarfonder: Rapport från en arbetsgrupp inom LO och socialdemokraterna*. Stockholm: Tiden/LO/SAP, 1982.

———. *Löntagarfonder och kapitalbildning: Förslag från LO-SAPs arbetsgrupp*. Stockholm: Tiden, 1978.

Lange, Peter. "Unions, Workers, and Wage Regulation: The Rational Bases of Consent." in J. H. Goldthorpe, ed., *Order and Conflict in Contemporary Capitalism*. New York: Oxford University Press, 1984.

Leber, Georg. "Vermögensbildung in Arbeitnehmerhand." *Gewerkschaftliche Monatshefte* 16 (1965).

Leber, Georg, ed. *Vermögensbildung in Arbeitnehmerhand: Ein Programm und sein Echo*. Frankfurt: Europäische Verlagsanstalt, 1964.

Leion, Anders. *Solidarisk lönepolitik eller löntagarfonder: Den svenska modellens sammanbrott*. Stockholm: Rabén & Sjögren, 1979.

Leminsky, Gerhard, and Bernd Otto, eds. *Politik und Programmatik des Deutschen Gewerkschaftsbundes*. Cologne: Bund Verlag, 1974.

Lester, Richard A. "Benefits as a Preferred Form of Compensation." In Richard L. Rowan and Herbert R. Northrup, eds., *Readings in Labor Economics and Labor Relations*. Homewood, Ill.: Richard D. Irwin, 1968.

Lewin, Leif. *Planhushållningsdebatten*. Stockholm: Almqvist & Wiksell, 1967.

Liebau, Edward, "Betriebswirtschaftliche Aspekte der Arbeitszeitverkürzung." In Hans Mayr and Hans Janssen, eds., *Perspektiven der Arbeitszeitverkürzung*. Cologne: Bund Verlag, 1984.

Lindbeck, Assar. "Reformera lönebildningen!" *SAFtidningen*, 17 March 1983.

———. *Swedish Economic Policy*. London: Macmillan, 1975.

Lindberg, Leon N., and Charles S. Maier, eds. *The Politics of Inflation and Economic Stagnation*. Washington, D. C.: Brookings, 1985.

Lindblom, Charles E. *Unions and Capitalism*. New Haven: Yale University Press, 1949.

Lindbom, Tage. *Den svenska fackföreningsrörelsens uppkomst och tidigare historia*. Stockholm: Tiden, 1938.

Lindroth, Bengt. "LO, framtiden och fonderna." *Tiden* 3 (1981).

Lipset, Seymour, and Martin Trow. "Reference Group Theory and Trade Union Wage Policy." In Mirra Komarovsky, ed., *Common Frontiers of the Social Sciences*. Glencoe, Ill.: Free Press, 1957.

Lóderer, Eugen. "Auszug aus einem hektographierten Manuskript der IG Metall ohne Orts- und Jahresangabe." In Gerhard Leminsky and Bernd Otto, eds., *Politik und Programmatik des Deutschen Gewerkschaftsbundes*. Cologne: Bund Verlag, 1974.

———. "Qualität des Lebens statt Vermögenspolitik." In Karl Heinz Pitz, ed., *Das Nein zur Vermögenspolitik*. Reinbek bei Hamburg: Rowohlt, 1974.

Lundberg, Erik. "Är vi verkligen solidariska?" In Landsorganisationen, *Lönepolitik och solidaritet*. Stockholm: LO, 1980.

244

———. "The Rise and Fall of the Swedish Model." *Journal of Economic Literature* 23 (March 1985).

Lundgren, Håkan. *Utjämning eller utveckling: Ett inlägg i den lönepolitiska debatten.* Stockholm: SAF, 1972.

Maier, Charles. *Recasting Bourgeois Europe: Stabilization in France, Germany, and Italy in the Decade after World War I.* Princeton: Princeton University Press, 1975.

Markovits, Andrei S. *The Politics of the West German Trade Unions: Strategies of Class and Interest Representation in Growth and Crisis.* Cambridge: Cambridge University Press, 1986.

———. "Trade Unions and the Economic Crisis: The West German Case." In Peter Gourevitch et al., *Unions and Economic Crisis.* London: Allen & Unwin, 1984.

Martin, Andrew. "Distributive Conflict, Inflation, and Investment: The Swedish Case." Cambridge: Council for European Studies, Harvard University, March 1980.

———. "The Dynamics of Change in a Keynesian Political Economy: The Swedish Case and Its Implications." In Colin Crouch, ed., *State and Economy in Contemporary Capitalism.* New York: St. Martin's Press, 1979.

———. "Trade Unions in Sweden: Strategic Responses to Change and Crisis." In Peter Gourevitch et al., eds., *Unions and Economic Crisis.* London: Allen & Unwin, 1984.

———. "Wages, Profits, and Investment in Sweden." In Leon N. Lindberg and Charles S. Maier, eds., *The Politics of Inflation and Economic Stagnation.* Washington, D. C.: Brookings, 1985.

Martin, Donald L. *An Ownership Theory of the Trade Union.* Berkeley: University of California Press, 1980.

Marx, Karl. "Value, Price and Profit." In Karl Marx and Friedrich Engels, *Collected Works,* vol 20: *Marx and Engels: 1864–1868.* New York: International Publishers, 1985.

Mayr, Hans, and Hans Janssen, eds. *Perspektiven der Arbeitszeitverkürzung: Wissenschaftler und Gewerkschafter zur 35-Stunden-Woche.* Cologne: Bund Verlag, 1984.

Meidner, Rudolf. "Deutsche Einflüsse auf die Schwedische Debatte über überbetriebliche Vermögensbeteiligung." In Hans Jochen Vogel, Helmut Simon, and Adalbert Podlech, eds., *Die Freiheit des Anderen: Festschrift für Martin Hirsch.* Baden Baden: Nomos Verlagsgesellschaft, 1982.

———. *Employee Investment Funds: An Approach to Collective Capital Formation.* London: Allen & Unwin, 1978.

———. "Limits of Active Labour Market Policy." Stockholm: Arbetslivscentrum, 1983.

———. "Några funderingar kring den solidariska lönepolitikens framtid." In Landsorganisationen, *Lönepolitik och solidaritet.* Stockholm: LO, 1980.

———. *Samordning och solidarisk lönepolitik.* Stockholm: LO/Prisma, 1974.

———. "Skölds ny giv i lönepolitiken." *Tiden* 5 (1956).

———. "Zur Problematik einer nationalen Lohnpolitik: Grenzen lohnpolitischer Nivellierungsbestrebungen in Schweden." Berlin: Wissenschaftszentrum, February 1980.

Meidner, Rudolf, and Berndt Öhman. *Solidarisk lönepolitik: Erfarenheter, problem, utsikter.* Stockholm: Tiden, 1972.

Mellor, Earl F. "Investigating the Differences in Weekly Earnings of Women and Men." *Monthly Labor Review*, June 1984.

Mertens, Dieter. "Quantitative und qualitative Beschäftigungswirkungen der Arbeitszeitverkürzung." In Hans Mayr and Hans Janssen, eds., *Perspektiven der Arbeitszeitverkürzung*. Cologne: Bund Verlag, 1984.

Mills, C. Wright. *The New Men of Power: America's Labor Leaders*. New York: Harcourt, Brace, 1948.

Montgomery, David. *Beyond Equality: Labor and the Radical Republicans, 1862–1872*. Urbana: University of Illinois Press, 1981.

——. *Workers' Control in America*. Cambridge: Cambridge University Press, 1979.

Moore, Barrington. *Injustice: The Social Basis of Obedience and Revolt*. White Plains, N. Y.: M. E. Sharpe, 1978.

Müller-Jentsch, Walther. "IG Bau-Steine-Erden: Juniorpartner der Bauindustrie." In Otto Jacobi, Walther Müller-Jentsch, and Eberhard Schmidt, eds., *Gewerkschaften und Klassenkampf: Kritisches Jahrbuch '73*. Frankfurt: Fischer, 1973.

——. "Die spontane Streikbewegung 1973." In Otto Jacobi, Walther Müller-Jentsch, and Eberhard Schmidt, eds., *Gewerkschaften und Klassenkampf: Kritisches Jahrbuch '74*. Frankfurt: Fischer, 1974.

Mulvey, Charles. *The Economic Analysis of Trade Unions*. New York: St. Martin's Press, 1978.

Nilsson, Gunnar. "Den solidariska lönepolitiken." In Landsorganisationen, *Lönepolitik och solidaritet*. Stockholm: LO, 1980.

Nycander, Svante. *Kurs på kollision: Inblick i avtalsrörelsen 1970–71*. Stockholm: Askild & Kärnekull, 1972.

Nyhlén, Erik, and Nils Viktorsson. *Stuvat: Spelet om hamnarna*. Stockholm: Tiden, 1975.

Offe, Claus. *Contradictions of the Welfare State*. Cambridge: MIT Press, 1984.

Offe, Claus, and Helmut Wiesenthal. "Two Logics of Collective Action." In Offe, *Disorganized Capitalism: Contemporary Transformations of Work and Politics*. Cambridge: MIT Press, 1985.

Ohlsson, Ingvar. "Den solidariska lönepolitikens resultat." In Landsorganisationen, *Lönepolitik och solidaritet*. Stockholm: LO, 1980.

Ohlström, Bo. *Vilda strejker inom LO-området 1974 och 1975*. Stockholm: LO, 1977.

Olson, Mancur. *The Logic of Collective Action: Public Goods and the Theory of Groups*. Cambridge: Harvard University Press, 1965.

Olsson, Anders, Madeleine Wänseth, and Tom Burns. *Det svenska löneförhandlingssystemet: Rapport 1, Projektet Löneförhandlingar i Sverige*. Uppsala: Sociologiska Institutionen, Uppsala Universitet, June 1984.

Olsson, Ulf. *Lönepolitik och lönestruktur: Göteborgs verkstadsarbetare 1920–1949*. Göteborg: Ekonomisk-Historiska Institutionen vid Göteborgs Universitet, 1970.

Organisation for Economic Co-operation and Development. *Wages and Labour Mobility*. Paris: OECD, 1975.

Palme, Olof. "SAF's nej till fondsamtal ett misstag." *Dagens Nyheter*, 15 September 1983.

Pfromm, Hans-Adam. "Einkommenspolitik und Verteilungskonflikt." Diss. Johann Wolfgang Goethe–Universität, 1974.

——. *Das neue DGB-Grundsatzprogramm: Einführung und Kommentar.* Munich: Günter Olzog Verlag, 1982.

——. *Solidarische Lohnpolitik: Zur wirtschaftlichen und sozialen Problematik tariflicher Lohnstrukturnivellierung.* Cologne: Europäische Verlagsanstalt, 1978.

Piecha, Manfred. "Tarifliche Stundenlöhne und Lohngruppenrelationen in ausgewählten Tarifbereiche 1960–1976." Düsseldorf: WSI-Tarifarchiv, 1977.

Piore, Michael J. "Fragments of a 'Sociological' Theory of Wages." *American Economic Review* 63 (May 1973).

Pitz, Karl Heinz. "Alternativen zur Vermögenspolitik: Der Beitrag der IG Metall zur vermögenspolitischen Diskussion." In Horst Günter Ptak, ed., *Ökonomische Probleme der Erfolgsbeteiligung von Arbeitnehmern.* Kassel: Gesamthochschule Kassel, 1978.

——. "Kein tragbares tarifpolitisches Konzept." *Wirtschaftsdienst* 12 (1976).

——. "Über die potentiellen Gefahren der 'grossen Lösung' des Vermögensproblems für die gewerkschaftliche Lohnpolitik." *Gewerkschaftliche Monatshefte* 21 (October 1970).

——. "Verbindungen zwischen Vermögenspolitik, Lohnpolitik und Sozialpolitik." In Klaus Schenke and Winfried Schmähl, eds., *Alterssicherung als Aufgabe für Wissenschaft und Politik.* Stuttgart: Kohlhammer, 1980.

——. "Zusammenhänge zwischen Vermögens-, Steuer- und Reformpolitik." *Sozialer Fortschritt* 4 (1972).

Pitz, Karl Heinz, ed. *Das Nein zur Vermögenspolitik: Gewerkschaftliche Argumente und Alternativen zur Vermögensbildung.* Reinbek bei Hamburg: Rowohlt, 1974.

Pontusson, Jonas. "Behind and Beyond Social Democracy in Sweden." *New Left Review* 143 (January–February 1984).

——. "Comparative Political Economy of Advanced Capitalist States: Sweden and France." *Kapitalistate* 10:11 (1983).

——. "Labor Reformism and the Politics of Capital Formation in Sweden." Diss. University of California, Berkeley, 1986.

——. "Radicalization and Retreat in Swedish Social Democracy." *New Left Review* 165 (1987).

——. "Sweden." In Mark Kesselman and Joel Krieger, eds., *European Politics in Transition.* Lexington, Mass.: D. C. Heath, 1987.

Popkin, Samuel K. *The Rational Peasant: The Political Economy of Rural Society in Vietnam.* Berkeley: University of California Press, 1979.

Projektgruppe Gewerkschaftsforschung. *Rahmenbedingungen der Tarifpolitik. Band 1: Gesamtwirtschaftliche Entwicklung und Organisationen der Tarifparteien.* Frankfurt: Campus, 1979.

——. *Rahmenbedingungen der Tarifpolitik. Band 2: Strukturdaten der Metallverarbeitenden, der Chemischen und der Druckindustrie.* Frankfurt: Campus, 1979.

——. *Tarifpolitik 1977: Darstellung und Analyse der Tarifbewegung in der Metallverarbeitenden, der Chemischen und der Druckindustrie sowie im öffentlichen Dienst.* Frankfurt: Campus, 1978.

——. *Tarifpolitik 1978: Lohnpolitische Kooperation und Absicherungskämpfe— Darstellung und Analyse der Tarifbewegung in der Metallverarbeitenden, der Chemischen und der Druckindustrie sowie im öffentlichen Dienst.* Frankfurt: Campus, 1980.

Ptak, Horst Günter, ed. *Ökonomische Probleme der Erfolgsbeteiligung von Arbeitnehmern.* Kassel: Gesamthochschule Kassel, 1978.

Rees, Albert. *The Economics of Trade Unions*. Chicago: University of Chicago Press, 1977.
Regalia, Ida, Marino Regini, and Emilio Reyneri. "Labour Conflicts and Industrial Relations in Italy." In Colin Crouch and Alessandro Pizzorno, eds., *The Resurgence of Class Conflict in Western Europe since 1968, vol. 1*. New York: Holmes & Meier, 1978.
Rehn, Gösta. "Finansministrarna, LO-ekonomerna och arbetsmarknadspolitiken." In Jan Herin and Lars Werin, eds., *Ekonomisk debatt och ekonomisk politik*. Stockholm: Norstedt, 1977.
———. "Idéutvecklingen." In Landsorganisationen, *Lönepolitik och solidaritet*. Stockholm: LO, 1980.
———. "Swedish Active Labor Market Policy: Retrospect and Prospect." *Industrial Relations* (Winter 1985).
———. "Unionism and the Wage Structure in Sweden." In John T. Dunlop, ed., *The Theory of Wage Determination*. London, Macmillan, 1957.
Reynolds, Lloyd G., and Cynthia H. Taft. *The Evolution of the Wage Structure*. New Haven: Yale University Press, 1956.
Robinson, Derek. *Incomes Policy and Capital Sharing in Europe*. New York: Harper & Row, 1973.
———. *Wage Drift, Fringe Benefits and Manpower Distribution: A Study of Employer Practices in a Full Employment Economy*. Paris: OECD, 1968.
Röttorp, Anders. "Löntagarfonder smygvägen." *Svenska Dagbladet*, 1 November 1982.
Roos, Patricia A. *Gender and Work: A Comparative Analysis of Industrial Societies*. Albany: State University of New York Press, 1985.
Ross, Arthur M. *Trade Union Wage Policy*. Berkeley, University of California Press, 1948.
Rossman, Witich. "Ohnmacht oder Gegenmacht? Gewerkschaftliche und politische Aspekte der Metaller- und Druckerstreiks." *Blätter für deutsche und internationale Politik* 29 (August 1984).
Runciman, W. G. *Relative Deprivation and Social Justice*. Berkeley: University of California Press, 1966.
Sabel, Charles F. *Work and Politics: The Division of Labor in Industry*. Cambridge: Cambridge University Press, 1982.
Sachverständigenrat. *Konjunktur im Umbruch—Risiken und Chancen: Jahresgutachten 1970/71*. Stuttgart: Kohlhammer, 1970.
———. *Zeit zum Investieren: Jahresgutachten 1976/77*. Stuttgart: Kohlhammer, 1977.
Scase, Richard. "Relative Deprivation: A Comparison of English and Swedish Manual Workers." In Dorothy Wedderburn, ed., *Poverty, Inequality and Class Structure*. Cambridge: Cambridge University Press, 1974.
Schacht, Konrad, and Lutz Unterseher. "Spontane Arbeitsniederlegungen—Krise des Tarifverhandlungssystems?" *Gewerkschaftliche Monatshefte* 25 (1974).
Schäfer, Claus. "Ist Vermögensbildung nur Vermögenseinbildung? Zur Brauchbarkeit von Vermögenspolitik als gewerkschaftliches Instrument." *WSI-Mitteilungen* 36 (July 1983).
———. "Zur gegenwärtigen vermögenspolitischen Diskussion." *WSI-Mitteilungen* 10 (1977).
Schager, Nils-Henrik. "Den lokala lönebildningen och företagens vinster: En

preliminär analys," from *Löntagarna och kapitaltillväxten 3: Tre expertrapporter från utredningen om löntagarna och kapitaltillväxten* (SOU 1979: 10). Stockholm: Ekonomidepartementet, 1979.

Schiller, Bernt. *Storstrejken 1909: Förhistoria och orsaker.* (Göteborg: Akademiförlaget, 1967.

Schmidt, Eberhard. "Die Auseinandersetzung um die Rolle der Vertrauensleute in der IG Metall." in Otto Jacobi, Walther Müller-Jentsch, and Eberhard Schmidt, eds., *Gewerkschaften und Klassenkampf: Kritisches Jahrbuch '74.* Frankfurt: Fischer, 1974.

———. "IG Metall 1966–1972: Von der Opposition zur Kooperation." In Otto Jacobi, Walther Müller-Jentsch, and Eberhard Schmidt, *Gewerkschaften und Klassenkampf: Kritisches Jahrbuch '72.* Frankfurt: Fischer, 1972.

———. *Ordnungsfaktor oder Gegenmacht: Die politische Rolle der Gewerkschaften.* Frankfurt: Suhrkamp, 1971.

———. *Die verhinderte Neuordnung 1945–1952: Zur Auseinandersetzung um die Demokratisierung der Wirtschaft in den westlichen Besatzungszonen und in der Bundesrepublik Deutschland.* Frankfurt: Europäische Verlagsanstalt, 1970.

Schmidt, Manfred. "The Welfare State and the Economy in Periods of Crisis: A Comparative Study of Twenty-Three OECD Nations." *European Journal of Political Research* 11:1 (1983).

Schmiede, Rudi, and Edwin Schudlich. *Die Entwicklung der Leistungsentlohnung in Deutschland: Eine historisch-theoretische Untersuchung zum Verhältnis von Lohn und Leistung unter kapitalistischen Produktionsbedingungen.* Frankfurt: Campus, 1978.

Schneider, Michael. *Streit um Arbeitszeit: Geschichte des Kampfes um Arbeitszeitverkürzung in Deutschland.* Cologne: Bund Verlag, 1984.

Schröder, Jürgen. "Betriebliche Vermögensbildung—Bleibt der DGB unbelehrbar?" *Der Arbeitgeber* 30 (1978).

Schudlich, Edwin. "Tarifpolitik ohne Kampfgeschrei: Die Tarifbeziehungen in der chemischen Industrie 1970–1979." In Ulrich Billerbeck, Christoph Deutschmann, Rainder Erd, Rudi Schmiede, and Schudlich, eds., *Neuorientierung der Tarifpolitik?* Frankfurt: Campus, 1982.

———. "Weniger Arbeit für mehr Beschäftigte: Historische Hinweise über den Zusammenhang von Arbeitszeit und Beschäftigung." *WSI-Mitteilungen* 4 (1983).

Schumann, Michael, Frank Gerlach, Albert Gschlössl, and Petra Milhoffer. *Am Beispiel der Septemberstreiks—Anfang der Rekonstruktionsperiode der Arbeiterklasse?* Frankfurt: Europäische Verlagsanstalt, 1971.

Scott, Franklin D. *Sweden: The Nation's History.* Minneapolis: University of Minnesota, 1977.

Scott, James C. *The Moral Economy of the Peasant: Rebellion and Subsistence in Southeast Asia.* New Haven: Yale University Press, 1976.

Seitenzahl, Rolf. *Gewerkschaften zwischen Kooperation und Konflikt.* Frankfurt: Europäische Verlagsanstalt, 1976.

Sen, Amartya K. "Rational Fools." *Philosophy and Public Affairs* 6:4 (1977).

Siebke, Jürgen. "Vermögenskonzentration." In Karl Heinz Pitz, ed., *Das Nein zur Vermögenspolitik.* Reinbek bei Hamburg: Rowohlt, 1974.

Skocpol, Theda. "Bringing the State Back In: Strategies of Analysis in Current Research." In Peter B. Evans, Dietrich Rueschemeyer, and Skocpol, eds., *Bringing the State Back In.* Cambridge: Cambridge University Press, 1985.

249

Sköld, Per Edvin. *Sparande och medinflytande.* Malmö: Arbetets debattforum, 1957.

Skogh, Göran. "Employers Associations in Sweden." In John P. Windmuller and Alan Gladstone, *Employers Associations and Industrial Relations: A Comparative Study.* Oxford: Clarendon Press, 1984.

Söderpalm, Sven Anders. *Arbetsgivarna och Saltsjöbadspolitiken: En historisk studie i samarbetet på svensk arbetsmarknad.* Stockholm: SAF, 1980.

———. *Direktörsklubben: Storindustrin in svensk politik under 1930- och 40-talet.* Stockholm: Zenit/Rabén & Sjögren, 1976.

Soskice, David. "Strike Waves and Wage Explosions, 1968–1970: An Economic Interpretation." In Colin Crouch and Alessandro Pizzorno, eds., *The Resurgence of Class Conflict in Western Europe since 1968: Volume 2.* New York: Holmes & Meier, 1978.

Spencer, Elaine Glovka. *Management and Labor in Imperial Germany: Ruhr Industrialists as Employers, 1896–1914.* New Brunswick: Rutgers University Press, 1984.

Spieker, Wolfgang. "Mitbestimmung im Unternehmen: Idee und Wirklichkeit." *WSI-Mitteilungen* 29 (August 1976).

Statistisches Bundesamt Wiesbaden. *Fachserie 16 Löhne und Gehälter, Reihe 2.1 Arbeiterverdienste in der Industrie.* Volumes for years 1960–1980.

———. *Fachserie 16 Löhne und Gehälter, Reihe 4.1 Tariflöhne.* October 1981.

———. *Statistisches Jahrbuch.* Volumes for years 1959–1976.

Statistisches Reichsamt. *Statistisches Jahrbuch für das Deutsche Reich: Jahrgang 1928.* Berlin, 1928.

Statistiska Centralbyrån. *Företagen 1981: Ekonomisk redovisning.* Stockholm: SCB, 1981.

———. *Löner 1981, Del 1: Industritjänstemän, handelsanställda m.fl.* Stockholm: SCB, 1982.

———. *Löner 1981, Del 2: Lantarbetare, industriarbetare, butiks- och lagerpersonal inom varuhandel m.fl.* Stockholm: SCB, 1982.

———. *Statistisk årsbok 1985.* Stockholm: SCB, 1986.

Stearns, Peter. *Revolutionary Syndicalism and French Labor.* New Brunswick: Rutgers University Press, 1971.

Steinkühler, Franz. "Angst vor den Freunden: Zerbricht das Bündnis von Gewerkschaften und Sozialdemokraten?" *Die Zeit,* 25 March 1988, 13.

Stephens, John D. *The Transition from Capitalism to Socialism.* London: Macmillan, 1979.

Sträng, Gunnar. "Avslutande kommentarer." In Kjell-Olof Feldt et al., *Ekonomisk politik inför 1980-talet.* Stockholm: Tiden, 1977.

Strasser, Arnold. "The Changing Structure of Compensation." *Monthly Labor Review* 89 (September 1966).

Streeck, Wolfgang. *Gewerkschaftliche Organisationsprobleme in der sozialstaatlichen Demokratie.* (Königstein: Athenäum, 1981.

Svenska Arbetsgivareföreningen. *Lönespridning: Arbetare tjänstemän 1972–1980.* Stockholm: SAF, 1981.

———. *Rättvis lön—lönepolitiskt programm.* Stockholm: SAF, 1979.

Svenska Metallindustriarbetareförbundet. *Kongressprotokoll Del 1: Svenska Metallindustriarbetareförbundets kongress 1981.* Stockholm: Metall, 1982.

———. *Protokoll: Svenska Metallindustriarbetareförbundets kongress 1973.* Stockholm: Metall, 1974.

——. *Protokoll: Svenska Metallindustriarbetareförbundets kongress 1977.* Stockholm: Metall, 1978.

Sveriges Industriförbund and Svenska Arbetsgivareföreningen. *Företagsvinster, kapitalförsörjning, löntagarfonder: Rapport från en arbetsgrupp inom näringslivet.* Stockholm: SIF/SAF, 1976.

Sveriges Socialdemokratiska Arbetarepartiet. *Motioner: 1978 års Socialdemokratiska Partikongress.* Stockholm: SAP, 1979.

——. *Motioner: 1981 års Socialdemokratiska Partikongress.* Stockholm: SAP, 1982.

——. *Protokoll: 1981 års Socialdemokratiska Partikongress.* Stockholm: SAP, 1982.

Sveriges Verkstadsförening. "Löneglidning och ackordsättning." Stockholm: VF, no date.

Swenson, Peter. "Beyond the Wage Struggle: Politics, Collective Bargaining, and the Egalitarian Dilemmas of Social Democratic Trade Unionism in Germany and Sweden." Diss. Yale University, 1986.

Teschner, Ekhart. *Lohnpolitik im Betrieb: Eine empirische Untersuchung in der Metall-, Chemie-, Textil- und Tabakindustrie.* Frankfurt: Campus, 1977.

——. "Zentralisierte Lohnpolitik und betriebliche Lohnbildung." In Otto Jacobi, Walther Müller-Jentsch, and Eberhard Schmidt, *Gewerkschaften und Klassenkampf: Kritisches Jahrbuch '72.* Frankfurt: Fischer, 1972.

Thompson, E. P. "The Moral Economy of the English Crowd in the Eighteenth Century." *Past and Present* no. 50 (February 1971).

Turner, H. A. *Trade Union Growth, Structure and Policy: A Comparative Study of the Cotton Unions.* London: George Allen & Unwin, 1962.

——. "Trade Unions, Differentials and the Levelling of Wages." *Manchester School of Economic and Social Studies* 20:3 (1952).

Turner, H. A., and D. A. S. Jackson. "On the Stability of Wage Differences and Productivity-Based Wage Policies: An International Analysis." *British Journal of Industrial Relations* 7 (March 1969).

Ullenhag, Jörgen. *Den solidariska lönepolitiken i Sverige: Debatt och verklighet.* Stockholm: Läromedelsförlagen, 1971.

Ullmann, Peter. *Tarifverträge und Tarifpolitik in Deutschland bis 1914.* Frankfurt: Peter Lang, 1977.

Ulman, Lloyd. *The Rise of the National Trade Union: The Development and Significance of Its Structure, Governing Institutions, and Economic Policies.* Cambridge: Harvard University Press, 1955.

——. *Wage Restraint: A Study of Incomes Policies in Western Europe.* Berkeley: University of California Press, 1971.

Vetter, Heinz Oskar. *Gleichberechtigung oder Klassenkampf: Gewerkschaftspolitik für die achtziger Jahre.* Cologne: Bund Verlag, 1980.

Victorin, Anders. *Lönenormering genom kollektivavtal.* Stockholm: Almänna Förlaget, 1973.

von Otter, Casten. "Swedish Welfare Capitalism: The Role of the State." In Richard Scase, ed., *The State in Western Europe.* London: Croom Helm, 1980.

von Sydow, Björn. "Löntagarfonder 1957 och 1977—och Per Edvin Sköld." *Tiden* 9 (1977).

Vorwerk, Wilhelm. "Wie entstand die Bundesvereinigung der Deutschen Arbeitgeberverbände?" *Der Arbeitgeber* 13 (January 1961).

Webb, Sidney, and Beatrice Webb. *Industrial Democracy.* London: Longmans, Green, 1902.

Weber, Hajo. "Konflikt in Interorganisationssystemen: Zur Konfliktlogik organisierter Arbeitsmarktparteien im Tarifkonflikt '84. *Soziale Welt* 37:2/3 (1986).

Weiss, Gerhard. *Die ÖTV: Politik und gesellschaftspolitische Konzeptionen der Gewerkschaft ÖTV von 1966 bis 1976.* Marburg: Verlag Arbeiterbewegung und Gesellschaftswissenschaft, 1978.

Weitzman, Martin L. *The Share Economy: Conquering Stagflation.* Cambridge: Harvard University Press, 1984.

Wende, Alexander. *Die Konzentrationsbewegung bei den deutschen Gewerkschaften.* Marburg: Marburg University, 1912.

Wickman, Krister. "Kapitalbildning och investeringsutveckling inför 1980-talet." In Kjell-Olof Feldt et al., *Ekonomisk politik inför 1980-talet.* Stockholm: Tiden, 1977.

Wiles, Peter. "Are Trade Unions Necessary?" *Encounter* 7 (September 1956).

Willey, Richard J. *Democracy in the West German Trade Unions: A Reappraisal of the "Iron Law."* Beverly Hills, Calif.: Sage, 1971.

William, Paul. *Fairness, Collective Bargaining, and Incomes Policy.* Oxford: Clarendon Press, 1982.

Wohlin, Lars. "Företagens soliditet och försörjning med riskkapital." *Ekonomisk debatt* 7 (1980).

Wredén, Åke. *Kapital till de anställda? En studie av vinstdelning och löntagarfonder.* Stockholm: Studieförbundet Näringsliv och Samhälle, 1976.

Zander, Erik. *Fackliga Klassiker: En antologi kring facklig demokrati, ideologi och lönepolitik.* Stockholm: LO/Rabén & Sjögren, 1981.

Zentner, Christian. *Das Verhalten von Georg Leber.* Mainz: v. Hase & Koehler Verlag, 1966.

Index